MW01285811

Praise for *Backbeat Gangsters*

"Jeffrey Sussman once again proves that he is the modern master of the mob. *Backbeat Gangsters* makes you question your dream of becoming a rock star and prepares you to turn down offers you can't refuse."
—**Daniel J. Glenn**, host of *Fascinating Nouns*

"Jeffrey Sussman has done an eye-opening job in exposing the mob influence on rock & roll. He further documents, in an entertaining but lucid style, the corrupting influence that the mob has had on an important part of American culture. Highly recommended."
—**Ron Chepesiuk**, author, screenwriter, and podcast host, *Crime Beat*

"Jeffrey Sussman's book *Backbeat Gangsters* shines a light on the mob's sinister role in deciding who the winners and losers would be in the music industry. With this book, an extremely dark chapter in organized crime history finally gets the in-depth attention it deserves."
—**Larry Henry**, author of *Mob in Pop Culture* and columnist for the Mob Museum, Las Vegas

"Exhaustively researched, compellingly written, Jeffrey Sussman's *Backbeat Gangsters* is a *must-read* for anyone in the recording business. It's also an eye-opening account of the dark underbelly of the 'innocent' music we all grew up with. Bravo!"
—**Tommy Sullivan**, composer, producer, and musical director of the original *Brooklyn Bridge*

"As an avid reader, I am truly fascinated by Jeffrey Sussman's book, *Backbeat Gangsters*. His research is extensive and pristine, with a thrilling prose that makes this book a tour de force!"
—**Joy Jan Jones**, singer, composer, and creator of JJJ & the Fiancés

Backbeat Gangsters

BACKBEAT GANGSTERS
The Rise and Decline of the Mob in Rock Music

JEFFREY SUSSMAN

ROWMAN & LITTLEFIELD
Lanham • Boulder • New York • London

Published by Rowman & Littlefield
An imprint of The Rowman & Littlefield Publishing Group, Inc.
4501 Forbes Boulevard, Suite 200, Lanham, Maryland 20706
www.rowman.com

86-90 Paul Street, London EC2A 4NE

Copyright © 2025 by Jeffrey Sussman

All rights reserved. No part of this book may be reproduced in any form or by any electronic or mechanical means, including information storage and retrieval systems, without written permission from the publisher, except by a reviewer who may quote passages in a review.

British Library Cataloguing in Publication Information available

Library of Congress Cataloging-in-Publication Data

Names: Sussman, Jeffrey, author.
Title: Backbeat gangsters : the rise and decline of the mob in rock music / Jeffrey Sussman.
Description: Lanham : Rowman & Littlefield, 2025. | Includes bibliographical references and index.
Identifiers: LCCN 2024030549 (print) | LCCN 2024030550 (ebook) | ISBN 9781538190265 (cloth) | ISBN 9781538190272 (ebook)
Subjects: LCSH: Music trade—Corrupt practices—United States—History—20th century. | Organized crime—United States—History—20th century.
Classification: LCC ML3790 .S8868 2025 (print) | LCC ML3790 (ebook) | DDC 364.1060973—dc23/eng/20240705
LC record available at https://lccn.loc.gov/2024030549
LC ebook record available at https://lccn.loc.gov/2024030550

♾™ The paper used in this publication meets the minimum requirements of American National Standard for Information Sciences—Permanence of Paper for Printed Library Materials, ANSI/NISO Z39.48-1992.

To my wife and best friend, Barbara

CONTENTS

Acknowledgments xi

Introduction 1
CHAPTER 1: Jukeboxes and Rock and Roll. 27
CHAPTER 2: Morris Levy: The Godfather of Rock
and Roll 45
CHAPTER 3: Alan Freed: Rock and Roll's Broadcast
Wizard 71
CHAPTER 4: Vincent "the Chin" Gigante: The Godfather's
Godfather 87
CHAPTER 5: Jimmie Rodgers: A Star Is Born and Reborn . . . 99
CHAPTER 6: Frankie Lymon: Sweet Voice Junkie 113
CHAPTER 7: Sal "the Swindler" Pisello: The Great Cutout
Swindle. 129
CHAPTER 8: Drugs, Music, and the Mafia. 145
CHAPTER 9: The Return of Payola. 167
CHAPTER 10: Pop to Doo Wop to Hip Hop. 187
CHAPTER 11: Scalping and Skimming 215

Appendix: List of Murdered Hip Hop Performers 231
Notes. 235
Bibliography 243
Index 245
About the Author 261

Acknowledgments

I am indebted to the following people: reference librarian and researcher Stephen Spataro, editor Becca Beurer, and lawyer Shelia Levine. And, of course, my wife, Barbara Sussman. There are numerous people who provided me with information for my books about the mob; though they did not want to be quoted, I am grateful to each of them.

INTRODUCTION

WHAT FOLLOWS IS AN INTRODUCTORY SYNOPSIS OF THE CONTENT of this book, which covers the 1950s to the present. The 1950s and early 1960s were a time when singers were paid a fraction of their royalties, if that, from record companies run by mobsters. Chapter after chapter deals with the various ways that organized crime controlled the rock music business. There are numerous marquee names, many of whom were victims of the mob, and names of those who preferred working in the shadows. The book concludes by noting the demise of the gangsters and the extravagant payment of hundreds of millions of dollars to retiring singers for their catalog of songs.

As rock and roll burst on the culture in the early 1950s, gangsters were there. They were like hungry lions on the lookout for easy prey. In the 1950s, when rock and roll became the music of teenagers, the major established record companies (that is, Decca, RCA Victor, Columbia, Capital) thought that the new music was just a passing teenage trend. Gangsters, both independent entrepreneurs and members of organized crime, pounced. They opened small independent record companies, signed ambitious young singers and musicians, and produced truckloads of 45 rpm records. To make sure that their records would be successful, the mob bribed disc jockeys in major cities to play the records. The deejays were given money, partial copyrights, and publishing rights to the songs they played; loans, mortgages, and prostitutes were made available. Whatever it took to gain air time and repeated plays of their songs, the mob made sure it happened. In addition to air time on hundreds of radio stations, the mob, which controlled jukeboxes throughout the country, made sure that their machines were filled to capacity with the new music.

The jukebox distribution business had been controlled by the mob long before rock and roll was around. Meyer Lansky, for example, had a company called Emby that had an exclusive license to distribute jukeboxes throughout the east. In Chicago, the Outfit controlled jukeboxes in numerous Midwestern states. If bar owners, restaurant owners, bowling alley owners, and diner owners didn't take their jukeboxes, they were ultimately persuaded to do so. It began with threats, then beatings, and, in several cases, murder. As an incentive, the mobsters explained to their prospective customers that everyone could profit from the installation of jukeboxes. The mob was willing to split the income from the machines 50/50, though in some cases the mob took 70 percent.

When it came to singers, however, mobsters had no intention of being generous to those who signed contracts with their record labels. Though they had paid young singers and musicians to sign contracts, sometimes even giving them cars, they rarely paid them the royalties that were due on hit songs. And when artists insisted on payment, they were told to get lost. If artists persisted in demanding royalty payments, they were met with threats. And if the threats failed to quiet the artists, beatings were sufficient to register silence. Some artists suffered severe beatings, including broken legs, broken arms, fractured skulls, or worse.

Working closely with deejays, the small record companies grew and became forces in the music industry. They spent small fortunes bribing those deejays, but they accrued large fortunes from the millions of records that were sold. The bribery eventually became a moral cause célèbre among prosecutors, and deejays were hauled before grand juries and senate investigating committees. Some deejays confessed and were obeisant in their apologies; others were recalcitrant, reciting their Fifth Amendment rights as if repeating song lyrics. Bribery of deejays had become known as payola, and prosecutors treated Alan Freed (who allegedly invented the phrase rock and roll) as if he were public enemy number one. When the trials were over, and Freed was fired from several radio stations, one after another, each one smaller than the last; he was a broken man, an alcoholic who died in poverty. Yet payola continued, though in clever, surreptitious ways, unspotted by prosecutors and IRS agents.

Among those singers who were victimized by greedy record companies, Frankie Lymon of the Teenagers stands out as a sad case. As a young man, he and his group had a major hit in 1956 with "Why Do Fools Fall in Love." It made a fortune for Gee Records and its owner, George Goldner, who took a writing credit for the song, though initial releases of the song listed Lymon and Teenager members Jimmy Merchant and Herman Santiago as the writers. Goldner eventually sold his music companies to Morris Levy, president of Roulette Records, in 1959, and Levy's name replaced Goldner's as cowriter of the hit song. Lymon, who died of a heroin overdose when he was twenty-five years old, never received royalty payments during his lifetime.

Morris Levy, who was a partner of Vincent "the Chin" Gigante, boss of the Genovese crime family, was notorious not only for not paying royalties to his artists but for threatening them if they attempted to leave his company. And when an artist attempted to hire a lawyer to sue Levy for unpaid royalties, no lawyer would take the case because of Levy's connections to mobsters, and not just the Genovese family but also to the DeCavalcante crime family of New Jersey. Mobsters hung around his offices as if they were part of the interior design. And their presence had the appropriate intimidating effect. It was not unusual for an angry songwriter or singer to be bounced out of the Roulette Records offices with a few bruises. Levy himself enjoyed delivering a beating as much as watching one. He was a large, overbearing bear of a man with a volatile temper and fists as big as neanderthal clubs.

Roulette was used as a front for criminals, especially capos in the Genovese crime family, whose members used it to launder money. It was the partnership of Morris Levy and boss Vincent "the Chin" Gigante that had cemented the mob's involvement in rock and roll. "Levy, the industry's lender of last resort, made his fortune draining the blood, figuratively and perhaps literally, from a succession of rock 'n' roll acts that began in the early 1950s and did not end until his death in 1991."[1]

Although Gigante was the most powerful mobster connected to Roulette Records, there were other mobsters whose presence was felt by singers, musicians, A&R men, producers, and others at the company. One was Gaetano "Corky" Vastola, a member of the DeCavalcante crime family of New Jersey. He had been a concert promoter and was part owner of a talent agency that booked such performers as Ray Charles, Redd Foxx, Sammy Davis Jr., and Aretha Franklin. As with Levy, he took songwriting credits for numerous songs, including the Valentines's recording of "Lily Maebelle," the Cleftones's "You Baby You," and the Wrens's "Hey Girl." In 1960, Vastola was convicted of trademark offenses, received a one-year suspended sentence, and was fined a mere $215 for not reporting some of his income.

During hearings before the House Select Committee on Crime in 1972, Vastola was identified by a New Jersey State Police criminal intelligence officer as having an interest in a New York talent agency called Queens Booking Agency, "which has booked many principal entertainment figures throughout the country." According to law enforcement and entertainment industry sources, Queens has booked concert appearances at Atlantic City, New Jersey, and casinos by such performers as Red Foxx, Ray Charles, Aretha Franklin, and Sammy Davis Jr. "One investigator described

Vastola 'as a tough character, very intelligent, with a background of violence.'"[2]

Copyrights, royalties, and trademarks were not the only targets of opportunity for mobsters: they made enormous sums from counterfeiting records and selling them to retailers at steep discounts. It became such a big business that millions of counterfeit records flooded the retail record market. To satisfy the mob's need for more outlets to sell their counterfeits, Levy opened a chain of record stores, seventy in all, named Strawberries, that not only sold counterfeits from every rock and roll recording company but also sold those of Roulette Records and the ones that Levy had counterfeited. Counterfeit records, though listing artists and composers on labels, never had the burden of paying royalties. It was such an underground market that very few people were ever able to do more than estimate the number of counterfeit records flooding that market.

Another scam involved cutout records, and Levy and Vastola were involved in one of the biggest cutout scams in the record business. Cutouts are unsold records that take up space in warehouses, and the corners of the albums have been cut off. To get rid of those records, the recording companies make deals with distributors to sell the records at a fraction of the original wholesale price. To sweeten the pot, the companies often throw in records by popular groups or singers. The cutouts are delivered by the truckload to distributors, who then sell the records to deep discount retailers. However, the middle men involved in negotiating those deals often keep the records of popular artists for themselves and sell those at prices higher than the cutouts. Once the companies that had agreed to buy the cutouts discover that they have been cheated by the omission of records by popular artists, they refuse to pay for the entire cutout shipment. Such refusals do not go unanswered. Mobsters intimidate the cutout buyers into paying for the full load of the records that they had originally agreed to purchase. If intimidation doesn't generate agreeable results, beatings often do. In some cases, the buyers' warehouses have been torched, leaving nothing but cinders.

One of the most surprising record companies to participate in a mob scam was the prestigious MCA Records. It involved a member of the Gambino crime family named Salvatore "Sal the Swindler" Pisello. He had been known to the FBI for various swindles but managed to escape the grip of the law. It wasn't until he was investigated by an assistant US attorney in Los Angeles, named Marvin Rudnick, that Pisello was finally convicted of tax evasion and sentenced to two years in prison, but that was years after he had received $700,000 in unreported income from transactions in the record industry. For two years, 1983 and 1984, Pisello had been dealing with MCA in various music deals. Though he was accused of being a member of the Gambino crime family and of being a drug trafficker, he denied it all. In court, he announced to the sentencing judge that he was "not a member of organized crime and never have been—I'll go to prison for 20 years if anyone can prove that," he said. "I go to church every Sunday and the only organization I ever belonged to was the Holy Name Society [a Catholic lay society]," he said.[3]

No one seems to know how Pisello initiated his relations with MCA. Though he had no experience in the record business, he was welcomed into high-level meetings with MCA record executives. Those meetings resulted in Pisello executing deals that earned him hundreds of thousands of dollars. When confronted by reporters and law enforcement officials, MCA executives said that they had no knowledge of Pisello's background and alleged ties to organized crime.

However, the company did admit that he first came to MCA in 1983, when, as a representative of Englewood, New Jersey–based Sugar Hill Records, Pisello helped arrange a deal in which MCA would act as distributor for the small record company. Yet Sugar

Hill's president Joe Robinson was quoted in the *Bergen County (N.J.) Record* saying that Pisello brought the MCA distribution deal to him. Sugar Hill's attorney then went on to say that he did not know how Pisello got involved. Pisello, not one of the most self-effacing men, proudly claimed that he confidently walked into the office of one of MCA's vice presidents and talked his way into making deal. No one has denied that account.

While MCA was unaware of Pisello's mob history, the IRS regarded him as a consummate con artist, whose scams had occurred primarily in the food service business. Prior to Pisello's dealings with MCA, the IRS had no record of his scamming anyone in the record business. By the early 1980s, the IRS didn't need evidence of record industry shenanigans. It had uncovered evidence that Pisello had filed only four income tax returns between 1965 and 1982, paying a modest $2,500 in federal taxes. He had apparently gotten away with his minimal payments. However, the IRS also learned that Pisello had a criminal record with the Italian National Police in which he was noted for defrauding a jeweler out of $102,000 at the Hotel Di Paris in Monte Carlo. In addition, there existed plenty of hearsay that he was a major heroin supplier. A thirty-nine-page DEA profile of Pisello noted that though he had no arrests for drug dealing, his closest associates were drug dealers in organized crime. The DEA, though unable to obtain hard evidence, believed that Pisello associated with mobsters in Italy and arranged for significant amounts of heroin to be smuggled into the United States via Turkey and France.

Always on the lookout for easy and quick ways to make an illegal buck, Pisello sweet-talked a group of wealthy doctors and businessmen into investing $500,000 in a restaurant he owned named Roma di Notte. The restaurant was later destroyed in a fire, along with its financial records. Fire officials listed the blaze as suspected arson, and the case has never been solved.

It was during an IRS investigation into a possible case of tax evasion that the IRS discovered Pisello's involvement at MCA. If he was dealing with the company, IRS agents suspected that a possible crime had been committed or was evolving. Agents contacted human resources executives at the company and were told that Pisello was neither an agent nor an employee of the company. That was in 1984. However, Pisello was at MCA's headquarters nearly every day during 1983 and 1984. He had the use of an office, phones, and secretaries. Pisello let it be known that he was there on behalf of a company named Consultants for World Records.

"He had the run of the place," one former top executive said. "It was unprecedented in all my years at the company. The managers of recording artists used to want to do that, and we wouldn't let them. They had to call and get an appointment; they couldn't just come in and hang out."

"Everyone in the office knew Sal," one MCA executive said. "And he stuck out so much, in terms of style and appearance. You know, the diamond rings and gold watch. . . . There was a standing joke around the office that you didn't know whether to shake Sal's hand or kiss it."

"According to MCA, Consultants for World Records was paid a commission of 3% on the net proceeds from the Sugar Hill distribution deal—amounting to $76,000 in 1984—despite the fact that neither Pisello nor Consultants [were] mentioned in the agreement."[4]

"According to MCA internal auditors, Consultants received a $50,000 advance against 1985 proceeds on the Sugar Hill deal at a time when Sugar Hill was in arrears to MCA to the tune of $1.7 million and it was 'doubtful' that MCA would ever owe the 3% commission."

"Pisello denied the prosecutors' allegations that he had made $700,000 on his various transactions with MCA, which he described as '1,000 % legitimate.'"

"Pisello said Friday that he simply 'walked into MCA and made an appointment with [MCA Records Executive Vice President] Myron Roth and said I represented Sugar Hill—I talked my way into it.'"

"He called MCA 'the nicest corporation in the world. There was nothing wrong in this on MCA's part. We're the victims here—me, MCA, Roulette and Levy.'"[5]

Pisello was referring to his cutout deal with Levy. And it was that deal that led to a major investigation and trial. Without any experience in the record business, Pisello had managed to become the guiding force in an MCA cutout deal that embarrassed the company and cost the freedom of several of those involved.

At the time that Pisello engineered his deal, which he thought would be worth millions of dollars, MCA had more than ten million cutout albums in its warehouse. Prior to Pisello's arrival, MCA had sold its cutouts through sealed bids to the highest per-unit bidder. Pisello, in order to make his deal work, changed that.

Not just the IRS but also the Justice Department attorneys in LA had begun burrowing into the mob's control of various aspects of the record industry. However, MCA and its head, Lew Wasserman, had powerful connections reaching right into the White House. Wasserman had been Ronald Reagan's theatrical agent and helped him obtain the union presidency of the Screen Actors Guild. As president of the Guild, Reagan opened the door for MCA to produce TV series, which talent agencies had previously been forbidden from doing. Wasserman was also an important contributor to Reagan's gubernatorial and presidential campaigns. It is not surprising that another door, the one to Reagan's White House, was always open to Wasserman. And following his retirement from the White House, Reagan was given a magnificent office in MCA's headquarters in Los Angeles, where his door—as expected—was always open to Wasserman.

Friends in high places can always be called upon to ease one's way in the world. Therefore, it not surprising that when investigators began shining spotlights onto MCA record deals, the Justice Department came to MCA's rescue and undermined the work of investigators by assigning them to other cases. William Knoedelseder, of the *Los Angeles Times*, provided detailed coverage about how the Justice Department pulled the rug out from under Marvin L. Rudnick's investigations; Rudnick had been acclaimed as one of the most effective prosecutors in the Department's Organized Strike Force. While creating a brick wall between Rudnick and MCA, the department nonetheless permitted him to prosecute Pisello for tax evasion. Because MCA had claimed that Pisello was neither an employee nor an agent for the company, his prosecution would not tarnish MCA's highly protected reputation.

Pisello's deal to sell millions of cutouts was based on the willingness of John LaMonte, a small-time distributor of cutouts who had served time in prison for counterfeiting, to buy the records. LaMonte was looking for a big score. He and Pisello cut a deal in which LaMonte would purchase 4.2 million albums and cassettes for $1.3 million. Pisello had led LaMonte to believe that the purchase would include recordings by some of the most popular artists as well as those who were long forgotten or who never made names for themselves at the outset of failed careers. LaMonte was being blindly led into a house of mirrors.

He was so eager to close the deal and collect a huge payout that deception and double-dealing were not in his mind's scenario of a big payout. Even when Pisello demanded off-the-books payments in cash and two sets of invoices, LaMonte couldn't imagine the final act of the con game in which he was the sucker. To add to the malodorous brew, Morris Levy showed up and guaranteed payment to MCA. Though LaMonte knew of Levy's unsavory reputation and his tight-fisted reluctance to part with money, he was only slightly suspicious. LaMonte figured he could control the situation, and Pisello assured him of the money he would make. And so LaMonte agreed to accept delivery of cutouts from sixty tractor trailers that arrived at his warehouse. However, his dreams of selling millions of cutouts erupted into a nightmare when he discovered that 600,000 records by popular groups and solo artists had been scooped off the top like cream off of plain milk. He now saw clearly that he was presented with a cornucopia of records by failed singers and decades-old one-hit wonders as well as vanity audition recordings by amateurs. Pisello had sold the most valuable records to one of LaMonte's competitors. Now Levy, as a guarantor of payment to MCA, demanded payment for the entire shipment. LaMonte angrily refused to pay for the shipment. The more Levy demanded payment, the angrier he became at LaMonte's steadfast refusal to pay.

A frustrated Levy called upon of his mob associates, including Gaetano "Corky" Vastola, to collect the money. Corky was not a man to waste words. He paid a visit to LaMonte and uncorked a punch that splintered LaMonte's jaw, fractured an eye socket, and crushed his sinus cavities. LaMonte, thereafter, needed very little convincing to become an undercover government witness, later entering the witness protection program. He gathered enough evidence that led to Levy and Vastola being arrested, indicted, and put on trial for extortion and conspiracy. As soon as the press began reporting on the events that triggered the arrests and trial, MCA washed its hands of Pisello. They were shocked (absolutely shocked!) that such a scheming scoundrel had taken advantage of MCA's good name.

But that wasn't all. The Justice Department now decided to bust those involved in payola, which is a scheme to bribe disc jockeys to play particular records. Prosecutors were encouraged to pursue payola culprits by MCA, which was pleased to have a judicial spotlight shined on those not connected to the giant music company. Payola had become a major influence, involving millions of dollars collected and spent by a loosely knit group of independent promoters, known as the Network. Each of its members spent tens of thousands of dollars to get a single record onto a radio station's playlist, and thousands more to keep it there. Fees varied according to the size of a station's listenership.

Indeed, the payola investigation was excellent PR for MCA because it was a much hotter news story than the Pisello cutout scam. Because the payola investigation became front-page news, Pisello was shipped off like second-rate cargo to the back pages and consigned to small paragraphs. And in case prosecutor Rudnick still wanted to go after MCA, he was warned that the company had very influential friends, not only in the LA legal community but also in Washington. To investigate and indict people at MCA would not only take him down a road of potholes and dead ends but would ultimately result in his driving off a high cliff. He didn't see that cliff until after he was summoned to Washington, where he was warned not to embarrass MCA. He soon was fired for insubordination and failure to follow orders.

Morris Levy did not fare well: he was found guilty of the extortion of John LaMonte, sold his music business holdings in 1990 for $70 million, and died before he could begin his ten-year sentence. Corky Vastola was sentenced to seventeen years in prison. "No MCA executives were ever charged with wrongdoing. MCA, Inc. was sold in 1990 to Japan's Matsushita conglomerate for $6.1 billion. Lew Wasserman made $300 million on the sale."[6]

The following is excerpted from the *Los Angeles Times*:

> *A report by internal corporate auditors of MCA Inc. indicates that MCA Records was more deeply involved with reputed organized crime figure Salvatore Pisello than previously revealed in court.*
>
> *The Los Angeles–based entertainment firm's auditors recently prepared a nine-page confidential report filled with de-*

tails of the record unit's dealings with Pisello, who last month was sentenced to two years in prison for income-tax evasion. The Times obtained a copy of the MCA internal report, which sources say was given to MCA directors at the firm's annual meeting in Chicago on Tuesday.

Law enforcement officials have previously identified Pisello as an "alleged high-ranking soldier" of New York's Gambino organized crime family. Before Pisello's sentencing April 22, a prosecutor had described in court records several dealings between Pisello and MCA Records.

MCA previously said that it had no knowledge of Pisello's background before his conviction and that it had cooperated fully with the Justice Department's investigation. Among other things, the MCA internal audit report says that MCA Records paid Pisello 3% of the net proceeds from a distribution deal that MCA had made with New Jersey-based Sugar Hill Records, even though the agreement makes no mention of Pisello or his fee, which amounted to more than $76,000 in 1984.

MCA executives are also holding a check from Pisello for another $50,000 but have not cashed it because of supposed insufficient funds, the report says. The check, which was submitted in January but postdated for April, was payment for about 140,000 so-called cutout, or out-of-date, records that were delivered to Pisello-arranged customers in December and January, according to the document.

Executives of the record company, who spoke only on the condition that they not be named, said the company's position is that the internal audit report clears MCA Records executives of any wrongdoing but not of bad judgment.

"We can't say we haven't been stupid; we accept the fact that we were conned," one executive said.

"Our guys simply got swindled out of $250,000," another said. "After the first deal went bad, they should have cut it off,

but, in the hope that they could eventually salvage things, they threw good money after bad."

A sentencing memorandum filed by the Justice Department's Organized Crime Strike Force disclosed Pisello's involvement in the 1983 Sugar Hill distribution agreement, the break-dance mats and Latin music deals, and his role as a middleman in the 1984 sale of 60 truckloads of cutout records valued at $1.4 million to New York-based Roulette Records.

The internal MCA report gives much greater detail on those transactions and discloses a subsequent $50,000 sale of cutouts directly to Pisello.

The MCA sources said that, based on Pisello's role as an "agent" for Sugar Hill, MCA agreed to have Pisello act as a middleman in the April, 1984, sale of nearly 5 million cutout albums and cassettes to Roulette Records. The report does not say whether Pisello was paid anything for his role in that deal.

The report says Roulette Records has paid MCA only about $600,000 of the $1.4 million it owes on the deal, supposedly because Roulette believes that it did not receive all of the cutout titles that it had been promised. According to the MCA internal audit report, there was no formal written agreement documenting the terms of the Roulette sale.

The report says MCA is attempting to retrieve the records it sold to Roulette.[7]

Because Levy, Vastola, and Pisello acted in concert to benefit of the Genovese, Gambino, and DeCavalcante crime families, *Backbeat Gangsters* will contain chapters about mob families and the men who inserted themselves into the music business. Here is a brief, concise description:

The Genovese crime family was run by Vincent "the Chin" Gigante, who was Levy's partner at Roulette Records, and in various other music-related enterprises, including a chain of record stores named Strawberries. William Knoedelseder writes in *Stiffed*,

> *In April 1984, FBI agents were told by a reliable informant that Gigante had developed a "stranglehold" on Levy's recording industry enterprises. Levy was an "earner," a source of ready cash for the organization and a front man in real estate investments, the informant said. He told the agents that a member of Gigante's family owned a substantial interest in Levy's Strawberries record store chain and was receiving large amounts of cash from him.*[8]

Gigante, who was considered one of the cagiest of gangsters, masqueraded as a lunatic, wandering around Greenwich Village in a tattered bathrobe and accompanied by a bodyguard posing as a caregiver. Gigante was labeled the Odd Father in New York tabloids. But behind the mask of insanity was a highly intelligent and devious gangster who controlled one of the largest crime families in the United States. His act of lunacy kept him from being arrested for many years, and just to make sure that his lunacy was confirmed by medical professionals, he regularly had himself checked into psychiatric facilities to update and confirm his diagnosis. Whether doctors were paid to provide fallacious medical opinions or whether Gigante was such a successful actor that he convinced doctors he was crazy remains unknown. One person who was impressed by Gigante's clarity of judgment was Morris Levy, who was not only frequently visited in his office by Gigante but was also seen on the streets of Greenwich Village engaging in walk-and-talks with Gigante.

Gigante had come a long way from his beginnings as a high school dropout and light-heavyweight professional boxer, who engaged in twenty-five bouts, winning seventeen, before eventually rising to be a capo for mob boss Vito Genovese. On his boss's orders, he attempted to assassinate rival gangland boss Frank Costello. The bullet only creased Costello's scalp, and Costello thereafter refused to testify against his assailant. Not wanting any unnecessary attention, Gigante was smart enough to position Fat Tony Salerno as head of the family, while Gigante wielded complete power behind the scenes. That power was not only exerted in the music business but also in the construction industry, labor relations, and any other industry where the mob could muscle its way in.

Beginning in 1997, Gigante's insanity act was investigated by prosecutors, and he was tried, convicted, and sentenced to twelve years in prison for racketeering and conspiracy. By 2003, facing additional criminal charges, Gigante admitted that his insanity act was a hoax. He agreed to accept a guilty plea and was sentenced to three additional years in prison. Following Gigante's sentencing, federal prosecutor Roslynn Mauskopf stated: "The jig is up . . . Vincent Gigante was a cunning faker, and those of us in law enforcement always knew that this was an act. . . . The act ran for decades, but today it's over."[9] Gigante died in the US Medical Center for Federal Prisoners on December 19, 2005.

A retired captain in the DeCavalcante family, Gaetano "Corky" Vastola was an associate of Morris Levy and was often in conversation with him at Roulette's offices. Early in his career he had made a name for himself by successfully promoting concerts by such popular performers as Ray Charles and Aretha Franklin. As noted earlier, he was listed as a songwriter on numerous hit records, such as "You Baby You," "Lily Maebelle," and "Hey Girl." In 1987, he was convicted of assaulting John LaMonte for not paying for a shipment of cutout records. Nevertheless, many people in show business regarded Vastola as a colorful figure, a good friend to top-drawer entertainers, such as Sammy Davis Jr. and others.

In addition to the Genovese and DeCavalcante families, the Gambino family, first under Paul Castellano, then under John

Gotti, had its share of the music business. Gotti, as mob aficionados know, was responsible for the hit on his boss, Castellano. Gotti then reigned supreme and took over his boss's music reins. He was seen at various music industry events, where he was observed in conversation with record company executives, record promoters, and, of course, other mobsters. One of those mobsters was Joseph "Joe Pinney" Armone, who acted as Gotti's go-to guy with record promoters and cutout dealers. In addition, Armone was deeply involved in the sale and distribution of drugs. On October 1, 1964, Armone and eleven other mobsters were indicted in what became known as the French Connection case. They were accused of transporting $20 million worth of heroin over a nine-year period. They had cleverly used US sailors, businessmen, and one corrupt diplomat as couriers. During Armone's trial, an alluring Playboy bunny, not in her bunny costume, seductively sidled up to one of the jurors. Using all of her charms, she attempted to get the juror to accept a bribe. Straitlaced, surprised, and annoyed by the woman's attempt to corrupt him, the juror reported the attempted bribe to court officials. The Playboy bunny, now a former Playboy bunny, was indicted, tried, and convicted of attempting to suborn a juror through bribery and was sentenced to five years in prison. Unable to fix his jury, Armone suffered the indignity of being convicted and was sentenced to fifteen years in prison and fined $820,000. The former underboss and consiglieri died in prison of natural causes on February 23, 1992.

Those and other gangsters of rock and roll could not have controlled so much of the music industry if they hadn't controlled the singers whose talents produced millions of dollars in revenue. Perhaps one of the saddest victims of the gangster overlords was Frankie Lymon. He was one of rock and roll's dazzling young stars. His ingenuously friendly face, big appealing grin, soprano voice, and youthful laughing eyes engaged young fans, who flocked to his concerts and bought his albums. His group, the Teenagers, was one of the earliest doo wop groups of the era. The five-member group released "Why Do Fools Fall in Love" in 1956. It rocketed up the pop charts and proved to be their most successful recording. It made Lymon a big star. Like so many young overpraised singers, Lymon decided he could succeed as a solo singer. Without the Teenagers, Lymon had several hits, but none was as big as the group's first recording. Lymon's initial stardom had inflated his ego, but as the air went out of his distended ego, a sense of failure made him feel like a derelict searching for water on desert sands. It was not water, however, that he found; it would be heroin. As a poor boy of fifteen, he had found an escape into a fantasy nirvana via heroin. By his early twenties, he was the drug's captive. Heroin was keeping his ego pumped up. But when sadly sober, he was circling in a whirlpool of failure, spiraling toward a drain. In 1961, his value greatly diminished, Lymon was no longer a valuable commodity, and Morris Levy cut him loose. Lymon now spiraled ever faster, heading rapidly for the drain of death. He finally went down from a drug overdose at age twenty-five. He died nearly broke. A year before his death, a desperate Lymon sang at my high school graduation for a fee of $50.

Lymon's hit song "Why Do Fools Fall in Love" was resurrected by Diana Ross, who turned her recording of the song into a major hit in 1981. Overnight, the song had a value that attracted potential copyright owners. Several women came forward claiming to be Lymon's widow. It was a tangle of confusing claims because Lymon—though married several times—had failed to divorce any of his alleged wives. They each contacted Levy, who controlled the copyrights and royalties of Lymon's songs. Levy was as eager to part with his copyrights as a lion is to give up the carcass of an animal it has killed. And so a blizzard of lawsuits interrupted the calm of Levy's life. Claims and counterclaims cluttered the files of lawyers. One widow was already married when she married Lymon. Another of the widows said she married Lymon in Mexico in

1965, but she could not produce a wedding license. Lymon's marriage to yet another woman was documented; however, Lymon was still married to two other women at the time, neither of whom he had bothered divorcing. Nevertheless, in 1989, a judge said that the last claimant was the legitimate wife and heir of Lymon's estate. The issue of who wrote "Why Do Fools Fall in Love," however, remained murky. The original single of the record credited Lymon, Herman Santiago, and Jimmy Merchant (members of the Teenagers) as coauthors. Later editions of the record credited Lymon and George Goldner as the writers. But Goldner sold his company to Levy in 1959, and Levy replaced Goldner as cowriter. In 1987, Santiago and Merchant sued Levy. In December 1992, the US District Court for the Southern District of New York ruled that Santiago and Merchant were indeed the coauthors of "Why Do Fools Fall in Love." However, in 1996 the ruling was reversed by the US Court of Appeals for the Second Circuit on the basis that the statute of limitations had expired: copyright cases must be brought before a court within three years of the alleged civil violation, and Merchant and Santiago's lawsuit was not filed for thirty years. Authorship of "Why Do Fools Fall in Love" currently remains in the names of Frankie Lymon and Morris Levy. Whoever said that crime doesn't pay was unfamiliar with the copyright machinations of the record business.

Another victim of Morris Levy's devious greed and that of his cohorts is Jimmie Rodgers, who suffered a severe beating following a dispute with Levy. Rodgers had three top 40 hits in the 1950s (that is, "Kisses Sweeter Than Wine," "Honeycomb," and "Oh-Oh I'm Falling in Love Again"). He not only wanted his royalty payments, but he was so angry at being cheated that he wanted to break away from Roulette Records. He no longer wanted to deal with a company that would withhold his royalties and charge him for expenses that he had not incurred. Morris Levy, however, held on to his profitable singers as if they had been chained to his desk.

Rodgers managed to break free from Levy and record with other labels. However, Levy felt as if he had been robbed of a valuable property. Levy had an eye for fresh new talents, and he had spotted Rodgers early on as a likely singer of hit records. Rodgers became an overnight success after winning a talent contest on the *Arthur Godfrey Show* on CBS television. He was awarded $700, but Levy told him he would earn a great deal more. Rodgers swallowed the bait, and Levy reeled in another hit maker. At Roulette Records, Rodgers produced his three big hit songs. His recordings were bought by millions of fans.

So successful and charming was Rodgers that he was invited to appear again and again on numerous popular TV variety programs with big name stars of the 1950s. He reached a huge audience of 48,500,000 when he appeared on the *Ed Sullivan Show* on September 8 and November 3, 1957.

Even without getting the royalties that Levy owed him, Rodgers's career was moving along with one success after another. It all changed, however, on December 1, 1967. He had been driving on the San Diego Freeway in Los Angeles when he was stopped by an off-duty policeman. Soon thereafter, he painfully awoke in his car with a fractured skull and other injuries that required several surgeries. Initial newspaper reports explained that Rodgers had suffered a severe beating with a blunt instrument. He was the victim of one or more assailants. When questioned in the hospital, Rodgers could not recall how he had been injured or who had beaten him or anything else that could lead police to arresting the perpetrators. The last things he could recall were a pair of blindingly bright lights suddenly appearing in the rear window of his car.

A few days later, the Los Angeles Police Department issued a statement claiming that an off-duty police officer named Michael Duffy (occasionally identified in the press as Richard Duffy) had stopped Rodgers for erratic driving. Once out of his car, Rodger had stumbled, fallen to the ground, and hit his head. The police statement noted that Duffy then called for assistance from two other officers, and the three of them put the unconscious Rodgers back into his car and left. That version was supported by doctors who had treated Rodgers. They had first said the skull fracture was caused by a beating, then changed their story to coincide with the police report. In his 2010 biography, *Me, the Mob, and the Music,* popular singer Tommy James wrote that Morris Levy had arranged the attack in response to Rodgers's repeated demands for unpaid royalties.

And Tommy James knew whereof he was claiming, for Levy owed James from $30 to $40 million in unpaid royalties, and he had been an up-close witness of Levy's relationships with mobsters. It took James years to get his royalties, and only after Roulette Records and its subsidiaries had been sold, following Levy's death. In fact, James did not write his book until Levy and his mob associates had all died.

James made clear that soon after meeting Levy, he realized that Levy used muscle and threats, when needed, to achieve his goals. James and many other singers, who had signed with Roulette, were only given a portion of the royalty money owed to them, and then only if Levy was in the mood to pay them, which was as frequent as the appearance of Hally's Comet. Because Levy was as tight fisted as if rigor mortis had set in, Roulette singers had to go on tour to make money.

But their tours would not have attracted thousands of fans if their records had not scaled up the list of hit records. And in the 1950s and 1960s, many of those records would not have even entered the parade of hits if it hadn't been for prominent deejays willing to play their records repeatedly and promote them as loudly as clanging cow bells. The most powerful of those deejays and a celebrity in his own right was Alan Freed, a beneficiary of enormous amounts of money spent on what came to be known as payola.

Freed started his career in Cleveland, where he was known as Moondog. When he was recruited to be the lead deejay at WINS in New York City, he had to abandon his Moondog sobriquet because a celebrated blind panhandler owned the name. Freed, looking for a name for the rhythm and blues records he played, came up with the phrase rock and roll, an expression in early rhythm and blues songs that referred to sexual intercourse. John A. Jackson writes, "The earliest instance of both rock and roll (yet not yet linked) appearing on a phonograph record label occurred in 1922 when blues singer Trixie Smith recorded 'My Daddy Rocks Me (With One Steady Roll).' The record inspired other blues songs about 'rocking,' including 'Rock That Thing' and 'Rock Me Mama.'"[10]

Freed took advantage of the need for extensive air play and charged a variable amount of money, which depended on how frequently a record was played. Because Roulette Records had the deepest pockets and the backing of the Genovese family, Roulette's records managed to top the charts. Freed benefitted not just by taking $500 here and $1,000 there but was able to buy a large, expensive house with a mortgage owned by Morris Levy. But it wasn't only payola that enriched Freed; he also took cowriting credits for popular songs. One, in particular, was the early Chuck Berry hit "Maybellene." Freed played "Maybellene" intermittently for two hours on his radio show. The record sold more than a million copies at a time when a popular R&B records sold around 100,000 copies.

Freed and Levy went on to produce Alan Freed's rock and roll shows at major theaters in Brooklyn and Manhattan. Each show would feature more than a dozen acts and attract hordes of screaming teenagers, who often got so excited that they would stampede toward the stage, where they would be pushed back by a phalanx of stone-faced cops.

I vividly recall that in the mid 1950s, I attended an Alan Freed rock and roll show at the Paramount Theater in New York. The concert ended with a wild, piano-banging performance by Jerry Lee Lewis as hundreds of teenagers surged like a tsunami toward the stage. Like many others, I was carried away and landed in front of a ruddy-faced cop who waved his night stick at my face. I said that I was helpless to retreat, and he snarled to get back. I was thankful that his club did not crease my skull.

Freed and Levy made hundreds of thousands of dollars from each concert. Indeed, Freed became so popular that he was given his own TV music and dance program named *The Big Beat*. However, the show came to an ignominious end as a result of 1950s racism. To wit: At the conclusion of each show, kids in the audience would come onto the dance floor and do the latest dance steps to a hit record. One day, after Frankie Lymon finished singing, he joined the dancers, grabbed a white girl, and the two began joyfully dancing. No one in the studio thought it unusual; however, the next day, ABC affiliate stations in the South were bombarded with complaints about a black boy dancing with a white girl. Advertisers responded by saying they would only continue to sponsor the show if Freed invited white performers only on his show. Freed, an ardent exponent of integration, refused to compromise. He said he would book whomever he wanted on the show, white and black. The show was quickly canceled.

In addition to being an enthusiastic integrationist, Freed was a carelessly generous man, whose money gushed out of his closets like water out of a broken dam. As a result, by 1958, he was short of funds and requested a $10,000 loan from Morris Levy. Though Freed had requested a loan, "Levy said the money was given to Freed with the 'tacit understanding and agreement' that Freed 'would continue to favor and expose records manufactured by Roulette' and that Freed 'could forget about repayment' of the $10,000."[11]

On such loans was Freed's payola road paved. Rumors abounded, and some executives from large record companies complained to the FBI; it did not take long for the FBI to open an investigation into Freed's activities. Others, eager to see Freed go down in flames, added combustible comments to a bonfire of outrage. Mitch Miller, of Columbia Records, stated that a certain disc jockey would not play records or book any acts that refused to pay him. Miller was careful not to mention Freed's name. However, he "insisted that payola was widespread in the pop music business and that one of the reasons Columbia Records was not heavily involved with rock & roll was the label's refusal to partake of the practice."[12]

Though Freed had been accepting hundreds of checks for playing records, he became cautious, not only because he heard rumors he was being investigated but also because of the quiz show scandals that revealed TV producers were feeding contestants answers to questions. Going forward, Freed would accept all payments in cash only. However, there still existed a paper trail of canceled checks, covering several years, and each of those checks was issued by a record company. Freed was eventually indicted and found guilty. His career in the music business had crashed and burned. Broke and depressed, Freed paid a fine for his participation in payola and retired to Palm Springs. However, that wasn't the end of his problems: the IRS claimed that he hadn't paid taxes for the years 1957 through 1959. He had no money to pay the government and attempted to drown his poverty-stricken state and loneliness in alcohol. In 1964 he was indicted by a federal grand jury for tax evasion and ordered to pay $37,920 in taxes on income he had allegedly not reported. Most of that income was said to be from payola sources.

Freed died at his home in Palm Springs on January 20, 1965. His cause of death was uremia and cirrhosis, likely brought on by years of heavy drinking. He was forty-three years old. He was posthumously honored by the Rock and Roll Hall of Fame, a victim and, some would say, a martyr to his unbridled enthusiasm for making hits. He truly loved rock and roll. After all, he created the phrase.

Years later a more sophisticated form of payola emerged, and it brought unappreciated attention to the Gambino crime family. There were eye-opening investigative reports by Brian Ross on television. Then came newspaper and magazine stories with screaming headlines. Record promoters ducked for cover, hoping that they would not be pursued by subpoenas. Record companies, fearful of being called before congressional investigators, broke ties with record promoters and claimed they had not paid promoters to bribe deejays. The promoters had, in fact, been bribing deejays at radio stations across the country. Like all good mobsters, the promoters had divided the country into individual territories. God forbid that a young, naïve entrepreneur should attempt to become a promoter in another promoter's territory. Unlike Freed, the new breed of promoters was making millions of dollars a year, producing hit records at a huge cost to record companies. Scurrying out of the liability lime light and into safe havens, some of the promoters found legal ways around new restrictions; others went into related music businesses.

The book goes on to describe how mobsters and record executives controlled musicians through the use of drugs; there were dozens of casualties from the use of heroin, not only performers but also record executives who were toppled from their corporate thrones after it was learned they had supplied performers with drugs. Three of the more famous drug deaths were those of Janis Joplin, Jimi Hendrix, and Jim Morrison. As bad as that was, there were also the dozens of murdered rap singers, who were shot to death by rivals, either in gangs or on other labels. Often drugs came into play in those deaths. In addition to the dozens who died from bullets, others wound up in prison, serving lengthy terms.

Many believed that the Mafia's last stand in the music business was the demise of the Westchester Premier Theater, which had been run by members of the Gambino crime family. Ten men, including the president of the theater, who was not a Mafioso, were indicted. The theater, which had been a pop, rock, and folk music emporium, was torn down and replaced by a rental property. It was not the end of the Mafia.

The Mafia has lost many of its top leaders, but it continues to operate. It's a many-headed hydra phenomena that never dies and often grows new heads. No matter how many mobsters are tried, convicted, and sentenced to long prison terms, the Mafia is so profitable and has its tentacles in so many businesses that it presents irresistible opportunities for those who like making money beyond the prohibitions of the law.

CHAPTER 1

Jukeboxes and Rock and Roll

A MUSICAL REVOLUTION ERUPTED IN THE 1950S. FOR TEENAGERS and preteens, the music blew away the benign, colorless, sexually modest music popular with their parents. Kids were not enraptured by the songs of Patti Page, Doris Day, Perry Como, and the cast of *Your Hit Parade* (Snooky Lanson, Gisele MacKenzie, et al.). There wasn't a crew-cutted ivy-leaguer in the rock and roll firmament. No button-down shirts, no khaki trousers, no brown penny loafers. Parents took one look at Elvis, Jerry Lee Lewis, Chuck Berry, and Gene Vincent, the Pied Pipers who would lead their kids into delinquency, drugs, and debauchery. The rockers had long greasy hair, side burns, skin-tight jeans, and black leather jackets and wore suggestive grins or rebellious sneers on their faces, provocations to suburban conformity and decency. Yet kids loved them, loved grooving to the blaring sounds, the strong beats of the new music. They tuned in to their favorite deejays such as Allen Freed, later a victim of the payola witch hunts. The new lyrics were sexually suggestive, all accompanied by obsessive, hard-driving rhythms that quickened heart rates. It was great dance music, great make-out music, great drag racing music. It was the beginning of the counterculture, a revolt against an old order.

In suburban and urban neighborhoods, kids sat at soda fountains or in booths and dropped their coins into tabletop, wall-mounted, or large Wurlitzer jukeboxes. They played cool doo wop records. They tapped their feet and kept beat with the latest Cleftones, Cadillacs, Danny and the Juniors, Platters, Ray Charles, Buddy Holly, Little Richard, Frankie Lymon, and Bo Diddley. Kids were a market for the mob, and the mob quickly filled a vacuum left by the major record companies, such as Decca, Capital, RCA Victor, and Columbia, whose top executives thought that rock and roll was a passing fancy. The mob, already in control of hundreds of thousands of jukeboxes, launched small independent record companies that recorded hundreds of kids who wanted to join an army of rockers. The mob was first out of the gate, the first to make millions from the new music.

Mobsters saw that rock and roll was no shooting star that would burn itself out and leave a dark sky in its wake. The audience for rock just kept on growing, and the number of singers just kept multiplying. During the 1960s, new groups and singers burst upon the scene. Out of nowhere they seemed to come: the Beatles, the Rolling Stones, the Animals, Jeff Beck, Otis Redding, Ten Years After, Rod Stewart, Dave Clark, the Supremes, Tommy James and the Shondells, and a host of psychedelic groups.

From small transistor radios to boom boxes, the music could be heard wherever one went. Kids, out for dinner with mom and dad, could be given a handful of coins to play their favorite songs. If parents were affluent, they might buy or lease a colorful Wurlitzer jukebox for their "finished" basements. The devices stood like science fiction gods, blinking and flashing an array of colorful lights, giddy invitations to enjoy the greatest new music born out of rhythm and blues. If a kid threw a party, all that was needed for a successful get-together was a Wurlitzer in the basement, a bowl of potato chips or pretzels, beer, soda, or a few illicit joints.

Though teenagers had become walking encyclopedias about the latest Top 40 hits, very few of them knew that the mob recorded the music, pressed the records, and distributed all those 45 rpm discs to jukeboxes and record stores. Following the wave of 45 rpm records, there came a stampede of albums. Jukebox owners were not happy about the advent of albums, but the single 45s kept coming and spinning in their machines.

For decades, nickels, dimes, and quarters were innocently fed into jukeboxes the way coins are fed into slot machines. From both devices, the mob collected millions of dollars, a cornucopia of untaxed cash. Jukeboxes were installed in diners, restaurants, bowling alleys, bars, clubs, pool halls, college dining areas, fraternity and sorority houses, recreation centers, and even in some private schools, and the mob took a minimum of 50 percent of all the money that was fed into the machines. In some cases, they even grabbed as much as 70 percent. It was a bonanza.

To fill the huge appetite for new records, the mob turned out songs as if recorded on an assembly line; they opened one record company after another, often fronts for other record companies, tax avoidance schemes galore. They popped up like mushrooms after a rain storm. The companies needed to maintain a steady flow of new records. They needed new talent, and talent flooded into their offices as if driven by hurricanes. Many teenagers wanted to get in on the exciting new music. It was one thing to listen to the music; it would be a great deal more exciting to sing and record the music. And so the record companies handed out contracts like Halloween candies. Aspiring rockers signed contracts and thought they were on a gilded ride to stardom and wealth. Broadway is known as a street of broken dreams, and many of the original rock labels were on Broadway. The mob made fortunes from the talents of naïve young singers, but they also left a detritus of smashed ambitions. Even for those who achieved success, wealth was often beyond their reach. Cheating was endemic.

Fredric Dannen wrote in *Hit Men*, "The pioneers deserve praise for their foresight but little for their integrity. Many of them were crooks. Their victims were usually poor blacks, the inventors of rock and roll, though whites did not fare much better. It was a common trick to pay off a black artist with a Cadillac worth a fraction of what he was owed. Special mention is due Herman Lubinsky, owner of Savoy Records in Newark, who recorded a star lineup of jazz, gospel, and rhythm and blue artists and paid scarcely a dime in royalties."[1]

The mobsters signed teenagers to exclusive contracts, locking them into musical servitude. The mobsters often told their naïve young singers that they couldn't pay royalties because it was extremely expensive to produce, promote, and market records. There was no money left over for royalties. The few who had tried to sue their labels for payment did not have the deep pockets to pursue a legal course of action; others were threatened and became quiescent. Once the mob had the records, they bribed disc jockeys to play the records and made sure the records were in every jukebox they controlled. Owning the records, the singers, and the jukeboxes gave mobsters the kind of monopolistic control they valued.

Though jukeboxes were a boon to rock and roll mobsters who grew small record companies into million-dollar enterprises, jukeboxes had been a source of cash for mobsters long before rock and roll was a dream in the mind of Elvis Presley. One of the original jukebox mobsters was Meyer Lansky, a founder—along with Lucky Luciano—of the National Crime Syndicate. He was the sole distributor of Wurlitzer jukeboxes on the East Coast. His company, Emby Distributing Company, held exclusive licenses to distribute the Wurlitzers, either tabletop or standalone models. Each machine was a signpost to fun, enclosed in a semicircle of rainbow-bright, neon-tube lights. In 1946, prices of a Wurlitzer began at more than a thousand dollars. It was a profitable business for Lansky, and he didn't tolerate competition. Those who maintained jukeboxes other than Wurlitzers were strong-armed by Lansky's emissaries to take only Wurlitzers. Many of Lansky's partners controlled exclusive territories for their jukeboxes. Joe Adonis (a capo in the Luciano crime family), for example, had all of Brooklyn, and Gerry Catena (an underboss in the Genovese crime family) had all of New Jersey. (Catena was also a secret investor in the Bally Manufacturing company, which was a major producer of slot machines. From 1955 to 1957, the company produced Bally Records to take advantage of the opportunities provided by jukeboxes.) No one wanted to sacrifice life and limb by competing with such tough guys, and so the mob's control remained unchallenged.

In his biography of Lansky, Robert Lacey writes: "But there was also the question of the official-looking sticker which every Emby Wurlitzer bore, a certificate claiming that [each serviceman] who stocked the machines with fresh records was a union member. Harold Morris, a serviceman-mechanic along one of Emby's routes in the 1940s testified to a Senate committee that he had not belonged to a union while working for Emby, and that, so far as he knew, some of his fellow servicemen were not union members either. The 'union approved' stickers were a fraud."

The Senate committee also discovered that it was an established practice for jukebox operators in search of new outlets to organize their own bogus union "locals," complete with nominee officials, and "union approved" stickers. Burly and aggressive-looking "members" of these locals would then picket outside bars that refused to take their own particular machines.[2]

By 1960, the mob's control of jukeboxes had not diminished. Indeed, it had grown. *Newsday* reported that "among the pinballs and jukeboxes, the [Senate's McClellan] Committee cited

Jimmy Hoffa's International Brotherhood of Teamsters and Long Island's Teamster local 266."

> *The committee said that 266 was typical of a national Teamster pattern of union-racketeer jukebox operations, in which officials of coin-machine locals either "worked hand-in-glove" with mobsters or else were "part of the underworld" themselves. The report said that such locals obviously had the "consent and approval" of Hoffa and other Teamster brass.*
>
> *The report said that the local's officers never gave "one thought" to aiding workers, but were concerned only with providing "fear and intimidation" to help crooked operators gain control of the industry. It said the local's chief business was the sale of union labels for jukeboxes and game machines in order to extort tribute.*[3]

Those who didn't join the fake unions were often beaten into submission. Some were killed. A Chicago entrepreneur, who controlled eighty-six jukeboxes, refused to pay tribute to the Outfit. For his recalcitrance, he was kidnapped, then murdered.

As part of its investigation of the mob's national control of jukeboxes, the McClellan Committee subpoenaed such mob witnesses as Mickey Cohen of Los Angeles and Russell Bufalino of Pennsylvania. Though intensely and aggressively interrogated, the two mobsters calmly relied on their Fifth Amendment right not to incriminate themselves. They gave up no information about their involvement in the jukebox business. Though steadfast in his redundant replies to questions, Cohen forcefully declared that he was never involved in shaking down operators who were not mob connected. And, of course, he would never attempt to shake down those operators who were mob connected. In other words, he claimed that he never shook down anyone. Bufalino was seen as a more important figure in the mob's control of jukeboxes, for he was a Mafia boss, while Cohen was head of a small Los Angeles gang. The *New York Times* reported, "the committee has received testimony picturing Mr. Bufalino as having left a jukebox business partnership with an alleged member of the Mafia, an underworld organization, to become head of local 985. He was also depicted as having used his union position to discriminate in favor of jukebox companies allegedly backed by the underworld."[4]

So violent and competitive were the battles to control the distribution of jukeboxes that gun fights often broke out between rival gangs fighting for territory. In 1961, one of the notorious Gallo brothers was marked for assassination for his attempt to take over a jukebox territory on Long Island. He and his brothers were primarily a Brooklyn gang with residences and offices on President Street in the Red Hook section of the borough. They owned a company named Direct Vending Machine Company, which placed jukeboxes in bars, restaurants, clubs, and pool halls.

The Gallos, like all gangsters, used violence or the threat of violence to get retail establishments to take their jukeboxes; when not threatening retailers, they were threatening jukebox distributors into making them partners. Sometimes the threats were not sufficient: when Sidney Saul, a jukebox distributor, refused to accept Larry Gallo as a partner, he was beaten by three thugs. When called to testify before a Senate racket's committee, Larry and his brother Joey recited the Fifth Amendment repeatedly. It sounded like a prayer of evasion. When asked if he controlled jukeboxes in New York City, Pennsylvania, Ohio, and West Virginia, Joey looked amused as he repeated his Fifth Amendment right not to incriminate himself. Following his appearance before the committee, Joey walked into Robert Kennedy's office and flirted with the attorney's secretary. Before leaving, he said he admired the room's carpeting and added that it would be ideal for a dice game. Kennedy, surprised to see Gallo in his office, told him to leave and commented that the guy dressed like a 1930s cinema hoodlum.

Though the Gallos dominated all those who got in their way, they nevertheless had to pay tribute to Joe Profaci, boss of one of New York's five Mafia families, a man who was often referred to in the media as the Olive Oil King for his vast distribution network of the oil. The Gallos did not like Profaci and hated having to pay him the lion's share of their jukebox money, but they had no choice. As Mafia soldiers in Profaci's crime family, the Gallos had to pay what was demanded of them. However, their resentment created a mounting fury, and it eventually resulted in a mob war.

On February 27, 1961, the Gallos kidnapped Profaci's underboss, brother, a capo, and a soldier. Fearing for his safety, Profaci made haste and boarded a flight to Miami, where he entered a hospital. With four of Profaci's top-ranking mobsters tucked away, the Gallos sent word to Profaci that they would release the four mobsters if the Gallos got to keep the bulk of their earnings. In addition, the Gallos demanded that Profaci pay them $100,000 before they entered into negotiations with the mob boss. As a demonstration of how far they would go, the Gallos threatened to kill one of the hostages. A few days later, perhaps realizing that the killing of a fellow Mafioso would result in contracts on their own lives, they rescinded the threat. Profaci next assigned Charles "the Sidge" LoCicero to negotiate a deal with the Gallos. They came to an agreement that satisfied the Gallos, and all the hostages were released. Negotiating with the mob is not exactly like a peace negotiation engineered by the United Nations. Back in Brooklyn after his humiliating hiatus, Profaci decided to kill all the Gallos. First on his list was gang member Joseph "Joe Jelly" Gioielli, to be followed by the murder of Larry Gallo. Gioielli was murdered while fishing, his body dumped into the Atlantic Ocean. Next came the attempted murder of Larry Gallo. While sitting at the bar of the Sahara Club, Larry was set upon by two men, who began strangling him with a rope. Fortunately for Gallo, a policeman entered the bar, and the panicked killers fled out a back door. Larry survived with a rope burn around his neck. Realizing they were targets of Profaci, the Gallos went to war with their former boss. The Gallo war erupted with guns blazing and bombs exploding, each side leaving bodies strewn on the streets of Brooklyn. The tabloids had a field day. Headlines blared and district attorneys said they would round up all the killers and shut down the mob in Brooklyn and anywhere else where bodies were dumped. The war was too much for the Gambino and Lucchese crime families, who preferred to operate out of the glare of publicity. Gangsters are not supposed to be cowboy gunslingers having shootouts on main streets; they are nefarious dealers in criminal activities, who stick to the shadows. The Gambino and Lucchese bosses attempted to engineer a truce, but Profaci would have no part of it. He thought those bosses were secretly scheming to take over his family. To his dying day, which was not long off, he remained furious at what he thought was their betrayal. The angry warlord died on June 6, 1962. He is interred in one of the largest mausoleums in St. John Cemetery in Middle Village, Queens, New York. His only satisfaction about the Gallos had been that Crazy Joey had been sentenced to prison in 1961 for murder. Ten years later, Joey was out and on the warpath again. He went to visit the new boss of the Profaci family, Joe Colombo, who generously lent his name to the family. Gallo demanded that Colombo give him $100,000 to cover his time in prison. Colombo refused and instead offered Gallo $1,000 dollars. Gallo scorned the offer, cursed the new boss, and stomped out of his office. Part II of the Gallo war (known as the Colombo war) soon erupted. Colombo knew how dangerous Joey Gallo could be and decided to have him killed before Joey could arrange for Colombo's death. A Colombo gangster named Vincenzo Aloi was ordered to kill Gallo. He failed, and instead Colombo was shot while addressing his Italian American Civil Rights League in Columbus Circle. He survived until 1978, paralyzed and mostly unconscious. Thereafter, Joey was not long for this world, and he was gunned down in 1972 while having dinner with wife and friends at Umberto's Clam House at 132 Mulberry Street in New York's Little Italy.

Murder and mayhem are part of the gangster milieu, but it's money that takes center stage. And none of the bloodshed that took the lives of a dozen gangsters during the two Gallo (Colombo) wars interfered with the mob's control of jukeboxes and records.

Mobsters, such as Morris Levy, president of Roulette Records (which was a Genovese crime family–connected company), continued to sign up one ambitious singer after another. Levy managed to tie up two of Roulette Records's biggest hit makers: Frankie Lymon and Tommy James. The singers were thrilled to get contracts and then to have hit records. Frankie Lymon and the Teenagers scored a big hit with "Why Do Fools Fall in Love," and Tommy James and the Shondells had their first big hit with "Hanky Panky." Levy, greedy for the value of copyrights and publishing rights, took those rights for himself. And when Lymon and James asked for their royalty payments, Levy's response was, "What royalties?"

One singer whose demands were adamant and relentless was Jimmy Rodgers. He said that if he wasn't paid the money he was owed, he would not only sue but leave Roulette Records for another label. He was threatened and promised a beating if he didn't acquiesce to Levy's demands. Rodgers had two big hits, "Honeycomb" and "Kisses Sweeter Than Wine," on Roulette Records in the 1950s. Levy was not only prepared to beat up Rodgers, he had gangsters from the Genovese and DeCavalcante families who regularly hung around in his office and who would be happy to do the beatings for him.

And, indeed, Rodgers was the victim of a terrible beating, but evidence about who may have ordered the beating has never existed. Rodgers had been driving near the San Diego Freeway on December 1, 1967. He was stopped by an off-duty cop. A few minutes later, he awoke slumped and bloody inside his car; the throbbing pain in his head was the result of a fractured skull. Local newspapers reported that Rodgers had suffered a severe beating from a blunt instrument used by unknown assailants.

The LAPD stated several days later that an off-duty police officer named Michael Duffy had stopped Rodgers for driving erratically. Having been ordered out of his car, Rodgers allegedly stumbled and, falling to the ground, he hit his head. The statement went on to report that Duffy called for assistance and two officers arrived on the scene. They put the unconscious Rodgers back in his car and departed. The treating physicians then changed their story and affirmed that Rodgers had hit his head as a result of a bad fall. Years later, in his autobiography, *Me, the Mob, and the Music*, singer Tommy James asserted that Morris Levy, president of Roulette Records, had ordered the attack. Roulette Record singers who thought they were owed royalty payments were silenced by fear of what Levy might do to them.

Another singer whose career was guided by the mob was luckier than Rodgers. He was Tommy Leonetti, who signed a contract with John Ambrosia, an alleged member of the Chicago Outfit. With Leonetti's signature in his pocket, Ambrosia paid a visit to Ted Sipiora, who owned a wholesale record company. Ambrosia insisted that Siporia carry one of Leonetti's records. Siporia refused, saying he didn't like the record, whereupon Ambrosia began tossing a bullet from hand to hand. "These things penetrate flesh, you know," he snidely warned. Siporia, unshaken by the implied threat, shook his head from side to side and said he still didn't like the record. Ambrosia proved to be cagier than a bullet-tossing thug. He created an incentive for Siporia to change his mind. Siporia's resistance vanished like a highway mirage after his jukebox customers started ordering the Leonetti record. Soon another organized crime figure, Joseph Glimco, a Teamster official and capo with the Outfit who had an impressive rap sheet, involved himself in Leonetti's career. Glimco (born Giuseppe

Glielmi), a close friend of Jimmy Hoffa, was known as speaking for the Outfit. If you disagreed with him, you disagreed with the Outfit, and penalties could be severe. While he owned several legitimate businesses not related to the music industry, he owned others that made him a force in the record business. He owned a recording distribution company and several jukebox leasing companies. While independent record labels were proliferating and signing young musicians, the Senate's McClellan Committee, investigating labor unions and organized crime, began an investigation of Glimco's jukebox businesses. At the conclusion of its investigation, the committee concluded that Glimco was the "boss of the jukebox rackets." The information was turned over to a grand jury, but Glimco was never indicted. It was later alleged that he bribed witnesses to avoid indictment and so was never prosecuted on these charges. Prior to the grand jury investigation, the Select Committee held a week-long hearing during which witnesses testified they had been threatened, assaulted, and intimidated by Glimco and his associates and that they had been forced to sign over portions of their wages to him; business owners testified that he had extorted them, that he had bribed witnesses to avoid prosecution and/or imprisonment, and that he had signed sweetheart deals to keep his jukebox empire thriving.

Undeterred by the law, Glimco called Robert Lindeloff, president of the Music Operators of Illinois, and firmly suggested that at the next meeting of the operators' association that Leonetti's record be accorded the honor of being named the "record of the day," thus making it the number one jukebox selection. "Lindeloff said that he refused the request."[5] Yet no one was an impenetrable fortress that could withstand a full-fledged assault by the mob. Leonetti got his record played and placed in jukeboxes, though his career was not one of numerous hit songs. In fact, he was known as a "one-hit wonder," though the epithet should have been corrected to two-hit wonder, for two of his songs, "Free" and "I Cried," made it onto *Billboard*'s pop charts. Perhaps to free himself from the mob's grip, Leonetti moved to Australia, had a successful career, and wrote music for movies and plays, there and here. Unlike Jimmy Rodgers, he suffered no injuries.

Without the limited success of Leonetti, the Chicago Outfit continued to make millions of dollars in the record and jukebox industries. The Chicago market had been ripe for Outfit harvesting. The city had more than one hundred jukebox distributors and more than ten thousand jukeboxes at the time Leonetti was trying to make a name for himself. The jukeboxes generated several million dollars a year, all cash, which is how the mob likes its funds.

In addition to Glimco, the Outfit had another star earner named Fred "Jukebox Smitty" Smith, a seasoned expert in the area of jukebox extortions. "He bullied and brutalized his way into orchestrating a massive industry shakedown that lasted decades and made him and his associates rich. In 1940, Michael Boyle, boss of the Electrical Workers Union, installed Smith as head of the union's jukebox division. Working as a business representative for Local 134, Smith introduced industry regulations that forced vendors to pay exorbitant fees or dues to operate. Vendors had to join an 'association' to protect their jukebox locations from outside competition. They were required to belong to a 'union' that acted as the association's enforcement arm. Smith also forced vendors to subscribe to the Commercial Phonograph Survey, a marketing and public relations firm. These fee-collection organizations offered no real benefits or services and were designed to simply fleece vendors. Smith's shakedown schemes were endless. Another popular scam was to force vendors to stock their jukeboxes with counterfeit or overpriced records sold from companies controlled by mobster Charles English [born Charles Inglesia]. Smith also required them to affix to their machines 'union stamps,' sold exclusively by him and renewable every quarter. Investigators determined that, between payoffs, salary kickbacks and regulatory fees, Smith and his associates split over $150,000 annually."[6]

The Outfit also made an arrangement with the Recorded Music Service Association, the jukebox operators, and distributors. It placed Sam Greenberg as president of the association and Hyman Larner as its executive secretary and general manager. Larner, who was a cautious man, wanted to maintain a low profile, so he changed his name to Thomas "Red" Waterfall, a name that caused some to think that the executive secretary was a Native American. Juke Box Smitty maintained his position with Local 134 of the International Brotherhood of Electrical Workers, a union, where he was the undisputed boss. It had been Larner and Smitty who decided that operators should be coerced into joining the union and pay tribute. The association handed out union labels and told jukebox operators that they could not gain union membership unless they put an Electrical Workers Union label on each of their machines. Without a union label, jukeboxes were subject to various electrical malfunctions and records would not arrive. If one refused to join 134 and pay the street tax, he would be met first with the destruction of his jukeboxes and then, if still recalcitrant, subjected to a beating. And so it went with numerous operators, many of whom were constantly forced to up their regular contributions. Either pay up or go out of business. Of course, they had to pack their jukeboxes with records forced upon them by the mob.

To increase the value of its jukebox racketeering, the Outfit's own company, Lormar Distributing, pressed records for jukeboxes. The frontman for the company was Charles English, who had regular dealings with Larner. English and Larner intimidated jukebox operators to buy records from their company. And many of those records were counterfeits of popular songs.

As cautious as Larner had been, he could not evade the pursuit of congressional investigators. On February 26, 1959, forty-four-year-old Larner, having been tracked down to his home in Florida, was forced to take the stand in front of the dour faces of the Senate McClellan Committee. Larner had claimed an annual income of $8,700. With accusatorial irony, the committee members asked Larner how, on such a modest income, he was able to buy six cars, two twenty-seven-foot cabin cruisers, a home in Florida, and a pair of apartments in Chicago. Not finished nailing him for tax evasion, the committee then asked if he hired thugs to beat up jukebox owners and to throw acid on their jukeboxes if they refused to join his association. Larner, like many others, refused to incriminate himself. He left the hearing a man undeterred. He continued to do business in the record and jukebox business, and he ventured into record counterfeiting and bootlegging. Whether selling stolen records or counterfeit records, he was making a fortune for himself and the Outfit.

> *Hyman Larner died at the age of 87 and was buried in a crypt in Waukegan, Illinois. He was convicted only once in his whole life . . . and never opened his mouth. In his prime he made a lot of money and had many connections, both in the underworld and in the upper world. One thing is for sure, Larner was the last one of the underworld's big leaguers [who] took a lot of the Outfit's dark secrets and its history to his grave.[7]*

While the mob generally preyed on young singers out to make names for themselves, they were also able to take advantage of well-established entertainers. One such person was singer/actress Debbie Reynolds. She was encouraged to record songs and videos for a device that was intended to be an advance on jukeboxes. It was an audiovisual jukebox named the Scopitone. Reynolds, eager to augment her income and reach a larger audience than she normally attracted, signed onto a venture that was controlled by Gerry Catena of the Genovese crime family and Vincent "Jimmy Blue Eyes" Alo, a gambling partner of Meyer Lansky. In 1964,

Reynolds was persuaded by her then manager to use a Hollywood production company to produce music videos for Scopitone machines. She and her manager did not know that Catena and Alo controlled Scopitone.

Scopitones, which were manufactured by a Genovese-owned company, would be sold for $3,500, plus $720 for the rights to thirty-six movies played by the machines. There was also a $60 monthly fee for removing old movies and replacing them with new ones. Altogether, ten thousand Scopitones were expected to be sold. One machine was even installed in the White House.

Reynolds and her manager produced four black-and-white and color movies per month for the machines in 1965. Their movies were aimed at an adult audience, and to add to the allure of the movies, Scopitone included as many sexually suggestive titles as possible. Scopitone also decided to focus on the large youth market. Major pop singers, such Frankie Avalon, Bobby Vee, and James Darren, were featured on Scopitone. But Reynolds continued to record songs from the standard American Songbook that were multigenerational in appeal.

Reynolds's smooth-running relationship with Scopitone was about to become a bumpy ride. In 1966, Tele-A-Sign, which owned Scopitone, became a target of a Justice Department investigation. When news broke in the *Wall Street Journal* that witnesses were being called to testify about Tele-A-Sign, investors couldn't dump their stock fast enough. What had seemed like a brilliant invention that would generate millions of dollars in sales was suddenly being portrayed as just another mob-run business. The company collapsed in 1969, and so ended the brief but promising audiovisual jukebox. Having reportedly lost hundreds of thousands of dollars, Reynolds blamed her husband for getting her involved with Scopitone. In fact, she went on to state that she had been robbed by all of her husbands. Yet she also said that Scopitone was twenty-five years ahead of its time. Indeed, it was so far ahead of its time that consumers didn't understand its value and so not enough people bought the machines.

After the plug had been pulled on Scopitone, Jimmy Alo was convicted of obstructing justice and giving false answers to the SEC. He was sentenced to five years in a federal prison. Robert Morgenthau, US district attorney for the Southern District of New York, stated that Alo was one of the most significant organized crime figures in the United States, and he went on to claim that he had been a longtime partner of Meyer Lansky, who stood at the apex of organized crime.

Gerry Catena received special mention, not from Morgenthau but from *Fortune* magazine, which surmised that Catena was the fourth richest mobster in the United States. It didn't note that Catena had been a secret investor in the famous slot machine company Bally Manufacturing. When that became publicly known, the company's president and CEO, William T. O'Donnell, resigned. Once he was gone, the company got a casino license to operate Bally's Atlantic City casino. When called to testify before the New Jersey State Commission of Investigation about his rackets, Catena (unsurprisingly) refused to incriminate himself. For his silence, he served five years at the Yardville State Prison.

The mob's involvement in the jukebox business continues to this day. Not only do they coerce, threaten, beat up, and kill non-mobsters who refuse to cooperate, but they also kill one another. In New York City recently, an ambitious young man named Anthony Zottola wanted to take over his father's real estate and jukebox empire. In order to do so, he hired a violent street gang of killers. The prize for Anthony of taking over his father's business would be millions of dollars. The father, Sylvester Zottola, an alleged Mafia associate, had not acceded to his son's ambitions. According to the *New York Times*, "As part of the plot, a group of brutal and bumbling assassins tracked Sylvester Zottola for about a year before fatally shooting him in late 2018 as he sat in his S.U.V.

at a McDonald's drive-through in the Bronx. Anthony Zottola was convicted last year of murder-for-hire and conspiracy, and on Friday, a federal judge sentenced him to life in prison, the mandatory minimum. The judge, Hector Gonzalez, said Mr. Zottola had subjected his family to a reign of terror."[8]

The *Times* did not note whether the McDonald's, where the elder Zottola met his end, had a jukebox.

CHAPTER 2

Morris Levy

The Godfather of Rock and Roll

HE WAS A LARGE, INTIMIDATING MAN. HIS HARD-EYED STARE
could bore holes in the confidence of youthful singers. His big
fists were like unpadded boxing gloves that could batter enemies
and deadbeats. He was Morris Levy, a mob-connected record producer, whose enormous greed was boundless.

He was born on August 27, 1927, in the Jewish section of
Harlem. There, his father died of pneumonia in 1928. The widow
Rachel Levy suffered from numerous maladies and barely earned
a living wage. She and her two sons, Morris and his older brother,
Zacharia (born 1922 and called Irving), subsisted on relief payments from the government. The family moved into a tenement in
the Bronx. It was a world where kids with the hardest, fearless fists
learned to use violence to get what they wanted. Gangs of street
delinquents proliferated, mugging defenseless youngsters and
oldsters, threatening peddlers and newsstand operators for weekly
retainers so as not to have their stands and carts incinerated. Those
who did not go in for muggings and protection rackets quit school
in their early teens to help support their downtrodden families.
Zacharia left school after completing the sixth grade and got a job
as a printer's apprentice. Morris, quick to anger and impulsively

45

violent, was destined to travel on a road paved with daring, unscrupulous deeds.

If many poor kids wore their resentments like epaulets on their shoulders, Morris had more than chips of anger on his shoulders. He had a pair of bricks, ready to crush the heads and hands of his enemies. He was a bright boy, bored by school, and impulsively violent. His anger turned into burning fury one day at school. He had been one of two students who had passed a math test, yet the small martinet who taught the class made all of her students stay after school to do extra math work. Morris naturally thought it unfair that he should be punished for not having failed the test. He rose to his feet and loudly protested. His protest was met with an attitude of "how dare you speak to your teacher so disrespectfully." She peremptorily ordered him to sit down and shut up. If not, she would make sure that his family's relief checks were stopped. A furious Morris leapt from his seat, ran to the front of the classroom, grabbed his teacher's wig, yanked it from her head, and flung it to the floor. While crushing the wig with one foot, Morris noticed a bottle of ink, snatched it, and poured its blue-black liquid onto the teacher's head. Outraged, she screamed and sputtered, throwing her arms up as if attempting to protect herself. Morris took off as fast as a getaway bank robber knowing the police were speeding to arrest him. He knew that, if caught, he would be treated to a few skull-cracking blows from a billy club. After that, he would be expelled from school. He might even wind up in reform school. He took off for a safe haven. By thumb and shoe leather, he made his way to Florida, where he talked his way into a job in a nightclub. He became a hat check boy and made his first acquaintance with mobsters.

Richard Carlin quotes Levy, saying, "When I was 14 or 15 I worked for people that were in the Mob because they were the people that owned the clubs. They liked me because I was smart, I was a hard-working, and I was a tough kid."[1]

After deciding that he was no longer in jeopardy, Levy returned to New York and got a job as a photographer in a nightclub, but soon World War II stalled his upward mobility. He enlisted in the Navy and was kept out of harm's way by being stationed in the city. Levy had no complaints, for he was getting to know many of the mobsters who ran the city's nightclubs. He saw the money that the mob was taking in from their nightclubs, and he was hungry to join the feast. The war soon ended, and Levy was discharged from the Navy. His time in service had been uneventful. The city was now bustling with activity; former servicemen, along with their wives or girlfriends, were living joyfully, glad to be alive, and spending money with celebratory abandon. Levy was primed to profit from it all. He learned of a nightclub, not a fast-food restaurant, with the unattractive name of Topsy's Chicken Shack located on Broadway and 47th Street. He went to his mobster friends and asked them to finance the purchase of the club. They agreed, taking the lion's share as expected but turning over the hatcheck concession to Levy. The club was renamed the Royal Roost, less of a barnyard sobriquet than its previous name. Levy had fallen in love with jazz while in Florida and convinced his partners to turn the club into a magnet for jazz enthusiasts. Within a few months, it became one of the hottest jazz clubs in the city. In addition to featuring some of the most talented bebop musicians, the club was noticed for not being on New York's commercial jazz street, West 52nd Street. Though successful, the club became a source of discontent for its owners, who argued frequently amongst themselves. Each had a different vision of how the club should be run. Levy decided to look around for another club that could become an even more powerful magnet for jazz, especially bebop. Levy, his brother, Irving, and several other investors purchased their new club from Joseph "Joe the Wop" Cataldo, a well-known New York mobster who owned several nightclubs, which were popular hangouts for wiseguys. The club was located below street level at

1678 Broadway and christened Birdland. There is some dispute about the origin of the club's name. Peter Eisenstadt and Marc Ferri write in *The Encyclopedia of New York City*, "Named by its owners Morris and Irving Levy for the alto saxophonist Charlie Parker (known as Bird,) who performed there."[2] However, others believe that the name was derived from Levy's previous avian-named clubs. Birdland opened on December 15, 1949, and became an immediate and dazzling success. Some of the original musicians who appeared that year and in 1950 included Hot Lips Page, Maxie Kaminsky, Charlie Parker, Harry Belafonte, Lester Young, Stan Getz, and Lennie Tristano. The club operated in its original Broadway location until 1964, when it closed due to a significant increase in rent. From 1949 to 1964, Birdland showcased a who's who of jazz talent and attracted famous writers, artists, actors, and socialites to its concerts. It advertised itself as the Jazz Corner of the World, and no one denied it. The club offered seating for five hundred attendees and charged a modest entrance fee of $1.50. Drinks were another matter.

While money nearly flooded in, so much so that there was not room enough in the club's safes, not all was giddy greedy glee at Birdland. Gloom descended on Morris in 1959, when his brother, Irving, was stabbed to death by a small-time hoodlum who took umbrage when Irving kicked the man's wife out of the club. Irving had assumed the woman was a prostitute soliciting customers in the club. Prostitutes were prohibited from soliciting in the club, and, when spotted, were unceremoniously shown the street. Several days after the murder, the *New York Times* reported that the killer was Lee Schlesinger and his wife, Terry, was indeed a prostitute. The killer had a lengthy rap sheet for robbery, forgery, grand larceny, and carrying concealed weapons; soon his résumé would include murder. After being arrested and tried, Schlesinger was found guilty and sentenced to life in prison. Some mobsters and gossip columnists speculated that Schlesinger had actually been hired to kill Morris Levy but got the wrong Levy. No evidence ever came to light to prove that possibility.

Morris may have cheated a few mobsters along the way, hence the suspicion that he may have been a target for murder. But it's unlikely that Morris was foolish enough to cheat mobsters. Instead it was musicians and composers he cheated. An early indication of Levy's glomming his name onto songs composed by others is "Lullaby of Birdland." Prior to its composition, he had been approached by representatives from ASCAP who wanted payment for the songwriters, whose music Levy had been playing at Birdland. It was an "aha" moment for Levy, who realized the potential wealth he could accrue if he owned the copyrights to all that music. He quickly formed a music publishing company, naming it Patricia Music to honor his wife, and he then proceeded to acquire by various means, deceitful and dishonest, the rights to songs played at Birdland.

Richard Carlin writes, "Levy quickly realized that owning the music that was played in his club would give him extra income. He began with the nightly radio broadcast from Birdland, which he sponsored. He decided that the show should have a signature theme song, and reasoned that it should be played to introduce each hour of the broadcast."[3]

The song was composed in 1952 by George Shearing with words by B. Y. Foster, a pseudonym for George David Weiss. Though Levy originally wanted Shearing to record a song that he wrote, Shearing refused, telling Levy he wouldn't be able to play such a song. It would make him feel uncomfortable. Gentlemanly Shearing never hammered home the point that Levy was neither a composer nor a lyricist. Instead Shearing generously agreed to share the rights to the song. Shearing's wife was furious that her husband had given up half the rights to a song that became a jazz standard, recorded by numerous musicians. It was the first in a long list of songs that Levy would claim as his own.

Levy's next step was to form his own record company, where his modus operandi would be listing himself as writer or cowriter of many songs. In 1956, he started Roulette Records with George Goldner. The company recorded jazz and rock and roll, and, to no one's surprise, Levy owned nearly all the songs Roulette released. Levy's mob partners and associates realized what a gold mine Roulette was fast becoming, and the company became a crime family enterprise. Very few people at the time knew that the Genovese crime family was Levy's dangerous partner.

In addition to the mob, Levy's partner in Roulette George Goldner was a brilliant record producer with a jeweler's eye for evaluating talent. He had begun his record business in 1948 before the great advent of rock and roll. His first label was Tico, which he marketed to Latin and Hispanic listeners. It featured such popular musicians as Joe Loco, Tito Puente, Machito, and Tito Rodriguez. Tico proved to be a top label for Goldner, selling not only to Latinos and Hispanics but also to black and white audiences. In fact, of all Goldner's labels, Tico would prove to be the most successful.

Goldner was riding high on his winning ability to generate hits. In 1953, he organized the Rama label to record jazz and rhythm and blues music. "He must've been astonished with what happened with one of his early releases, the fifth record in the company's history; in fact, a group harmony number by an act called the Crows, entitled 'Gee,' featuring an arrangement co-written by veteran R&B singer-pianist Viola Watkins. 'Gee' was issued in the spring of 1953, and by the summer was charting high not only as an R&B release, but as a pop number. Goldner and just about everyone else in the business was surprised, not only by the *legs* that 'Gee' showed but by the fact that it was being bought by a surprisingly large number of white teenagers."[4]

Like a batter who can only hit home runs, Goldner went on to discover Frankie Lymon and the Teenagers and Little Anthony and the Imperials, all of whom recorded major hits with Goldner.

And like Levy, he didn't just record and market his records, he also added his name as a cowriter of the many hit songs he recorded. Perhaps the most well known is "Why Do Fools Fall in Love," first recorded by Frankie Lymon, then by Diana Ross, which became a major hit.

Though Goldner had a flexible standard for his ethics, he was nevertheless a major force for making popular music popular. Bruce Eder writes on the *All Music* website that George Goldner "discovered more talent, both in front of the microphone and behind the scenes, than most producers get to record in a lifetime. Moreover, in the decades since, much of the music that Goldner recorded and released has retained an astonishing appeal to generations of listeners."[5]

On the dark side, Goldner was something other than a record producer and a soi-disant lyricist. He was a perfect sap for the mob, for he was an obsessive gambler, just what mob loan sharks feed on. As a result, Goldner was often swimming in an ocean of debt, and it often seemed as if he would drown or be taken down by the sharks to whom he owed money. To save himself, Goldner agreed to sell his shares in Roulette to Levy. In addition, Levy temporarily sated his voracious appetite by gobbling up labels that Goldener had owned independently, including not only Tico but Rama, Gee, and later on End and Gone. Levy had prepared a feast of musical properties that he and his mob partners could gorge themselves on for years, at least until the law put an end to the banquet.

Having covered his gambling debts, Goldner, the intrepid entrepreneur, started two new labels: End Records and Gone Records, both of which would be distributed by Roulette. As expected, Goldner's eye for seeing future hits remained as sharp as ever. With the Flamingos and the Chantels, Goldner produced hits that shot up the charts. Never satisfied with yesterday's successes, Goldner started forming a new label named Firebird. Before the bird could take off, Goldner fell off his perch and dropped dead of a massive heart attack on April 15, 1970, at age fifty-two. In the annals of twentieth-century popular music, Goldner holds a place as a visionary who could see hits while others attempted to follow his lead. Among those he discovered and promoted were the Crows, the Cleftones, the Teenagers, the Flamingos, the Chantels, the Valentines, and the Shangri-Las, all of whose CDs continue to sell, while hexagenerians, septuagenarians, and octogenarians listen to their old vinyl albums.

Goldner was an important partner for Levy, but Levy had his own visions of what could generate large sums of money. He did so by sending his musicians out on tour. Not only did he receive a percentage of what his musicians earned, he was also able to sell copies of their records wherever they performed. And wherever they performed there were disc jockeys who would be happy to play the performers' records, over and over again. The disc jockeys were incentivized to do so by being paid by Roulette. It became known as payola. The more they played, the more money they received. It was a good investment, for increased air time meant increased record sales.

The man who gave payola a bad name was Alan Freed, a popular disc jockey and impresario in Cleveland. He was the most popular radio personality among teenagers who loved the rhythm and blues songs he played. Many of the songs had been recorded by black musicians, and most white-owned radio stations refused to play the songs. Freed was one of the first disc jockeys to realize that black and white kids loved the same music. And when he produced concerts of black and white rhythm and blues singers, the audiences were completely integrated. Nobody had seen anything like it. To staunch traditionalists, Freed was a dangerous provocateur who was said to be lighting a fuse that would erupt in explosive race wars. Instead it resulted in a booming rock and roll record business and sell-out concerts.

Freed's reputation spread like an uncontrolled forest fire, burning down old cultural myths. In New York City, radio station owners heard of the crazy disc jockey from the Midwest, but none of them wanted him in their studios. One man, however, was desperate to save his near bankrupt station. The station was WINS. The station needed a shot of show business magic to turn red ink to black. Freed was the magician who could it. In New York as in Cleveland, he became as popular as the singers on his program, *The Big Beat*—so much so that he was able to put on rock and roll concerts featuring top acts with himself as master of ceremonies. To help finance his early operations, he brought in Levy as a partner. Together, they were making hundreds of thousands of dollars from concerts at the Brooklyn and Manhattan Paramount Theaters. Thousands of kids, black and white, flocked to the concerts. As the singers performed, kids danced in the aisles, jumped up and down on their seats, or rushed toward the stage. In some cases, mayhem erupted and cops had to hold back waves of surging bodies, eager to join the entertainers on stage. Levy and Freed were a perfect match. (Please see chapter 3 about Freed.)

Whether Freed knew about Levy's mob connections is not known. But he would have found out in 1958, when *Billboard* magazine announced that Gaetano "Corky" Vastola, a member of the DeCavalcante crime family of New Jersey, was an investor in Roulette Records. It was soon whispered about that Levy had introduced Vastola to Freed, and that Vastola became his manager. Vastola knew the music business, for he was a concert promoter of numerous top acts, including Ray Charles and Aretha Franklin. He was also seen playing eighteen holes of golf with pal Sammy Davis Jr. Of course, like other investors in Roulette Records, Vastola was occasionally listed as a songwriter, particularly of doo wop records of the 1950s and 1960s, such as "You Baby You," "Lily Maebelle," and "Hey Girl." Though indicted in 1960 for trademark offenses, Vastola got away with a mere slap on the wrist: a one-year suspended sentence and a $215 IRS fine.

The singers recorded by Roulette Record may have thought that Vastola was just another tough producer, but he was also an important member of the DeCavalcante crime family, which consisted of about sixty members, including a boss, an underboss, a consiglieri, capos, and soldiers. Most Mafia families hate having their activities spotlighted to the public. And in 1969, Sam "the Plumber" DeCavalcante was deeply embarrassed when the FBI released a 2,300-page report about his crime family members' activities. From 1961 to 1965, the FBI had been eavesdropping on the Plumber, who received his sobriquet as the owner of a plumbing supply business. The eavesdropping tapes revealed not only the problems faced by a conscientious Mafia boss who tried to keep his members fully employed but also his marital problems. To have such problems made public was a challenge to the Plumber's machismo. To add to his embarrassment, the tapes also revealed that he was conducting an affair with his secretary, who was married to his partner in the plumbing business. In movies such as *The Godfather*, made men often speak in Italian to one another. On the FBI tapes, however, one can hear the Plumber speaking Yiddish to his partner, though the Plumber was not Jewish. In addition to his secretary, the Plumber carried on numerous affairs; and when he wasn't romancing, he was bemoaning his problem finding work for the soldiers in his organization. He was quoted saying, "Most of [our soldiers] ain't making much. Those making money give me one third. Say, one makes $600, then he gives me $200 and I don't split with anyone else."[6] On another section of the tapes, a man named Frank Cocchiaro tells the Plumber that he has money problems. He gives his wife $50 a week and pays rent of $125. The Plumber sympathizes, but what can he do? Vastola, however, was a member whose finances didn't worry the Plumber.

Vastola, though a valuable member of the DeCavalcante family and partner in Roulette Records, managed to rock the boat by assaulting a record company executive who refused to be extorted. As a result, Vastola went to prison in 1987. While serving time in the Metropolitan Correction Facility, Vastola had the misfortune of sharing a cell with John Gotti, the boss of the Gambino crime family. Gotti believed that Vastola was a government witness, a rat. He wanted to have him killed, but Vastola survived Gotti's murderous intention, for Gotti got nailed by prosecutors who charged him with conspiracy to murder Vastola, plus loansharking, bribery, tax evasion, and obstruction of justice. As of this writing, a very fortunate Vastola has celebrated his ninety-fifth birthday, living as a free man.

Another long-lived mobster who worked with Levy was Sonny Franzese, who died at age 103. In 1967, Franzese obtained a financial interest in a newly established record company, named Buddah Records. It was an ideal vehicle for Franzese to launder mob money and to pay off disc jockeys. There was an additional company for Franzese to use; it was Calla Records, founded by Nate McCalla, Levy's bodyguard and muscle collector. If someone owed Levy money, McCalla was sent to collect, either with his fists, a weapon, or simply by a few verbal threats. He never returned to Levy's office empty handed. Levy hated having debts on his books, unless, of course, the debts could be written off as tax deductions. McCalla went from strong-arming deadbeats and producing records to promoting concerts. He was able to get some of Levy's partners in the Genovese family to underwrite a concert in Maryland. Unfortunately for McCalla, receipts from the concert disappeared like a magician's rabbit. And like Levy, the Genovese family did not tolerate debtors. Unable to pay off his investors, McCalla took off for Florida, hoping to put distance between himself and mob retribution. Several months after his hasty departure, his decomposing body was stinking up a house in

Fort Lauderdale. In typical Mafia style, McCalla had been shot in the back of his head. Mobster insiders claimed that Levy had no choice but to give McCalla up to his Genovese partners. Some said that Levy actually ordered the hit on McCalla as a favor to Vincent "the Chin" Gigante. The black-owned Calla record company had ceased operations three years before McCalla's death.

Though Vastola and Franzese were powerful mobsters, there was none more powerful at Roulette than Vincent "the Chin" Gigante. He quickly rose to fame, not for his abbreviated boxing career but for his attempted assassination of mob boss Frank Costello. Gigante had been instructed to assassinate Costello by mob boss Vito Genovese, but when Gigante shouted to Costello in the lobby of his apartment building, "This [bullet] is for you Frank,"[7] Costello turned his head and was only grazed. At Gigante's trial, Costello refused to identify the man who fired a gun at him. While leaving the courtroom, Gigante whispered his thanks to Costello. Such is the etiquette of mob bosses.

Though Costello resigned as a mob boss after the attempted assassination, he and his associates, Meyer Lansky, Lucky Luciano, and Carlo Gambino, set up Genovese in 1958 to be arrested as a drug dealer. It was the kind of payback that the more cerebral mob bosses indulged in and had a long history, going back to the arrest of bootlegger Waxey Gordon in 1933. Lansky and Luciano had provided documents to prosecutor Thomas Dewey, who was able to win a conviction against Gordon for tax evasion, resulting in a ten-year prison sentence. To nail Genovese for his attempt to kill Costello, Luciano paid $100,000 to a drug dealer named Nelson Cantellops to sell drugs to Genovese and then testify against him at trial. On April 17, 1959, Genovese was sentenced to fifteen years in prison. Ralph Salerno, a New York City organized crime investigator with the NYPD, told the author that "it is unbelievable that a crime boss would let himself be set up for a drug deal. Bosses keep themselves too isolated to let something like that happen" (interview with author 1991). On February 14, 1969, Genovese died in a prison hospital.

Shortly after Genovese was sent off to prison, Gigante became the boss of the Genovese crime family and a partner of Morris Levy. Gigante and Levy had known each other from their boyhood days in the Bronx and had an easy, mutually cooperative relationship. In the Genovese crime family, however, no member could ever refer to Gigante by name. One either had to create the letter c with a rounded forefinger and thumb or just point to one's chin when referring to him. To protect himself from arrests and indictments, Gigante pretended to be crazy by wandering around Greenwich Village in a tattered bathrobe and mumbling to himself. He was often accompanied on his outings from one of his social clubs by a young man who held his arm and helped him cross streets. Gigante's act was effective for years in preventing the government from prosecuting him, a man who many said was too crazy to run a mob family. It resulted in tabloids naming him the Odd Father.

The man was as crazy as a fox and as voracious as a shark, the perfect partner for Morris Levy. When Levy decided to open a chain of record stores called Strawberries, it was financed by the Genovese crime family and its CEO Gigante. According to Richard Carlin, "Levy's partners in Strawberries were drawn from the Mob. In secretly recorded tapes, Joe Buonanno stated that 'the GIGANTE faction of the Genovese LCN Family owns a share of Levy's . . . Strawberries.' He added that one of Gigante's brothers 'has a piece of Strawberries on the books' as a means of 'getting it that way and also the green'—i.e., the Gigantes planned to take total control of the business and the money it generated."[8]

The chain of more than seventy stores generated millions of dollars that Levy, Gigante, and various mobsters invested in large real estate holdings. Raw land, country estates, and urban buildings, both residential and commercial, were added to their portfolios. Construction contracts of every variety were always nonunion and mob connected. From Massachusetts to Pennsylvania and areas in between, Strawberries was a bank that dispersed funds where needed. In addition to the stores, Levy started a now defunct record label (Tiger Lilly) and would press a limited number of records by unknown singers that no one would buy. Though he would press only a small number of records, he would claim to have pressed a much larger quantity, then dump the records into a warehouse. At the end a year, he would have the records destroyed and use an inflated number to declare a significant tax loss.

One of those who benefitted from Levy and the money generated by Strawberries was Father Louis Gigante, brother of Vincent Gigante. Father Gigante was honored for building low-income housing in the Bronx, but often with mob-connected, nonunion contractors. He also served as a New York City council member. The following appeared in an article titled "The Priest and the Mob" in the *Village Voice* on March 7, 1989. It was written by William Bastone:

> *Morris Levy, the president of Roulette Records, has been a long-time source of ready cash for the Genovese family, particularly Chin Gigante and his live-in companion, Olympia Esposito. According to a 1985 FBI affidavit, Levy money was also "funneled" to Father Gigante in the form of a gift of a piece of upstate property and a low-interest mortgage.*
>
> *The property, located on the edge of Levy's sprawling horse farm in the town of Ghent, was given to Father Gigante in August 1979 with an accompanying $32,000 mortgage at 5 per cent interest. At the time, prevailing rates were between 10 and 11 per cent. In addition to the house loan, records show that Levy also gave the priest a $15,000 "business loan" in 1981.*
>
> *When the Voice first tried to question Gigante about the 1979 transaction in April 1988 (when the FBI affidavit was*

made public), he did not return phone calls. He finally told his tale just before Levy was sentenced last year on federal extortion charges.

On September 20, 1988, Gigante wrote to Stanley Brotman, the federal judge sentencing Levy, and termed the FBI's account of the house deal "a bold lie." Gigante claimed that Levy actually donated the land to Gigante so that the pair could build a home for one of the priest's former secretaries.

In his letter, Gigante explained that he uses a "large part" of his earnings "to take care of my dear friend and loyal assistant" Erma Cava. The priest's former secretary, 55, who is partially paralyzed and confined to a wheelchair, has had a SEBCO senior citizens project named after her. Gigante went on to state that since 1980, Cava "has been living full-time at the farm" and that there she is cared for by "another of my secretaries," who Gigante claimed he also supports. The spacious ranch-style home, which sits on about an acre of land, features a sun room, two-car garage, and a backyard that slopes down to a large pond. "Morris and I visit frequently and I often bring children from the parish to visit and spend time in the country. Erma is still paralyzed on her right side, but we see continued improvement. She is even beginning to speak although she is aphasic," Gigante wrote. He concluded: "I am not involved with organized crime and it is an insult to mischaracterize Morris' kindnesses to me and others as the funneling of money to organized crime. I believe Morris' greatest contribution was the idea to build a home for Erma . . . an unfortunate person who might have been forgotten without us." While appearing heartfelt, Gigante's letter borders on total fiction.

Not only is the deed, mortgage, and phone at the property in the name of Louis Gigante, when the Voice visited the home last year, two cars registered to the priest were in the driveway, but nobody was home. In addition, Department of Motor Ve-

hicle records show that the priest currently registers his Cadillac from the Ghent address as well as three cars owned by his real estate management firm. When a neighbor was asked if he knew where the "Gigante house" was, he immediately pointed it out.[9]

An FBI investigation has shown that since before 1963 Morris Levy has been a lucrative source of cash and property for leaders of the Genovese LCN family. Levy's dealings, the document alleged, had been "primarily through and for the benefit of (Gigante) to whom Levy has passed large cash payments, property and shares in Levy's recording enterprises."[10]

In addition to his other scams, Levy got involved in purchasing cutout albums (records that couldn't be sold except at steep discounts) and forcing distributors to pay inflated prices for buying the cutouts. An entire later chapter will be devoted to a deal to buy cutouts from MCA, then sell the records to a distributor, but not provide what was promised in the original purchase order. The buyer was, nevertheless, threatened and forced to pay MCA for records he did not receive. The entire case turned into a huge scandal that resulted in the indictments of Levy and major mob figures.

The following article by William Knoedelseder Jr. appeared in the *Los Angeles Times* under the title "Head of N.Y. Record Firm Charged with Extortion; 16 Others Arrested in Sweep":

After a two-year probe of alleged mob infiltration of the record business, FBI agents on Tuesday arrested the president of a New York City record company and 16 other people on charges ranging from cocaine and heroin trafficking to extortion.

Among those seized in a dawn sweep were Morris Levy, president of New York City-based Roulette Records; Howard Fisher, Roulette's controller; and Dominick Canterino, reputedly a leader in New York's Genovese crime family.

The arrests were announced at a packed news conference at the U.S. attorney's office in Newark, N.J., on Tuesday morning, soon after 60 FBI agents fanned out across metropolitan New York and New Jersey to make the arrests. The agents were acting on a 117-count indictment handed up Friday by a federal grand jury in Newark. Agents originally set out to pick up 21 individuals, but four remain at large, including Gaetano (Corky) Vastola, identified as a chieftain in the DeCavalcante organized crime family of New Jersey, and Rudolph (Rudy) Farone, allegedly a DeCavalcante soldier.

The Newark probe is one of at least five federal grand jury investigations looking into suspected Mafia infiltration of some segments of the $4-billion-a-year record industry. The other investigations are based in Los Angeles, New York, Philadelphia and Cleveland.

Tuesday morning's raids and arrests were the first public action in the Newark case, which was launched in November, 1984. The investigation utilized extensive wiretap surveillance—including one on Roulette's office phones, it was learned.

Law enforcement sources say the Newark case began as a "classic racketeering investigation" of individuals involved in traditional organized crime activities such as gambling, loan sharking and narcotics trafficking in New Jersey. But the scope of the investigation was broadened to include the record industry in the spring of 1985, when investigators began picking up information that members of the DeCavalcante, Gambino and Genovese crime families had become involved in certain record business transactions.

At Tuesday's press conference, Thomas W. Greelish, the federal prosecutor in Newark, said Levy, Fisher and six alleged organized crime figures named in the indictment were "charged with conspiring to use extortionate means to collect a $1.25-million debt" owed to Los Angeles-based MCA Records *by John LaMonte, the owner of a Philadelphia-area budget-record distributorship called Out of the Past Inc.*

. . . that debt was incurred through LaMonte's 1984 purchase of nearly 5 million so-called cutouts, or out-of-date, recordings from MCA. According to the indictments, the cutouts were sold to LaMonte on credit, with Vastola and Levy guaranteeing LaMonte's payment to MCA. However, after MCA shipped the records to Out of the Past in the summer of 1984, "LaMonte determined that the order had been creamed, meaning that the more valuable items had been taken out," Greelish told the press conference.

When LaMonte subsequently refused to pay MCA for the records, Vastola, Levy, Canterino and Fisher used "physical violence and threats to take over LaMonte's company to enforce their guarantees of payment" to MCA, according to the indictments.

Greelish alleged that the investigation shows that "after a series of discussions among Levy, Vastola and Canterino," LaMonte was severely beaten by Vastola in May, 1985.

Vastola's ties to Levy and the music business go back at least 20 years. According to published transcripts of FBI wiretaps on the phones of Sam (the Plumber) DeCavalcante, Vastola earned half a million dollars from a record counterfeiting deal in 1965.[11]

Levy not only cheated distributors such as John LeMonte but also singers who recorded with Roulette. One of those was popular rockabilly singer Buddy Knox, who had recorded his song "Party Doll" for a small Texas label. Unable to generate national sales, the Texas record company sold the rights to the song and its master recording to Roulette Records. Levy spent a considerable amount of money, including payoffs to disc jockeys, to popularize the song. In each of numerous major cities, "Party Doll" was given extensive air time, played frequently throughout the day, week after week. Levy's investment paid off, for the recording reached number one on the *Cashbox* charts. Though "Party Doll" had sold 1.2 million records, the royalty statement that Levy issued listed a sale of 600,000 records. In addition, or by subtraction, Levy withheld funds from Knox, saying that he had spent a fortune promoting the record and that cost would have to be deducted from royalties. Knox wanted his contract with Levy torn to shreds, but Levy—unsurprisingly—would not oblige Knox and his bandmates. The contract not only tied Knox to Roulette, but it also gave Levy publishing rights and ownership of the master recording. For a number one hit that should have produced about $400,000 in royalty income, Knox and his bandmates received a measly $8,000. He was ultimately able to leave Roulette and signed a contract with Liberty Records. He was voted in the Rockabilly Hall of Fame, and "Party Doll" was named one of five hundred songs that contributed to the shape of rock and roll. Knox died in 1999 of lung cancer at age sixty-five.

Even more badly treated than Knox was Jimmy Rodgers. The record industry became aware of Rodgers after he won a talent contest on the Arthur Godfrey talent show on CBS-TV. He also appeared on TV programs hosted by Jack Benny and Ed Sullivan. It was not surprising that he was a potentially hot property for a record label. The songwriting team and record producers Hugo Peretti and Luigi Creatore nabbed him for Roulette Records. Hugo and Luigi (as they were known throughout the record industry) had an illustrious career in the record industry, especially after leaving Roulette; they produced hits by Sam Cooke and Elvis Presley among various other formidable talents and produced popular Broadway musical albums, such as *Bubbling Brown Sugar*. At Roulette, however, they not only produced Rodgers's number one hit, "Honeycomb," but also his other hits, such as "Kisses Sweeter Than Wine," "Oh-Oh, I'm Falling in Love Again," and

"Secretly." Though Rodgers's records were big-hit money makers, his royalties were tiny. Frustrated by being put off by Levy's excuses, Rodgers finally demanded that Roulette pay what he was owed. He hired accountants who went over Roulette's books, all with varying numbers. Though the accountants provided enough evidence for Rodgers to sue for the money owed to him, he ultimately decided against suing because of Levy's reputation for being connected to the mob. In response to Rodgers's accountants, Levy said he had spent more to promote Rodgers than he generated in royalties. As with Buddy Knox, Rodgers was offered a settlement of $8,000.

Rodgers no doubt knew the dangers of suing Roulette. The menacing presence of mobsters hanging out in Levy's office created an aura of danger for anyone who had the temerity to make demands on Levy. There had been singers thrown out of the office; others were threatened with guns and fists. Nevertheless, the drive to obtain what was owed lived on in the angry hearts of many cheated singers. Rodgers, years after leaving Roulette, still had the option of suing for his royalties. It is why some thought Rodgers had been the victim of a Levy hit in 1967. In his own autobiography, *Me, the Mob and the Music*, another Roulette singer, Tommy James, claims that the attack on Rodgers was paid for by Levy in response to Rodgers's relentless demands for the royalties he had earned.

Here's what happened: While driving in Los Angeles, Rodgers was stopped for erratic driving by police officer Michael Duffy. What happened next are differing two stories without backup evidence. Duffy said that Rodgers stumbled out of the car, fell, and hit his head, resulting in a fractured skull. Rodgers, however, claimed that Duffy, and perhaps two other officers, beat him. Regardless of who was telling the truth, no one could deny that Rodgers was found unconscious in his car. Physicians who treated Rodgers initially said that Roders's skull fracture was the result of a beating; however, they changed their story and concluded that Rodgers had fallen, and the fall had caused his injuries. He required two operations.

Rodgers subsequently sued the city of Los Angeles for eleven million dollars; the three policemen and the Fire and Police Protective League then turned around and sued Rodgers for slander and defamation. Both suits were eventually dropped; in 1973, the city of Los Angeles paid Rodgers $200,000. Both before and after the settlement, rumors flew that Rodgers had been beaten because of his unrelenting demands that he be paid his outstanding royalties. Following his injuries, he suffered from spasmodic dysphonia for a number of years and could hardly sing. Spasmodic dysphonia, also known as laryngeal dystonia, is a disorder in which the muscles that generate a person's voice go into periods of spasm. For a singer it can be a career-ending malady as it manifests in frequent voice interruptions. Even without the interruptions, a singer's voice may suddenly sound strained and off key. The condition is lifelong and may get worse. Though there is no cure for the condition, it may be mitigated by the injection of a botulinum toxin right into the muscles of the larynx, but the benefits usually last for only a few months. That Rodgers continued to perform before large appreciative audiences is a testimony to the love of his music and to the courage he demonstrated in the face of embarrassing on-stage episodes of his condition. After a 2012 concert, he returned home for open heart surgery, following a heart attack he had suffered three weeks earlier. He died from kidney disease on January 18, 2021, at the age of eighty-seven. Curiously, Rodgers's wife died after a fall at her home in 1977.

In 1993, one of the officers who was alleged to have beaten Rodgers, Raymond Virgil Whisman, was arrested for assaulting his wife and threatening to kill her. Sheriff's deputies had to storm his house after being told that Whisman was holding his wife hostage at gunpoint. Following the arrest, the deputies found eleven rifles, four shotguns, and two handguns in the house.

Another sad case was the one that ended in the death at age twenty-five of one of rock and roll's early boy stars, Frankie Lymon, lead singer of the Teenagers. His death was due to a heroin overdose. But years earlier, when he was only fourteen years old, he and his group recorded their biggest hit song, "Why Do Fools Fall in Love." In 1956, the song went to the top of the charts; it was a million-dollar hit. The Teenagers should have received hundreds of thousands of dollars in royalties; instead they were paid nothing.

Franklin Joseph Lymon was born into a poor family in 1942; his mother was a maid, his father was a truck driver. They sang in a gospel choir, and young Frankie sang in a junior gospel choir. But at age fourteen, he heard a doo wop group on the streets of Washington Heights, and he fell in love with the music. He befriended the group's lead singer, Herman Santiago, and was invited to join the group that called themselves first the Ermines and then the Premiers.

In 1955, two members of the Premiers, Santiago and Jimmy Merchant, were given a small stack of love letters that had been sent to one of their friends. The friend thought the love letters might inspire the duo to write doo wop songs. Merchant and Santiago were, indeed, inspired by one of the letters and wrote the song "Why Do Fools Fall in Love." No longer satisfied with the name Premiers, the group decided to call themselves the Teenagers. The group sang their song for Richard Barret of the group called the Valentines. Barrett was impressed and thought the group had come up with a potential hit. He introduced the Teenagers to George Goldner, who set up an in-studio audition. The clock was ticking, costing Goldner money, and he refused to wait for latecomer Santiago to show up. Is there anyone else who can sing the lead? asked Goldner. Lymon, as eager as a young otter, said he could do it. Not only could he sing the lead, he said, but he claimed that he had helped to write the song. Goldner was impressed by what he heard and quickly signed the group to his

Gee label. It shot up like a rocket not only on the *Billboard* pop singles chart but also on the *Billboard* R&B singles chart. Goldner had discovered gold, as in gold records, and he produced a series of hits for *Billboard's Hot 100* for the group that included "I Want You to Be My Girl," "The ABCs of Love," "I'm Not a Juvenile Delinquent," "Who Can Explain," and "I Promise to Rember."

Lymon, as did many lead singers in groups (think of Diana Ross), broke out on his own and developed a solo act. He and his producer knew he was a hot commodity, and the spotlight of fame loved him. He moved to Roulette Records, where he was promised riches galore. It didn't quite work out the way he had anticipated. In July 1957, he lip-synced a song on Alan Freed's *The Big Beat* television show. Toward the end of show, the kids in the audience were invited to dance to the closing music. Lymon left the stage, grabbed the hand of a white girl, and the couple happily danced as the closing credits rolled. No one in the studio thought anything of Lymon dancing with a white girl, but flames of anger and indignation were ignited among Southern viewers. Three years after the famous *Brown vs. Board of Education* case that outlawed segregation in public schools, *The Big Beat* was canceled.

Addicted to heroin more than to stardom, Lymon's career slid from peaks of popularity to dark valleys of sadness and disappointment, which led to ever more dependency on heroin. Levy thought Lymon's career was over, and in 1961, his contract with Roulette was over. Lymon was reduced to accepting singing gigs for whatever he could get. He was a desperate young man, who couldn't stop singing and couldn't stop his downward spiral. In 1960, he sang at my high school graduation for fifty dollars. Many of my fellow students and I were stunned that such a major star of rock and roll had been reduced to singing for a handout.

Though his charisma had fallen away from him, Lymon continued to attempt to breathe life into his terminal career. On June

21, 1966, he was arrested and charged with heroin possession. Give a choice between jail and the Army, he chose the latter. The Army was not to his liking, and he often went AWOL. While on leave from Fort Gordon in Georgia, he met, fell in love with, and married Emira Eagle, a local school teacher. The Army did not regard Lymon as an asset as he seemed to go AWOL whenever the impulse to escape inspired his departures. Not surprisingly, the Army dishonorably discharged him. Attempting to restart his career, Lymon went to New York in 1968, where he met with Sam Bray of Big Apple Records. Bray signed Lymon. Levy learned about it and figured that there was still money to be made from Lymon. He approached Bray, and the two decided that Lymon would record his earlier hits and Roulette and Big Apple would release the records. Lymon figured his career was about to take off, and he went to his grandmother's house to celebrate by taking heroin. He killed himself with an overdose of the drug.

Lymon died a polygamist; he had three former wives, none of whom he had divorced. And each of them arose, claiming to be Lymon's legitimate widow, and thus his heir. And each wanted a piece of his estate. Because Levy had taken over Goldner's record companies, he also owned Lymon's copyrights. He was sued not only for the rights but also for all the royalties that were owed to Lymon. The widows wanted what they were entitled to. One widow was already married when she married Lymon, so her claim was dismissed. A second widow claimed to have married Lymon in Mexico, but her file cabinet contained no record of the marriage. When Lymon married Eagle, his third wife, he hadn't bothered divorcing the other two. One can image a big smile stretching across Levy's face.

But not so fast. One court ruled that wife number one was a legitimate heir. Then in 1989, the Appellate Division of the Supreme Court in New York declared Eagle the legitimate heir. Levy's smile vanished. But he still hung onto the songwriting credits. Though the original recording of "Why Do Fools Fall in Love" credited Lymon, Santiago, and Merchant as the song's writers, later releases had Lymon and Goldner as the writers. And then when Levy bought Goldner's companies, Levy's name appeared as cowriter of the hit song. Merchant and Santiago now sued Levy. It was like watching a bouncing ball, not knowing where on the Roulette wheel it would land. First, a District Court ruled that Merchant and Santiago were the legitimate writers of the song. Four years later, in 1996, the US Court of Appeals said that the statute of limitations had run out: Merchant and Santiago were twenty-seven years too late in filing their suit. A broad smile returned to Levy's countenance as he learned that he would continue to share authorship of "Why Do Fools Fall in Love" with the deceased Frankie Lymon.

Though Levy was the beneficiary of numerous lawsuits, his obituary was being written by the FBI in 1984 when the agency began its investigation into the Genovese's control of Roulette Records. Feeling the heat of the investigation and knowing that he might be arrested, Levy sold Roulette Records and his publishing rights for between twenty and fifty million dollars. Levy was arrested in September 1986 at the Ritz Carlton Hotel in Boston. The arrest was televised nationally. Levy was indicted on three of 117 count indictment against him and twenty-one others. In an interview with Brian Ross on NBC-TV, Levy said, "There is no connection between the mob and the music business. The charges are not true. They wouldn't have been filed yesterday if I had joined the witness protection program." He then claimed that the FBI told him he would be killed if didn't join the witness protection program. "I said I would not join the witness protection program." Why not, he was asked. "Two reasons. I do not believe in the entire thing being constitutional. And the other one is there is nothing I could tell them about a mob. And the third is there's nothing I could do. I just wouldn't join. I don't believe it's right. I don't believe that people should be paid to testify. I don't believe in the whole program. I don't think it's constitutional." He went on to say that the charges against him were ludicrous. "Actually, if I joined the program there would be no charges." He thought the three charges against him were ludicrous. He was particularly annoyed that he had been accused of usury, saying that if he lends money he doesn't charge any interest. Levy then said he would enter a plea of not guilty.[12]

A story in *Jersey Magazine* noted that "Levy's conviction was based upon FBI wiretaps that had been covertly recorded of his conversations." Levy had a sign behind his desk that read, "O Lord! Give me a Bastard with talent." It was into that sign that the FBI placed a tiny microphone in the letter O where it could not be seen. In addition, the FBI had secreted a camera in the ceiling of Levy's office. In December 1988, Levy was convicted of two counts of conspiring to extort. He insisted to reporters that he had known mobsters as a result of his long history as a Broadway entrepreneur. He added, "I knew Cardinal Spellman, too. That don't make me a Catholic."[13]

As he was about to be sentenced, his attorney asked the court to consider Levy's extensive philanthropic activities. It made no difference. In 1988, he was sentenced to ten years in prison and fined $200,000. During his appeal, Levy remained free on bail secured by Sunnyview Farm, his large working farm in upstate New York. In 1989, Levy's conviction was upheld by the US Court of Appeals for the Third Circuit in Philadelphia. In 1990, Levy petitioned to have his sentence eliminated because he was terminally ill. He was granted a ninety-day stay and scheduled to report to prison on July 16. He died, still a free man, on May 20, 1990.

CHAPTER 3

Alan Freed

Rock and Roll's Broadcast Wizard

HE WAS THE P. T. BARNUM, THE ST. PAUL, THE PIED PIPER OF rock and roll. He was a wizard of promotion, a disc jockey who used the radio better than any carnival barker. He was Alan Freed, who loved rhythm and blues and married it to rock and roll. He took what radio programmers thought of as black music, and he made it interracial. From his nightly radio program, he may have done more to bring black and white teenagers joyfully together than any government program, many of which bred resentment and resistance. He gave a back beat to a burgeoning youth culture and died a broken man.

Alan Freed was born in 1921 in Johnstown, Pennsylvania, to a Jewish father and Welsh Catholic mother. In 1933, the family moved to Salem, Ohio, where—in high school—Freed became a musical magnet. He led a band called the Sultans of Swing in which he played trombone. Having worked in Armed Forces radio during World War II, he was bitten by the broadcasting bug and decided on a postwar career as a disc jockey. He worked at numerous local Ohio radio stations, where he played jazz and rhythm and blues records, much to the consternation of conservative radio owners. However, the owners couldn't argue with the success

Freed generated by attracting large numbers of teenage listeners. Sponsors rushed to place commercials on his programs, and Freed hyped the products of his sponsors. From small Salem stations, he moved to a larger one in Cleveland. There he continued his one-man whirlwind marathon. White kids were tuning into the music Freed played on the air. Record stores saw a huge rise in sales of black-recorded music. Yet record companies supplied stores with white cover renditions of black music, all sanitized to be free of sexual references. Many loyal Freed listeners dismissed the discs as pale imitations of the original black renditions and bought only the records that Freed played on the air. The discs of white recordings of songs made popular by Chuck Berry, Little Richard, and Fats Domino would never be played by Freed. For Freed, his choices were sacrosanct. Record companies took notice and realized that Freed and his loyal listeners were changing the way the record companies did business.

Freed's ego was as big as his influence. It is not surprising then that he claimed to have originated the term rock and roll, though he was unable to trademark the phrase. Not only wasn't he permitted to trademark it, but its origin existed long before Freed came on the music scene. It can be traced back to black music in the early part of the twentieth century, where it had strong sexual connotations. In 1923, for example, Trixie Smith recorded a song titled "My Man Rocks Me." Other sexually suggestive titles are "Rock Me, Mama" and "My Daddy Rocks Me With a Steady Roll." Beginning in the 1950s, many rock and roll songs with sexually suggestive titles proliferated: "It Ain't the Meat," "Keep On Churnin'," "Pay Before You Pump," "Great Balls of Fire," "Lay Lady Lay," "Big Long Slidin' Thing," "Willie and the Hand Jive," "My Ding-a-Ling," "Wynona's Big Brown Beaver," "Afternoon Delight," "The Girl Can't Help It," and the list goes on. Rock and rollers of the 1950s had a new vehicle for joyous rebellion, for thumbing their noses at the strictures that governed the pop songs of the 1930s and 1940s. It's not an exaggeration to suggest that rock and roll gave birth to the sexual revolution of the 1960s, which may have found its most suggestive expression in the title "Why Don't We Do It in the Road?" Fifty-eight years earlier, the esteemed actress Mrs. Patrick Campbell was quoted as saying, "Does it really matter what these . . . people do, so long as they don't do it in the streets and frighten the horses."[1]

On radio, Freed called himself Moondog, and when he moved to New York, he discovered that there was a famous blind musician and composer who already owned the name Moondog. It belonged to Louis Thomas Hardin, who was often seen on Sixth Avenue and 52nd Street. With his long hair, beard, and robe he was a Christ-looking figure. To dissuade passersby from thinking of him as Christlike, he began wearing a Viking helmet with horns shooting out each side. He also carried a long stringed instrument.

When in 1954 Moondog heard Freed calling his radio program *The Moondog Rock and Roll Matinee*, he brought suit. The New York State Supreme Court ruled against Freed, who had also been playing "Moondog's Symphony" on his program; it was the Moondog's first recorded piece of music. Testifying on Moondog's behalf were Benny Goodman and Arturo Toscanini, both of whom testified that Moondog was a serious composer. Not only did Freed have to cease using the name Moondog and playing the "Moondog's Symphony," he had to apologize on air, stating that Hardin had adopted the name Moondog long before Freed had. Once again, Freed was denied the opportunity to register a name that had become synonymous with his mission to be the loudest advocate of rock and roll.

The lawsuit led to considerable publicity for Moondog, who was interviewed by print and TV reporters. Even the actor James Dean would spend time with Moondog, discussing the music that had influenced the young Hardin when he visited Indian reservations with his father. To those who learned of Moondog, they found him to be a unique celebrity, an unusual presence on the streets of the city, who supported himself by selling copies of his music and poetry.

Tourists coming to New York would often be invited by tour guides to see the composer/poet while touring the city. They were told that Moondog came to New York from Wyoming in the late 1940s. He was the son of an Episcopal minister, and when he was sixteen years old, he picked up a blasting cap while wandering in a field near his parents' home in Fort Bridger. He didn't realize what he had in his hand, and the cap exploded into his eyes, leaving him permanently blind. As a youth, he studied music in schools for the blind and decided to become a composer. He is one of the city's unusual attractions, tourists were told.

Moondog lived in an apartment in upper Manhattan until 1972, when he left the city for his country home in Candor, New York, which had a population of 825 in 2000. Moondog died in 1999 at age eighty-three. Following his death, he was credited with having influenced the minimal music of composers Philip Glass and Steve Reich. It was not the kind of music that would have engaged the enthusiasm of Freed, who had arrived in New York in 1954 when the owner of radio station WINS needed a force of nature that would deliver his company from spiraling downward into bankruptcy.

Freed immediately became the voice and star of WINS. According to John A. Jackson, "WINS owner J. Elroy McCaw could not have been happier. Thanks to Alan Freed and rhythm and blues, his radio station showed a 42 percent rise in advertising sales, compared to the same period the previous year. Overall, WINS showed a substantial profit for the first time in its history."[2]

Freed's music had become so popular and ever present in the culture of teenagers that entertainment trade publications began referring to Freed as Mr. Rock and Roll and the Pied Piper for a generation of listeners. The trades also stopped referring to Freed's music as rhythm and blues and began calling it rock and roll. Alan Freed, wrote one columnist, was the Tom Paine of music and had initiated a revolution for hundreds of thousands of teenagers who were marching to the beat of a different drummer than the one their parents had heard. Freed's music was the new big beat for a young generation.

Like many who followed in his footsteps, Freed did not promote singers without some sort of quid pro quo. In the case of Chuck Berry, Freed took a cowriting credit for the hit "Maybellene" (1955). Having donned the hat of cowriter, Freed gave the song extensive air play. His efforts rocketed the song up the pop charts. While Morris Levy was known as the godfather of rock and roll, Chuck Berry has been known as the father of rock and roll, and Freed readily identified with Berry's mission of turning rhythm and blues into the new rock and roll, for they both had the same ambition. However, Berry was not happy to share a cowriting credit with Freed, and had his lawyer bring suit. After a lengthy court battle the writing credit was given to Berry. Without referring to Freed, Berry commented on the explosive popularization of rock and roll in the 1950s: "Well, actually they began to listen to it, you see, because certain stations played certain music. The music that we, the blacks, played, the cultures were so far apart, we would have to have a play station in order to play it. The cultures begin to come together, and you begin to see one another's vein of life, then the music came together."[3]

Though Freed would lose his cowriting credit, he knew how important Berry was and hired him to perform in his live concerts. And Berry proved to be more than a one-hit wonder, he went on to write and record other hit songs, including "Roll Over Beethoven" (1956), "Rock and Roll Music" (1957), and "Johnny B. Goode" (1958).

And when it came time to recognizing Berry's unique achievement, the Rock and Roll Hall of Fame chose Berry as one of its first inductees. He was cited for having "laid the groundwork for not only a rock and roll sound but a rock and roll stance. After Elvis Presley, only Chuck Berry had more influence on the formation and development of rock & roll. The St. Louis native internalized country, blues and R&B influences to create a singular guitar technique."[4]

With an ever-growing audience for his radio program, Freed was moved from the late evening slot to prime-time evening. Teenage listeners loved the new time slot. "It keeps us off the streets at night," one teen told the *New York Daily News* during the spring of 1956, "because from six thirty to nine is the rock and roll party with Alan Freed."[5]

I vividly recall tuning our AM radio to 1010 as soon as dinner was over to listen to Freed holler and exclaim, cow bell ringing, of the latest Jerry Lee Lewis, Chuck Berry, Fats Domino, or Little Richard song. My parents, who thought little of rock music, ascended to their den where they watched the latest sitcoms, quiz, and variety shows.

Meanwhile Freed was using his program to broadcast and promote his rock and roll concerts. The first concert, named "The Rock 'n' Roll Jubilee Ball," was held at the St. Nicholas Arena (more often a venue for boxing matches than for rock and roll concerts), where more than six thousand teenagers showed up to hear the singers whose music Freed was championing on his radio program. The place was packed. Though the concert took place in the middle of winter, the arena was as hot and humid as a terrarium. Morris Levy, who financed the show, complained that the ceiling was dripping, if not from human sweat, then from condensed moisture. As uncomfortable as the arena's weather, audiences ignored their discomfort for two nights of concerts on January 14 and 15, 1955. After giving WINS 10 percent of the concert profits, Freed and Levy split the rest. After such an unanticipated success, Freed and Levy realized their next concert would have to be in a much larger and more prominent space than the arena offered.

The next stop was the Brooklyn Paramount Theater, where Freed staged his "Rock 'n' Roll Easter Jubilee," beginning on April 12, 1955. According to John A. Jackson in his biography of Freed, "His week-long Brooklyn Paramount run drew ninety-seven thousand people and produced a box-office gross $107,000 that shattered the theater's all-time house record set in 1932 by crooner Russ Colombo."[6] The gross was nearly four times as large as the gross from the St. Nicholas Arena concert. The show set a holiday pattern: from then on, Freed would produce concerts on Christmas, Easter, and Labor Day. Having proven the financial value of his concerts, Freed was invited by numerous theater owners to produce rock and roll concerts for them. Freed and Levy, however, stayed with the owners of the Paramount and would soon produce a concert at New York's Paramount Theater in the heart of Times Square, often referred to as the "Crossroads of the World" and "The Heart of the Great White Way," a perfect place to have a concert that would generate national publicity. Freed and Levy would sell thousands of tickets. It was considered a breakthrough venue for singers, for it was on the stage of the New York Paramount Theater on December 30, 1942, that a skinny young Frank Sinatra sent thousands of bobbysoxers into near paroxysms of ecstasy. Girls flung their panties and bras onto the stage.

During Freed's concert at the New York Paramount, which featured six shows a day, more than sixty-five thousand teenagers paid to see one of the most exciting rock and roll concerts ever produced in New York. I vividly recall attending one of those concerts. The concluding act was Jerry Lee Lewis, wildly hammering his piano's keyboard, kicking over his piano stool, and shouting out the lyrics of "Great Balls of Fire." The performance seemed to have ignited an explosive reaction in the audience as thousands of kids rushed toward the stage, some of them mounting it, before being tossed aside or escorted off by NYC cops. A few kids got into fights with cops as other kids surged around the wrestling bodies in the aisles. When the show was over, there was a sense of post-orgasmic relief among the audience. They seemed transformed, either in a state of beatific wonderment or let down that reality had descended like a gray cloud portending a cold rain.

As expected, Levy and Freed raked in a small fortune. Never-theless, as successful as their partnership was, it was destined to fail: Freed wanted to own a larger percentage of Roulette Records than Levy had promised, and Levy was not about to turn over money to anyone without a fight. Freed felt betrayed, without understand-ing the depths of Levy's love of money. Levy loved making deals in which he was able to take advantage of the person with whom he was negotiating. And throughout his relationship with Freed, Levy had often taken advantage of him by getting Freed drunk before negotiating a business deal. So the two parted ways, but not as enemies. Levy still needed Freed to feature his singers in his shows and on his radio program. And Freed could always depend on receiving noncollateralized loans from Levy, which did not have to be repaid. Those so-called loans would come to be seen by prosecutors as nothing but bribes.

In addition to his radio program and stage shows, Freed appeared as himself in numerous movies that increased the number of fans who attended his concerts. Listenership of his radio program also increased, firmly putting him on the throne as New York's king of rock and roll. The movies in which Freed appeared and to which teenagers flocked were *Go, Johnny, Go!*, *Rock Around the Clock*, *Don't Knock the Rock*, *Mister Rock and Roll*, and *Rock, Rock, Rock*. The movies did not receive positive reviews, but that hardly mattered to teenagers who loved the excitement generated by the pounding beats of the music. Rock and roll had become a movement that revolutionized their lives, not only inspiring them to thumb their noses at the culture of their parents but also to rebel against the constraining sexual mores that valued virginity until married and accepted only petting as the acceptable standard for teenage sexuality. Rock and roll blew an old order to smithereens. Not only the lives of teenagers but also those of their parents would be radically altered by the sexual revolution.

But it wasn't only the old order that crashed: Freed's career, like a jet plane losing power, was also about to crash. The first thing to go was his TV dance show, *The Big Beat*. The show premiered, amid much fanfare, on ABC on July 12, 1957. It proved to be immensely popular with teenagers and advertisers, and ABC was prepared to extend its run for the next year. However, a storm then arose without warning. ABC canceled the show. *The Wall Street Journal* reported that the show were canceled because the black teenage singer Frankie Lymon "was seen on TV dancing with a white audience member."[7]

That incident ignited a fire storm of protest in the South. Two episodes after Lymon innocently ignited the anger of segregationists, the show went dark. Freed was unbelieving that such innocence could lead to the cancelation of his show. His disbelief turned to fury, but there was nothing he could do. Fighting ABC would be like going up against an infantry brigade with a water pistol.

Though Freed was initially unaware of it, the FBI had begun an investigation into Levy and Vincent "the Chin" Gigante. Because of his close relationship with Levy and his tangential one with Gigante, Freed came under the agency's microscope. The agency soon learned that the mortgage on Freed's Connecticut house was owned by Levy. That meant, according to investigators, that Freed was owned by Levy and perhaps by Gigante. Investigators followed clues like pigeons following a trail of breadcrumbs. Their final tidbit was that the mortgage payment must have been a bribe, which was named payola in the media.

Payola was as much a part of the record business as pressing records. Record companies paid disc jockeys to play certain records, and all parties profited handsomely. Hank Bordowitz relates the following anecdote: "A guy who will go unnamed, he was the music director up at WINS when Alan Freed was there," muses Joe Smith, "It was a hot radio station. The guy was making $125 a week as the music director. And he was living over on Sutton Place, wearing fancy suits, driving a fancy car, going off to Europe on his $125 a week. The station manager, oblivious to all this, said, 'You're doing a great job. We're going to promote you to the news department and give you $200 a week.' He begged him, 'Please don't do that to me!'"[8]

News spread to congressional representatives about the FBI investigation. Having enjoyed the benefits of the immense amount of publicity generated by the congressional investigation that led to the quiz show scandals, which had found contestants were fed answers prior to being asked questions, a congressional committee decided the time was ripe to investigate disc jockeys and the role of payola in the record industry. The ensuing publicity would be a great catalyst for raising campaign funds. With the zeal of an inquisition, congressmen shot withering questions like poison-tipped arrows at Freed and others. Freed was not about to let his career be killed off by haters of rock and roll. Though his bosses would have preferred that he adopt an air of obeisance and apologize and promise like a good little boy not to participate in payola, Freed refused. His position as the king of the hill, rock and roll's supreme impresario, would not permit him to bow and scrape like Steppin' Fetchit in front of the committee. Freed blasted the pomposity and self-righteousness of the committee, thus igniting their fury. They were prepared to burn him at the stake of rock and roll. Unfortunately, Freed was too full of himself to interpret the reality before him. He was a dead man walking. He believed strongly in himself and thought the practice of payola was simply a respected way of doing business. After all, hundreds of record companies admitted that they paid disc jockeys anywhere from \$20 to \$200 to play their records. Furthermore, it was not illegal as long as disc jockeys reported the extra income to the IRS. What was the big deal?

Record companies and disc jockeys understood that without payola neither party would be able to control what would become a hit. In today's jargon, disc jockeys were influencers; indeed, they were the most powerful and pivotal influencers in the record business. Those who made laws, however, were incensed by payola and the arrogance of people like Freed, so they would make sure that new laws would put an end to the practice of payola. And so it happened: but not until 1964 when Freed was indicted by a federal grand jury for tax evasion and ordered to pay \$37,920 in taxes on income he had allegedly not reported. Most of that income was said to be from payola sources.

First Freed had to be portrayed as a satanic manifestation of greed and dishonor before he could be tied, blindfolded, and stood before a firing squad. Richard Wagoner writes: "Freed never admitted taking payola. But the big targets were Freed and another popular DJ named Dick Clark. Freed refused to sign a statement for WABC denying that he took it, and he was fired. His last show was in November 1959. Interestingly, payola was not illegal at the time; that wouldn't happen until 1960. But like the quiz shows—which also broke no laws at the time—the negative publicity took its toll. Freed—the man who helped spawn a new generation of music and a new type of radio—could not get a job at any of the major radio stations, New York or elsewhere."[9]

"At 6:00 PM, November 27, 1959, Alan Freed vanished from New York airwaves. Pop singer Richard Hayes, who already had his own television show, was set to take over Freed's 'Big Beat' telecast. At WABC, disc jockey Freddie Robbins was already presiding over Freed's old radio program."[10] Then, in December 1962,

Freed was charged on multiple counts of commercial bribery. He finally pled guilty to two counts of commercial bribery and was fined $300 and given a suspended sentence. But his career had flamed out.

What was the point of nailing Freed if you couldn't nail Levy as well? Levy had given Freed $20,000, claiming it was a loan and not payola. However, Levy was brought before a grand jury and given immunity; as a result, if he didn't honestly answer questions he could be held in contempt and jailed until he relented and agreed to testify. So squeezed, Levy had no choice but to admit that the $20,000 was a bribe, which was paid to Freed to ensure that Roulette Records would receive the lion's share of airtime on Freed's program. Though the New York DA was gunning for disc jockeys to shoot off their privileged perches for accepting bribes, he had no intention of indicting record company executives who paid those bribes. And because Freed was the biggest celebrity disc jockey in New York, his conviction would generate reams of news coverage for a DA, who acted like a sheriff in an old western town, driving the bad guys into jail.

Freed had a difficult time understanding that he was no longer a glittering star in the galaxy of rock and roll. Like many celebrities who believe that they are indestructible adornments in a world of admirers, Freed thought he would spend the rest of his days celebrated as rock and roll's greatest impresario. It was a bitter surprise for him when he was found guilty of accepting bribes, amounting to $30,650. Though the punishment was mild, a mere $300 fine and a six-month suspended sentence, Freed's career as a top New York celebrity disc jockey was over. He had been toppled by forces he could not control. Always a prolific drinker, he attempted to blot out reality by increasing his heavy drinking. The IRS attacked his assets, claiming that he had not paid taxes from the years 1957, 1958, and 1959; he was billed $37,920. He had to borrow money just to stay alive. Every day, he called friends to ask for money. Of all the people he solicited, Levy came through with money until the day Freed died. It was surprising generosity from a man who took great pleasure in not paying royalties and cheating singers. For Freed, it was humiliating, a drink in one hand, the other clutching his lifeline phone. He was not only living on borrowed money but on borrowed time. Alcohol was slowing destroying his liver.

He sold his beloved Connecticut house and moved into a small, banal house in Palm Springs. Embarrassed to be living in it, he referred to it as a nothing house. Hoping to kick start his career, he got a job at KDAY radio in California; he thought he could use his program to promote the kind of concerts that made oodles of money in New York; however, the head of KDAY would not let him use his broadcast for any other purpose than for playing music. Disgusted and disappointed, he quit and sought out another station that would have a more flexible policy about his outside ventures. He signed on with WQAM in Miami, but that gig didn't work out either. In 1964, he was hired by KNOB/97.9 in Long Beach, California. He had gone from making $200,000 a year in New York to $25,000 in California. He was truly a broken man, a has-been, a shadow of his former self. His fans may have mourned the loss of their champion, but New York radio stations just moved on to the other popular disc jockeys, though none would be credited with the influence that Freed wielded.

Though one thinks of Palm Springs as an area populated by movie stars and other celebrities, it has its run-of-the-mill houses and working-class residents. And though Freed lived in a neighborhood called Raquet Club Estates, no one who visited him was impressed by its nonluxury. Freed continued to drink heavily. Rather than relieving his many disappointments, alcohol fueled his despondency. On January 20, 1965, he died from uremia and cirrhosis of his liver. His daughter said he died of a broken heart. He was only forty-three years old. He was cremated, and his ashes would be as itinerant as the last years of his life. He was initially interred in

Ferncliff Cemetery in Hartsdale, New York. Then in March 2002, Freed's daughter-in-law, Judith Fisher Freed, brought his ashes to Cleveland, Ohio. There the ashes would be installed in a position of honor in the Rock and Roll Hall of Fame. Then on August 1, 2014, the RRHF asked Lance Freed, Alan's son, to remove the ashes permanently. That the man who brought rock and roll music to millions of teenagers would be evicted was in keeping with the rest of Freed's downfall. From there the ashes were taken by Freed's family to Cleveland's Lake View Cemetery, where they were interred beneath a jukebox-shaped headstone that had Freed's face on one side and the image of a jukebox on the other.

The following story appeared on the website www.cleveland .com:

> *A brushed brass urn containing the ashes of the iconic disc jockey Alan Freed was evicted from The Rock and Roll Hall of Fame and Museum in 2014, but his remains will not be traveling far.*
>
> *Freed is staying in Cleveland, and will be interred permanently on May 7 at a monument in Lake View Cemetery, his son Lance announced today. "We are holding a celebration of Alan Freed's life—his coming home," Lance Freed said in a news release.*
>
> *More than 50 years after Alan Freed's death, he will finally be put to rest in a beautiful and natural memorial setting that is designed to invite the public to visit now and in the years ahead. The granite monument will be located in a prominent plot at the cemetery near Wade Chapel, and in the vicinity of the tombs of other Northeast Ohio icons such as President James A. Garfield, John D. Rockefeller, Carl and Louis Stokes, and Eliot Ness.*
>
> *The monument will be inscribed with a tribute to Freed's life and historical contributions to music in America, and will*

include an epitaph of his signature sign-off: "This is not good-bye—it's just good night."

Freed is widely credited with coining and popularizing the term "rock 'n' roll" as a popular DJ at WJW-Radio in Cleveland in the 1950s. He hosted what is considered the first rock 'n' roll concert, the Moondog Coronation Ball, in 1952 at the Cleveland Arena, and was one of the reasons the Rock and Roll Hall of Fame is located in Cleveland. When Freed died in 1965 at age 43, he originally was interred at the Ferncliff Memorial Mausoleum in Hartsdale, N.Y. But in 2002, the rectangular receptacle containing his ashes was brought to Cleveland. It originally was kept in a wall at the Hall of Fame, and later was put in a display case along with other Freed memorabilia, including his microphones. The marble marker from his vault was hung for years in the lobby at the Hall of Fame.

Freed's public exhibition ended in August 2014, after Rock Hall President and CEO Greg Harris told Lance Freed to remove his father's ashes. The urn has been kept in a locked vault at Lake View Cemetery since then.[11]

More stories abounded throughout the country about Freed's new resting place. The following one was written by Tom Ferran for the *Cleveland Plain Dealer*:

Alan Freed always enjoyed drawing a crowd. He did it again Saturday, 51 years after his death, with a celebrity-studded and respectfully rocking memorial unveiling at Lake View Cemetery.

About 400 people—family members, friends, fans and the curious—watched on the lawn behind Wade Chapel as Freed's son Lance drew the cover from a gleaming granite monument depicting Freed on [one] side and a jukebox on the other. It be-

comes, at last, the permanent resting place of the disc jockey and impresario proclaimed "the father of rock 'n' roll."

In the hour earlier, the mostly over-60 crowd heard Freed remembered in speech and song from a portable stage. The event opened in bright sunshine, but a soft rain began to fall—"like teardrops," one watcher whispered—as Freed's children spoke. Lance said that the odyssey of his father's ashes after his death on Jan. 20, 1965—from California to a mausoleum in New York to 12 years on display at the Rock & Roll Hall of Fame—echoed the concert tours that kept him on the road in the 1950s.

"Dad, what I want to say to you is, 'Welcome home,'" he said. "You don't need to travel any more."

Only 43 when he died, his father had told him he regretted nothing, but wished he had more time and dreamed of getting back on top in radio.

"The fact that we're all here today is living proof that he did carry on," Lance said.

"Rock on, Dad," said Freed's daughter Sigie, who wondered "how much more Dad would have been able to accomplish had he lived a long and healthy life."

"I'm the baby," said son Alan Jr., who was 9 when his father died. He said his strongest memories of Freed involved his feelings about "how we should treat each other and how the races should get along."

Between speakers, the Drifters sang "This Magic Moment," "Stand by Me" and "Smoke Gets in Your Eyes."

Musician Steve Van Zandt of the E Street Band, longtime friend of Lance, was credited for suggesting the design of the memorial stone jukebox.

"I'm honored to be part of this sacred ceremony," he said. "For those of us whose religion is rock 'n' roll, I do mean sacred."

"Freed was special," said former Rock Hall CEO Terry Stewart. "He had the passion. He had a vision."[12]

CHAPTER 4

Vincent "the Chin" Gigante

The Godfather's Godfather

Though Morris Levy was known as the godfather of rock and roll, it was to Vincent "the Chin" Gigante that Levy paid tribute.

The Chin (a shortening of Vincenzo or Vincinzo) was not your typical gangster. He devoutly attended Catholic Mass every Sunday, and for those who only saw him genuflecting, he looked to be a humble parishioner in touch with God. Yet this devout gangster led all but one of his brothers into the ranks of the mob. The exception was Father Louis Gigante, who was a political powerhouse on his own terms. He regularly received encomiums from numerous politicians and community organizations for his success in providing low-income housing to thousands of families in the Bronx. Father Gigante was praised by Cardinal O'Conner, the Catholic bishop of New York, as "a great master builder," who had done more to provide homes for poor people of the Bronx than any other individual in the city. In addition to being a priest, he served as a NYC councilman, introducing bills to benefit his low-income housing ventures. When not campaigning for low-income housing, he was a vociferous defender of Italian American civil rights, lending his prestige to Joseph Colombo's Italian American

Civil Rights League, which staged a fateful demonstration in Columbus Circle in 1971. It was there that Colombo, head the eponymous Colombo crime family, was assassinated by a gunman pretending to be a journalist. Shortly after the assassin was assassinated by Colombo's bodyguards, Father Louis ran to the podium. He told the crowd to remain calm: police and doctors would do their duty. Father Louis stretched out his arms in a Christlike pose and asked the crowd to join him in prayer. As he recited the Lord's Prayer, an ambulance with its wailing siren carried away the stricken Colombo to a brief life in a vegetative state.

The Chin, gangster and devout Catholic, was a man of many faces: he had been a light heavyweight boxer who had won twenty-five bouts, mostly by outpointing his opponents. He proved himself a tough guy, who let it be known that he would not be hesitant in using violence to achieve his ends and for those he chose to work. He quickly became a valued member of the Genovese crime family, where he eventually ascended to being the boss of the biggest Mafia family on the East Coast. No underlings, no associates, not even his lawyers were permitted to use his name. Who knew who might be listening? When referring to him, one had to point to one's chin or make the letter C by curving one's thumb and forefinger to resemble the letter. If anyone close to him made the mistake of speaking his name, the speaker would no longer be close to anyone. For such a grave injury, the speaker would be confined to a swampy grave.

In addition to being a crime boss, the Chin was an actor of impressive abilities; he dressed as a derelict in a tattered bathrobe and worn slippers, pretending to be insane as he wandered through the Greenwich Village streets near his social clubs. The FBI photographed him muttering to himself or to the young man who guided him on his peregrinations. For years, he fooled the FBI, local police, district attorneys, and federal prosecutors. They could not tear away the Chin's mask of insanity. To create a paper trail proving his insanity, the Chin would often check himself into psychiatric facilities, which confirmed that the Chin suffered from a variety of mental illnesses. He never stepped out of character. He was the mob's Brando, always performing for the government's prying cameras. In the nineteenth century, famous actors made careers out of playing the same part for decades. The Chin followed in their theatrical footsteps. He mastered his part so thoroughly that he could have given lessons at the Actor's Studio. In fact, any actor who is cast to play him in a Mafia movie would need to watch police surveillance films just to master the outward ticks, gestures, facial expressions, and the Chin's way of walking.

The Chin never missed an opportunity to confirm his insanity. One day he stepped into the shower in his mother's bathroom as FBI agents entered the apartment with a search warrant. There they found the Chin standing under a hot shower, dressed in a raincoat as he held an umbrella above his head. Charlie Chaplin, Buster Keaton, or a 1930s surrealist performer could not have put on a more ludicrous performance.

Though Chin was a brilliant actor with a sense of the absurd, he would put away his tattered bathrobe and worn slippers and put on an elegant Italian silk shirt, perfectly tailored trousers, and slip his feet into a pair of handmade loafers to visit Olympia Esposito, the woman he lived with in an expensive Upper East Side townhouse. As night descended in the city, Chin was chauffeured by a driver whose serpentine gymnastics on the city streets would have made him the most in-demand getaway driver in the in the city. The townhouse was the Chin's escape from disguises, excessive caution, and mob camaraderie. Not only were love and relaxation the components of life with Esposito on the Upper East Side, but the townhouse was the manifestation of the various financial arrangements that the Chin had with Morris Levy. The house had been a vehicle for moving cash and deeds around. The money that was laundered out of Roulette Records had been effectively used for a variety of financial transactions, including loans, mortgages, and real property purchases. Levy was Giganti's magician, and Roulette Records was the source of many financial magic tricks.

The two men seemed an odd couple. Yet there were many Jewish associates of the Italian Mafia families. And Jewish and Italian members of the National Crime Syndicate served with equal authority. The two men had met when they were young, each on the make, each looking for scams, schemes, and hustles. While Levy was a capitalist adventurer who picked up or discarded partners as needed, the Chin was a CEO of a vast corporation whose employees owed not only their wealth to him but also their very lives. Those employees, following a nod of the Chin's head, would kill, maim, threaten, or do whatever was asked of them. They were his private army of soldiers and capos. Unlike John Gotti, who lived in the spotlight of celebrity, the Chin clung to dark corners and walked in shadowy alleys, where he was like a feral cat on a tightrope ready to leap to safety and land noiselessly on his feet. He was also a lot cagier than his predecessor, Vito Genovese, who was so power hungry that his enemies were able to manipulate him into realms of self-destruction.

The Genovese crime family often competed with the Gambino family for recognition as the biggest Mafia family on the East Coast. But the Genovese family, other than under its power-greedy boss, Vito Genovese, proved more subtle than the Gambinos, when it was headed by John Gotti, who exulted in his celebrity status. Like a movie star, he referred to the public as his fans. His thumb-in-your eye defiance of the ethics of caution and concealment was a challenge to prosecutors to nail him. And they did.

The Genovese crime family, founded in 1931, was traditional in keeping a low profile and avoiding media coverage. It had originally been the Luciano family, following the assassinations of Mafia bosses Salvatore Maranzano and Joe "the Boss" Masseria. Luciano, with the instincts of a Fortune 500 CEO, operated as boss of the family and was smart enough to never use his surname as a sobriquet to identify his family. Though Thomas Dewey nailed him to a fifty-year sentence for pimping, Luciano, with the craftiness of a legal fox, was able to win parole and spend the rest of his years exporting heroin from Italy to the United States. Following his postprison deportation to Italy, Luciano appointed Frank Costello to be the family's boss. Costello, like Luciano, was primarily a businessman, who was determined to shed his reputation as a gangster. He was a man who dealt in politics and power and never carried a gun. His appointment infuriated an envious and ambitious Genovese, who in 1957 ordered the Chin to assassinate Costello. The attempted assassination took place in the lobby of the Majestic apartment building on Central Park West as Costello entered and pushed the elevator button to be transported to his apartment. Gigante had pumped up his weight to three hundred pounds so that he wouldn't be recognized. He pulled a pistol from his jacket, pointed it at Costello's head, and said, "This is for you Frank," and pulled the trigger. Hearing his name, Costello turned his head just as the bullet rocketed out of the barrel of Gigante's pistol. There was a momentary flash and loud explosion. The bullet did not penetrate Costello's skull; it just left a bloody crease. Impatient to make his getaway, the three-hundred-pound assassin took off like a lumbering sumo wrestler. He thought he had successfully achieved his mission. When he later learned that he hadn't, Gigante immediately went on a diet. Yet the law ran him to ground. A slimmed down but beefy Gigante appeared at trial. He had been charged with the attempted murder of Costello. When Costello took the stand and was asked if he could identify the man who had shot him, he said he could not. Gigante breathed a sigh of relief. As the case was dismissed and Gigante was leaving the courtroom, he turned to Costello and said, "Thanks Frank." Not wanting to wind up a dead Mafia boss, Costello decided that retirement was in the cards for him. He could attend to his lush gardens on Sands Point on Long Island. Genovese accepted that Costello would no longer be a rival and uncharacteristically let him enjoy his retirement.

Costello, unsurprisingly, was not about to go quietly into Mafia oblivion. Mafioso are not known for their Christian forgiveness. Revenge is woven into their psyches. Costello and his partners, the deported Luciano and cagy Meyer Lansky, did not need to silence Genovese with two bullets fired into the back of his head. Humiliation followed by incarceration would be more corrosive to Genovese's self-importance than a quick murderous end to his reign. It would begin by so embarrassing Genovese and so angering mob bosses that Genovese would lose standing with other Mafia families.

Like the head of a government, Genovese called for a summit meeting of mob bosses to take place in Apalachin, New York, at the home of Joseph Barbara. At the meeting, Genovese, like Napoleon crowning himself emperor, was prepared to announce that he was now the boss of bosses. He knew that his reputation for cold bloodedness and deviousness, based on his having gotten rid of Albert Anastasia, Willie Moretti, Frank Costello, and others, would shield him from potential objections.

And among the men in expensive silk suits there was not a whisper of disapproval. The mobsters had arrived in elegant Cadillacs and Lincoln Continentals, eager for a good time. And Barbara would not disappoint them: he had ordered the finest meats, fish, fresh fruits and vegetables, expensive liquors and wines, and delicious Italian pastries. As the one hundred mob bosses from the United States, Canada, and Italy were drinking and laughing, a sudden loud knock was followed by the announcement that police were at Barbara's front door. Suddenly, festivities turned into panic. It was as if someone had fired a gun at a herd of startled cattle. Some had run out of back doors, others dove through windows. They stampeded through the surrounding woods. They cursed and yelled; their fine suits were cut by thorns, thickets, brambles, and pine needles. Their handcrafted thin-soled Italian shoes were sloshed with mud. The guest of honor, Vito Genovese, was immediately demoted in the minds of running mobsters to the level of being a jerk. Why hadn't he paid off the cops to leave them alone? Where was their protection? Fifty-eight of the running mobsters were picked up by cops, who corralled them, each furious and embarrassed and muttering about revenge. Names that would become Mafia marquee names were on new arrest records: Trafficante, Profaci, Genovese, Bonanno, Gambino, Catena, Civello, Galante, and many more. Now that it was made public, an embarrassed J. Edgar Hoover, head of the FBI, had to admit for the first time that there existed a national criminal syndicate that posed a threat to all law-abiding Americans.

News outlets reported that cops had seen the large number of expensive cars arriving at the Barbara estate. Police checked license plates and discovered that a number of cars were registered to men with significant criminal records. A police spokesman said that the gathering of a such a large number of criminals is what caused them to come to the house. However, no one with mob knowledge believed that explanation. Some savvy reporters noted that Lansky, Costello, and Doc Stacher were not at the meeting. How strange that such mob bigwigs would not have been invited or chose not to attend. Indeed, it was those three, plus Luciano living in exile in Italy, who had planned for the event to be raided. A brief phone call to local police about a convention of criminals would be sufficient to ring alarm bells.

After Apalachin, Genovese was down but not out. He could still make a comeback. The plotters needed one more event to foreclose Genovese becoming boss of bosses: they would set him up to be busted. They paid $100,000 to a Puerto Rican drug dealer named Nelson Cantellops. He was given the mission of selling drugs to Genovese, enough drugs so that Genovese would spend the rest of his life in prison. "The bait was set by one of Meyer's couriers, Nelson Cantellops. Meyer had been angry with Nelson after he got himself mixed up running drugs at the same time he was working for Meyer. When Nelson was caught, Meyer refused to help him and he was sent to Sing Sing on a narcotics conviction. Then, using his brother Jake, Meyer passed a message to Nelson that he would forgive him if he would take on a little job. Cantellops was promised a pension for life. So poor sap Nelson Cantellops, despite the danger he would be in, asked for an interview with the Narcotics Bureau in New York and told an agent, George Gaffney, that he would provide information about how Genovese and his partners were smuggling narcotics from Europe to the United States."[1] The government had been looking for ways to nail Genovese, and they didn't care where the impetus came from. They certainly didn't care about the reliability and veracity of Cantellops. They wanted a conviction, and they finally got their man. On July 7, 1958, Genovese was convicted of drug dealing. He would need a lot of money for his defense and appeals. Much of the money came from Gigante and Roulette Records. Money, however, could not buy Genovese absolution. He was a doomed man. Judges and prosecutors felt like heroes, having nailed the bad guy. Hanging judges denied numerous of Genovese's appeals. With all legal routes posted with dead-end signs, Genovese traveled the only road left open to him. It led directly to prison. On February 11, 1960, he began to serve a fifteen-year term. He knew he had been set up, and he would take the only revenge available to an imprisoned mob boss: he would have the betrayers killed. First there was Anthony Carfano, who Genovese believed had supported Costello. So Genovese ordered one of his capos Anthony (aka Tony Bender) Strollo to kill Carfano. On the night of September 25, 1959, Strollo invited Carfano to dinner at Marino's restaurant. During the meal, Carfano received a phone call that left him suddenly nervous. After hanging up, he announced that he had to leave. An urgent matter had come up. In fact, the call was from Costello, warning Carfano that he would be hit that night. A jittery Carfano got into his new Cadillac, turned the ignition key, and peeled out. Gunning the car's powerful engine, he was hoping to outrun whoever might be on his tail. Exceeding the speed limits and ignoring red lights, he was racing to a plane that would fly him to Miami. He could imagine safely breathing in the hot, humid air of Florida. Right now, however, he was sweating to reach safety.

Strollo, a killer with a chess grandmaster's long-range vision for anticipating his opponents moves, had hidden a pair of gunmen on the floor of Carfano's Caddy just behind the front seats. Before Carfano could deposit himself at one of the airport's terminals, he felt a cold gun barrel against the back of his head. He was told to drive to a quiet deserted street near the airport. A few minutes later, police received an anonymous phone call. Whoever called wanted to make sure that Carfano's demise would be quickly reported. Police discovered Carfano's corpse, a single bullet hole in the back of his head. This is what happens if you betray Vito Genovese.

In typical Mafia fashion, where killers are killed and their killers may also be killed, a contract was issued on the life of Anthony Strollo. A Mafia gossip, either intending to ingratiate himself with Genovese or a man simply attracted to murder and mayhem, whispered into Genovese's ear that Strollo had conspired with Carlo Gambino to set up Genovese for his drug arrest and conviction. The grandmaster's ability to anticipate the future failed Strollo, for on April 8, 1962, he vanished after departing his residence in Fort Lee, New Jersey. Unlike the Carfano hit, no one called the cops, and Strollo's body was never found

Instead of broadcasting his happiness over the disappearance of Strollo, Genovese let mob snitch Joseph Valachi know, with a smile and a chuckle, that his was the hand that guided the fate of Strollo. Genovese, though initially unable to control his pride, later

decided it was necessary to get rid of Valachi too. A man of paranoid convictions, Genovese now believed that Valachi would testify
against him. Observing old world, traditional Mafia mores, Genovese planted a kiss of death on Valachi. That was all Valachi needed
to become a government informant and witness. He testified not
only against Genovese but also against everyone else in the mob.
His words generated reams of news print but no convictions. And
ultimately it didn't matter to Genovese, who died of heart disease
in prison on February 14, 1969. His successor, Vincent "the Chin"
Gigante, would attempt to avoid all of his predecessor's failings.
Roulette Records and the Strawberries Record stores, so pivotal in
advancing rock and roll and the burgeoning youth culture, would
be his secret banks and fronts for laundering money.

The Chin did not want to wind up like Genovese. He would
be a man of the most purposeful caution. He was the opposite of
Morris Levy, who was boisterous, domineering, threatening, and
in your face. The Chin tended to speak softly, never even speaking on a phone. He was extremely difficult to pick up on wiretaps.
Because he knew that the FBI would attempt to bug his apartment, he never left it unoccupied. If he had to leave, he made sure
someone he trusted was there to guard it. His cautious behavior,
however, was not a wall against indictments. In May 1990, he was
indicted along with members of New York's five Mafia families
for rigging bids and exacting extortion payments in their efforts
to control multi-million-dollar window installation contracts. The
New York City Housing Authority was the target of their efforts.
At his indictment, the Chin showed up in his ratty bathrobe and
worn slippers. His defense attorneys claimed that their client was
mentally ill and too incompetent to stand trial. While his attorneys
vigorously argued their case, Gigante mumbled to himself, seem-
ingly unaware of what was going on around him. Prosecutors were
determined to prove that the Chin was not crazy, that it was all a
clever act to avoid prison. Defense attorneys put on a performance

of outrage at such a conjecture, not that it was absent of any empathy for a fellow human being in the throes of mental illness. Lawyers being lawyers somehow didn't bother to threaten their adversaries with lawsuits about defamation and slander. Was the Chin being defamed? Slandered? Not settling for the windows case alone, prosecutors charged him in 1993 with ordering the murders of six mobsters and conspiring to have John Gotti, boss of the rival Gambino family, assassinated. A cliché of the legal profession is that the wheels of justice turn slowly, but never stop. On April 7, 2003, a prosecutor named Roslynn Mauskopf was set to play tapes in court that would prove that Vincent Gigante was as articulate as any corrupt politician running from an indictment. Poor Gigante: his defense imploded. He pled guilty to obstruction of justice and was sentenced to three years in prison. Mauskopf stated, "The jig is up . . . Vincent Gigante was a cunning faker, and those of us in law enforcement always knew that this was an act. . . . The act ran for decades, but today it's over."[2]

A man who rose through the ranks of organized crime and was considered the cagiest of bosses would now spend the rest of his days in a cage. In court, he still looked like an escaped inmate from a mental institution. He was gaunt and disheveled, his gray hair looked as if it were unfamiliar with the tender mercies of a comb. His scraggly beard could have been worn by a nineteenth-century California gold miner who had gone bust. Instructed to raise his right hand and be sworn in, he raised his left hand: the last gesture of a failed performance. He was no longer muttering or mumbling to himself. He spoke clearly and succinctly: "Yes, your honor." "I can hear you, your honor." To questions after questions, the Chin spoke clearly and crisply. No interlocutor needed to point to his chin or make the letter C with thumb and forefinger.

Afterward, his defense lawyer, Benjamin Brafman, said that while his client was coherent enough to enter his plea, he was "clearly suffering from dementia. . . . I think anyone who has seen

'A Beautiful Mind' will tell you that the person could be very seriously mentally ill and still have some degree of rational thought."[3]

Vincent "the Chin" Gigante died at age seventy-seven, on December 19, 2005. He outlived his pal, Morris Levy, by a little more than fifteen years. Their partnership did much to shape the early years of rock and roll. In fact, one could say that the triumvirate of Levy, Gigante, and Alan Freed shaped much of the culture of 1950s, generating hit records and boosting careers of young singers eager for stardom. Of course, they also cheated many of those singers, not paying royalties and stealing song writing and publishing credits. The singers were angry about it, but for many it was the price they paid for rock and roll stardom.

CHAPTER 5

Jimmie Rodgers

A Star Is Born and Reborn

IF THERE WAS EVER A LIFE THAT SHOULD BE THE SUBJECT OF A movie, it is that of Jimmie Rodgers, a singer from nowhere who almost ended up nowhere.

When I phoned Jimmie's youngest daughter, Katrine, she was excited to talk about her dad. For her, he was not only a profoundly gifted musician but also a devoted, loving father. In his last years, while his wife and daughter provided all the care Jimmie needed, he nevertheless struggled with numerous maladies. He had learned at an early age never to give in to self-pity. His father, Archie, taught him not only how to hunt and fish but also how to deliver a right cross and never land on your ass.

Jimmie was born in 1933 in Camas, Washington, a town with a population a bit over 4,200 in that year. Today, the town has a population of 27,000. His family was poor, but Jimmie and his older brother, Archie (aka Bus), never realized it or felt any deprivations. Jimmie graduated from the local high school, where he was known as a musical whiz for his skillful guitar and piano playing and admired for his smooth style of singing. He picked up his love of music from his mother, Mary, who played piano accompaniments for silent movies in local theaters. So in demand was Mary that a movie could not be shown without her fingers dancing over the ivory keys.

Though Jimmie wanted to have a career in music, he did not think he was sufficiently talented. In addition, he had no connections to the world outside of Camas. Instead of pursuing a career in music, Jimmie worked briefly at the large paper company, Crown Zellerbach, which has since been absorbed into ever larger companies. Jimmie's escape from Camas and a life of drudgery was brought about by the war in Korea. Jimmie joined the US Air Force, and it was among his fellow soldiers that he continued honing his musical skills. Soldiers loved his singing and often told him that after the war, he should get a manager and strike out for a career. Jimmie nodded in agreement, and his friendly but inscrutable smile disguised his burning ambition to make it as a singer. Soon thereafter, fate sent to him to an Air Force base in Nashville, where he was a member of a group called the Melodies. He got a job in a nightclub, where he sang and played guitar for five dollars a night, plus a few free drinks to assuage his economic woes. It was during this time that he heard the song "Honeycomb," which would become his first major hit and make millions of dollars for his record label. It was millions of dollars that would settle into the accounts of Roulette Records but never find a home in the accounts of Jimmie Rodgers. Though he enjoyed singing in a nightclub and attracted some fans, no one was opening any doors for Jimmie in Nashville. He had served his time in the Air Force and was honorably discharged. It was time to go back to Camas and figure out his future.

Back home, Jimmie wed the beautiful Colleen McClatchey, a local girl whose career as an actress was proving more successful than Jimmie's noncareer. Colleen had already appeared in a few films being cast in credited and uncredited roles. She can be seen in Universal Pictures's *Written on the Wind* and *Francis in the Haunted House*. Though without even a first step upon the ladder of success,

Jimmie was happy to spend his days and nights with his stunning new wife. On the night May 12, 1956, Jimmie was performing in a club in Vancouver, and Colleen was attending a dance in Seattle. They could not have been happier and were looking forward to getting together. Colleen and a friend left the dance shortly after midnight. Colleen was a gay and effervescent passenger in the car. She couldn't stop talking about what a wonderful future was out there for her and Jimmie. An elderly couple, driving in the opposite direction, had trouble seeing the lights of an oncoming car in the dense fog. The couple's car crossed the highway dividing line and was aimed like a torpedo at the car carrying the two young women. The cars collided with a loud crash, glass shattered, metal crunched, and a horn ceaselessly blasted like a scream in the night. Colleen's head had hit the metal dashboard. Bones in her face were broken, some crushed, others mashed into powder, or shredded into sharp shards. For a beautiful actress whose looks had a been a passport in and out of casting offices, Collen's future was as dark as an abandoned theater. Soon afterward, Universal—noting that its investment was now without value—canceled Colleen's contract. She would undergo numerous surgeries to restore her beauty, but for the Hollywood studios it was too late. There were hundreds of other beautiful young women hungry to be movie stars. They arrived every day in Hollywood, disembarking from trains and buses, their heads filled with glorious dreams of stardom; most of them—after years waiting tables and/or being transient guests on casting couches—would return home, accompanied by fading dreams that had gone stale and pitiful. Their fantasies engendered by *Photoplay* and other Hollywood fan magazines would lie in coffins, ready to be buried, but perhaps not forgotten. There is a certain nostalgia for the successes that might have been. And Colleen's addiction to painkillers created an aura not of nostalgia but of a future where success was just beyond the reach of her outstretched fingers. It now seemed as if it had all been an illusion.

Years later, Jimmie told an interviewer:

When my career started, I was married and had two kids. I was a very responsible kid. I really was. I worked very hard to keep that marriage together even though the marriage finally did disappear. My wife was sick. She passed away, my first wife. We were married 12 years. She died in brain surgery. I supported her and took care of her, but I didn't live in the house because her mother, father, and brother all moved into the house. So, I moved out. Her life was a tragedy. I didn't mess around with girls on the road. I was called the "Angel of the Road" in those days. I didn't play any of the games basically.[1]

Jimmie's good friend and fellow musician, Chuck Miller, wanted to yank Jimmie out of his depression about Colleen's accident and suggested that the couple go to New York City, the home of many major record companies. If Jimmie was going to succeed as a singer/musician, there was no place better suited to rocket his career into orbit than a New York record company. Jimmie had heard the song "Honeycomb" and made it his. It is a habit in the pop music industry to take the songs of others, mold those songs to fit one's talents, and come up with a version that perfectly fits a singer's personality. "Honeycomb" became Jimmie's calling card. The song had been written by Bob Merrill and recorded on Decca Records by Georgie Shaw three years before it would become Jimmie's rocket to success. However, Jimmie had to get noticed before he could even consider signing a recording contract. Jimmie and Colleen arrived in New York with dreams of success bubbling in their brains. But Jimmie didn't know anyone and had no connections in the record business. One day, while carrying his guitar, he saw a sign advertising the Arthur Godfrey Talent Show. He got in line with a number of other musicians who wanted to perform for Godfrey. As each singer got to the head of the line, he was asked his name and song. When it was Jimmie's turn, he gave his name and was told his name was not on the list of those who would be competing that day. Not wanting to lose an opportunity, Jimmie said he was filling in for another entertainer. He was granted admission. When it was his turn to perform, he rocked the audience with his rendition of "Honeycomb." Godfrey was transfixed, and Jimmie not only won the contest, he also received a prize of $700. He thanked Godfrey and ran back to his hotel, exclaiming his good fortune to Colleen. They would be able to pay their hotel bill and have enough money to travel home to Camas. But Morris Levy had heard the song and seen Jimmie on television. Jimmie was golden: a teen idol, a handsome kid with a great voice. Levy would make him a star and himself richer. And so Jimmie began his recording career with Roulette Records in the summer of 1957. His recording of "Honeycomb" shot up to number one and owned that position for twenty-two weeks. That recording was followed by "Kisses Sweeter Than Wine." Jimmie was a hit-making and money-making machine, recording twenty-one hit records in three years. His version of "Honeycomb" became so popular that three months after he recorded it, Ricky Nelson also recorded the song, but his version suffered from anemic popularity. Jimmie stated:

> *I think one of the things is that I was a good-looking young kid with black curly hair and the girls liked me a lot. After Honeycomb came out and started to get some play, I did the Ed Sullivan Show right away and that boosted the record sales tremendously. Just one little thing led to another. Nobody could really categorize what I was doing. It was sort of a combination of country, folk, and pop. You know, I did all the rock 'n' roll shows. I worked with Little Richard, Buddy Holly, The Diamonds and everybody that was out there. We did these rock 'n' roll shows and I didn't like them. I was not comfortable.*

Yeah, well, it was very innocent. We were all kids just trying to make a buck. None of us had any idea that any of this 50's music would catch on and stay around like it did. We were just a bunch of 18, 19, 20-year-old young kids having a good time. We didn't have any drugs and no booze of course. Really, very few people even smoked in those days. We got out once in a while. I used to put on an old coat and a hat and got out in the audience, but you were taking your life in your hands. One day I got out and a cop was out there on horseback in those days. If it hadn't been for him I probably would've really been hurt, because the kids recognized me. I got behind his horse. He was up against the side of a building with me behind his horse and about 500 screaming girls trying to tear my clothes off. (Laughs). They would just go nuts. A man by the name of Chuck Miller who recorded for Mercury. Chuck had a record out called The House of Blue Lights which was a huge hit for Mercury Records in those days. Chuck walked into this club one night and heard me. He told me he was gonna set up an audition for me with Roulette Records in New York. Roulette Records was an affiliate of Mercury. So, through one hook or crook or another, I managed to work my way back to New York City and auditioned for Roulette. The first song I sang for them in the first part of 1957, was Honeycomb. They basically said, don't go any further, that's great. They took me in at 2 a.m. after Chuck had been recording some things. I went out and got me a 6 pack of beer 'cause I was so nervous. I drank a couple of beers, recorded Honeycomb and it became a hit. It was Number One in 4 weeks.[2]

Jimmie, like many other Roulette artists, soon realized that he was not going to be paid his royalties. He consulted a number of lawyers who refused to take his case because of Roulette's ties to the Genovese crime family. Jimmie figured he would wait for an opportune time down the road, assuming there would ever be such a time and such a road. Meanwhile, he was not about to record more songs for Roulette, letting Levy make millions of dollars, none of which would be given to Jimmie.

Instead of suing Roulette and Levy, Jimmie decided to leave with two years to run on his contract. He wouldn't be able to record with another label for two years, but that was better than having his talents used to make someone else rich. One day, Jimmie walked into Levy's office and told him he was leaving the company. Levy fumed and cursed, threatened to kill Jimmie, break his legs. He concluded his tirade by telling Jimmie that he would never work in the music business again. Levy then changed tactics and offered Jimmie a more generous contract with a handsome signing bonus, but a skeptical and determined Jimmie turned him down. He knew that Levy already owed him more than a million dollars in royalties and would never part with more than a few thousand. He had sized up Levy as being all bluster and bullshit. Jimmie, feeling relieved and somewhat nervous about his safety, left Levy's office. Levy and his attorneys then produced bogus contracts that they claimed Jimmie had signed. Jimmie denied that he had signed those contracts. Thereafter, he would receive anonymous phone calls at 2:00 a.m., 3:00 a.m., 4:00 a.m., in which a harsh, whispered voice would say, "We know you signed those contracts, and you better watch your back when out on the street."

Nevertheless, Jimmie went his own way, guided by his scruples and his determination not to give in. He knew he could not record with another label for two years, so he ventured into acting in a movie. The picture was titled *The Little Shepherd of Kingdom Come*. The movie was not a hit in urban areas and did not inspire teenagers to fall in love with a handsome young star. Though Jimmie would appear in another movie, *Back Door to Hell*, his trajectory was aimed at music not cinema. In 1962, legally free from his obligations to Roulette Records, Jimmie signed with Dot Records, whose owners Randy Wood and Gene Nobles were eager to have the young singer on their label. Free from the frenetic hustle and bustle of the New York record scene, Jimmie would go to the headquarters of Dot Records in Gallatin, Tennessee, where he recorded. His songs were popular but did not rise to the level of popularity generated by "Honeycomb" and "Kisses Sweeter Than Wine."

In addition to recording, Jimmie was making good money by touring the country and putting on concerts. He not only appeared in concerts that he headlined but also in the concerts of other popular artists. He was a profitable asset for concert promoters and for musicians who wanted to attract large audiences. Jimmie was riding high. Everywhere he turned he was in demand. His popularity was compounding. One day, while waiting to go on stage with Herb Alpert at Carnegie Hall, he saw a young woman who was crying. He walked over to her, asking what was wrong. She told him that the man she loved was a musician with the Herb Alpert band, but the man no longer loved her. Jimmie spoke with the young woman, offering bromides of sympathy. The woman told Jimmie that she loved her boyfriend so much that she couldn't give him up, even though he no longer loved her. Jimmie told her it was all over and there was nothing that could be done. According to Jerry Singer's documentary about the life of Rodgers, the singer returned to his hotel room and wrote the song "It's Over." It was recorded by Glen Campbell, Dusty Springfield, Roy Orbison, and—most famously of all—by Elvis Presley.[3]

From Dot Records, Jimmie moved on to A&M Records. His future looked brighter than ever. He had money, fame, and confidence that his career was on track to bring him cornucopias of rewards. On the morning of December 1, 1967, at around 2:00 a.m., Jimmie left a party in Los Angeles with his pal Eddie Samuels. They each departed the party in their own car. Eddie followed Jimmie, who had had perhaps two or three drinks. It was not a lot, but Jimmie rarely drank liquor. On the way to Jimmie's home, Samuels missed the turnoff from the San Diego Freeway. As Jimmie made his way toward home, a car with its brights on pulled up behind him. Jimmie thought it was Samuels. It was not. Jimmie rolled down his window, and before he could say anything, he was hit on the head with a tire iron. It crashed through his skull. Doctors later said that Jimmie had been hit several times. He lay bleeding and semiconscious on the front seat of his Cadillac. He heard a voice just outside of the car say, "Damn, Duffy, you killed this man."[4]

When Jimmie didn't show up at his house, Samuels searched the roads that Jimmy would have traveled on. He finally spotted Jimmie's Cadillac, and just as he pulled up to it, Samuels saw a white Volkswagen and a police car leaving the scene. To Samuels's shock, Jimmie lay in a puddle of blood on the front seat. Jimmie was taken by ambulance to the Glendale Community Hospital. Doctors weren't sure they could save the savagely beaten singer. His skull was badly fractured in several places. Surgery left the right side of his head exposed. He began having grand mal seizures and on December 5, he suffered cerebral bleeding and underwent additional surgery. Emerging from surgery, he could barely walk or talk and was bedridden for two years. During that time, he was cared for by a male nurse who seemed intent on keeping Jimmie drugged and dependent on him. It was a good job that came with room and board, plus the proximity of a celebrity. The nurse would not permit friends and relatives to visit his patient, often telling those who phoned that Jimmie was sleeping or not feeling well enough to have visitors. Jimmie was reduced to being an emaciated figure. His hair was neither cut nor combed. He was not shaved, and his beard had grown into a wild untrimmed bush. Finally, one of Jimmie's friends who had not been permitted to visit called Jimmie's brother Archie, who quickly arranged to fly to his stricken brother. He rented a car at the Los Angeles airport and sped to Jimmie's house. An angry Archie banged on the front door, impatiently waiting for the nurse to respond. The male nurse attempted to bar Archie from seeing his brother, but Archie pushed the nurse aside, for nothing would keep him from rescuing his brother. Archie was shocked to his see his once handsome, robust brother reduced to 118 pounds, his face surrounded by a shaggy tangled beard, the hair on his head matted and filthy. A desperate but excited Jimmie gripped Archie's hand and in a faint voice whispered, "They're trying to kill me."

On June 17, 1968, surgeons inserted a twelve-inch metal plate in Jimmie's head. To cover the plate, surgeons took skin grafts from Jimmie's buttocks. Though the plate set off metal detectors and occasionally caused computers and microwaves to either switch on or off, Jimmie felt grateful. In fact, he felt reborn. He was engaged to perform at the Coconut Grove nightclub. Newspapers reported on Jimmie's recovery and return to entertaining. Shortly thereafter, those reporters got word that Jimmie's head injury was not the result of a car accident or drunken fall as they had originally been told by police. An off-duty policeman named Michael Duffy had stopped Jimmie on the night of the so-called accident and beat him with a metal rod. Duffy claimed that he had seen Jimmie driving the wrong way on the San Diego Freeway and pulled him over. Jimmie got out of his car, fell backward, and hit his head, said the officer. Two other cops who had arrived in a patrol car claimed they never saw Jimmie, and Duffy told them that Jimmie was sleeping on the front seat of his car. In their police logs, the two cops wrote that Jimmie had departed by the time they arrived. As the investigation into police misconduct got underway, however, the two cops admitted that the information in their logs was not true. Now questions began to be asked about if Jimmie was beaten by a corrupt cop on behalf of Morris Levy and Roulette Records. And was it the cop's intention to beat Jimmie or to kill him? When a popular singer dies, sales of his records skyrocket. And Roulette controlled Jimmie's most popular recordings. Tommy James, who had recorded numerous hits with Roulette, believed that Levy had arranged for the hit on Jimmie. "If you cross Levy, you could end up like Jimmie Rodgers, left for dead on the LA Freeway."[5]

Though newspapers had changed their stories from portraying Jimmie as an accident victim to a possible crime victim, they still did not have enough information to write more than Jimmie was the victim of a beating by an unknown assailant. Soon the stories became more detailed and Duffy's name began appearing in print. Yet when asked who may have beaten him, Jimmie said he had no memory of the actual beating. All he could recall was that he had seen a pair of bright lights in his rearview mirror and thought they were from Samuels's car, and so he stopped. He sat behind the wheel of his car, waiting for Samuels to get out. Then everything went dark until he awoke in a hospital.

The police had closed ranks and their spokesmen asserted that LAPD officer Michael Duffy (occasionally misidentified as Richard Duffy), while off duty, had stopped Jimmie's car after witnessing the car being driven in an erratic manner. Once he was stopped, Jimmie was instructed to get out of the car. Outside, an inebriated Rodgers stumbled and hit his head on the pavement. Rather than arresting Jimmie for drunken driving, Officer Duffy called for assistance, and two officers arrived at the scene. The three of them managed to lift Rodgers's unconscious body from the pavement and lay him on the front seat. There, they figured, the singer could sleep off his drunkenness. Once Rodgers was safely sprawled out, the three cops agreed not to press charges and left the scene. Though the doctors who had originally examined Jimmie said that he was the victim of a vicious attack by an individual wielding a pipe or metal rod, they now agreed that the singer had fallen to the pavement, thus injuring himself. Jimmie was not about to buy into a story that was filled with contradictions and was as changeable as a chameleon's camouflage. The following month, he filed an

$11 million lawsuit against the City of Los Angeles, claiming that the three officers had beaten him. Though the police and the LA County district attorney rejected the claims, the three policemen (Michael T. Duffy, Raymond V. Whisman, and Ronald D. Wagner) were suspended for two weeks for using improper procedures and leaving the injured Rodgers alone in his car. Duffy had had a previous four-day suspension for using unnecessary force; he had used a blackjack on a juvenile. In 1993, Raymond Virgil Whisman was arrested for assaulting his wife and threatening to kill her. The arrest occurred after sheriff's deputies stormed his house after being informed that he was holding his wife at gunpoint. Deputies found eleven rifles, four shotguns, and two handguns in the home. Whisman was charged with two counts of assault and two counts of making terroristic threats.

In the spirit that the best defense is an aggressive offense, the three policemen and the Police Protective League filed a $13 million dollar slander suit against Rodgers for his public statement accusing the cops of brutality. Their supporters stated that the three officers had their professional reputations besmirched. They refused to believe that Jimmie was receiving late night phone calls warning him to drop his lawsuit. However, they could not deny that Jimmie's beautiful red Chevy Corvette convertible had been incinerated while parked in his driveway. Of course, the media loved it all: the story had a celebrity, possible police violence and corruption, and the possible involvement of an East Coast Mafia family.

Though the newspapers may have wished that both sides would keep fighting to generate a cornucopia of newspaper headlines, the two lawsuits died with barely a whimper. Not wanting to incur further legal costs and perhaps suffering a loss at trial, which would have been a public relations disaster, the Los Angeles City Council proposed giving Jimmie $200,000. In addition to the settlement, the slander suit against Jimmie would be rescinded. In 1973,

Jimmie agreed to accept the payoff. There was no point, he felt, in going on: even if a trial resulted in the police being found guilty, the case would be appealed. It could go on for years. However, without a trial, there was no definitive answer as to what happened the night that Samuels found his friend bleeding and unconscious. Jimmie's supporters continue to believe that he was set up and beaten by corrupt cops who may have been paid by emissaries of Morris Levy. And certainly Tommy James, as a recording artist for Roulette Records and a victim of Levy's cheating and threats, believes that Jimmie was a victim. In his 2010 biography *Me, the Mob, and the Music*, James writes that Levy had arranged the attack in response to Rodgers's repeated demands for unpaid royalties. After Roulette was sold to another record company, Jimmie's estate began receiving past-due royalty payments. However, the amounts were rather small.

Jimmie continued to perform, though he would frequently lose his voice and at other times he would not be able to walk. He suffered from spasmodic dysphonia, also known as laryngeal dystonia. It is a malady in which one's voice suffers from periods of spasm. The spasms cause interruptions in a speaker's or singer's voice and can occur as rapidly as every few sentences or lyrics. The onset is often gradual, and the condition lasts for a lifetime. It was a sad outcome for a singer whose voice was sweeter than wine.

Though Jimmie was vastly changed from the young man who turned "Honeycomb" and "Kisses Sweeter Than Wine" into major hits, his fans still treated him as a great entertainer. One night, he was performing on a stage in a Midwest theater. Because he had difficulty walking, he sang while sitting on a chair. All of a sudden, as he neared the end of the song he had been singing, he went as silent as a radio without electricity. One of his friends walked onto the stage and led Jimmie off. His fans gave him a standing ovation. His father had told him never to land on your ass, and Jimmie never would. He remained an optimist and fighter the remainder of his life. Following a concert in 2012, Jimmie had a heart attack. It did not kill him, but he desperately needed open heart surgery. The optimistic trooper survived the surgery and the damage to his heart. He would also survive two bouts of prostate cancer, colon surgery that resulted in his having to wear a colostomy bag, and kidney disease that resulted in regular dialysis treatments. He had a long and fruitful life, dying at age eighty-seven on January 18, 2021, from COVID. His old friends and neighbors from Camas showed their support by having his hometown name a street in Jimmie's honor.

His third wife, Mary, told me that there was nothing phony about Jimmie. He was absolutely genuine, a loving, kind man, whom people admired. He loved animals, loved fishing, and especially loved his children. He was also a man of deep religious faith, and he and Mary regularly attended services at a nondenominational church in Palm Desert. When asked about his relationship with Roulette Records and Morris Levy, Mary said Jimmie was such a young man then, naïve and trusting, and knew nothing about organized crime. They took advantage of him, and when he began making money again after leaving Roulette, they arranged to have Jimmie beaten.

Frankie Lymon

Sweet Voice Junkie

A THIRTEEN-YEAR-OLD SINGER WITH THE VOICE OF AN ANGEL, who was also a heroin addict. What would come first? His stardom, or his suicide?

Frankie said of himself: "I never was a child, although I was billed in every theater and auditorium where I appeared as a child star." Lymon told Art Peters, a reporter for *Ebony* magazine, in 1967:

> *"I was a man when I was 11 years old, doing everything that most men do. In the neighborhood where I lived, there was no time to be a child. There were five children in my family and my folks had to scuffle to make ends meet. My father was a truck driver and my mother worked as a domestic in white folks' homes. While kids my age were playing stickball and marbles, I was working in the corner grocery store carrying orders to help pay the rent."*

> "I looked twice my age," Lymon told *Ebony.*

> *"I was thin as a shadow and I didn't give a damn. My only concern was in getting relief. You know, an addict is the most pathetic creature on earth. He knows that every time he*

sticks a needle in his arm, he's gambling with death and, yet, he's got to have it. It's like playing Russian Roulette with a spike. There's always the danger that some peddler will sell him a poisoned batch—some garbage."

Here young Frankie knocks on wood. "I was lucky. God must have been watching over me."[1]

Franklin (Frankie) Joseph Lymon was born on September 30, 1942, in Washington Heights. His father, Howard, was a truck driver, and his mother, Jeanette, was a maid. They were singers who performed with a gospel group known as the Harlemaires. With his sweet soprano voice, young Frankie, along with his siblings, sang with the Harlemaires Juniors. Anyone who saw the pint-sized Frankie immediately was taken by his stage presence: he radiated confidence, joy, and stardom. He had the ingratiating energy of a six-month-old puppy. If ever a kid was suited to be in the spotlight, it was Frankie Lymon.

The Lymons were a poor family, and each member had to contribute to its upkeep. Frankie, at age ten, did his part by taking a job in a local grocery. Though he worked diligently, his heart was in music: it was both his escape and his future. And in the 1950s, a new, inviting style of music known as doo wop had sprung up like mushrooms after a rain storm. Groups of singers consisting of four or five boys or young men would gather in subway stations, where the acoustics were terrific. One day, on his way home, Frankie heard one of those doo wop groups. It was the Coupe De Villes. Frankie could have imagined himself as its lead singer, backed up by members Jimmy Merchant, Sherman Garnes, Joe Negroni, and Herman Santiago; the group was a handsome blend of black and Puerto Rican talents. Frankie's soprano voice as endearing as a bird's love song was just what the group needed. With Frankie as a new member, the group changed its name to the Premiers. By 1956, the group, soon to be known as Frankie Lymon and the

Teenagers, stood on the threshold of stardom. It came with their recording of "Why Do Fools Fall in Love."

The genesis of a hit song is often as fortuitous as the success of the song itself. A friend of the group showed them a series of love letters that he had received from his girlfriend. Jimmy Merchant and Herman Santiago read the letters and were inspired to write their own kind of love song. They showed the song to Richard Barrett, who sang with the Valentines. Barrett was sufficiently impressed to take the song to George Goldner, a record producer who owned several labels. He, too, was impressed and decided to have the Teenagers record the song; he had them and their parents sign contracts with one of his companies, Gee Records. On the day of the recording, Santiago was detained and could not get to the session on time. This was young Frankie's moment: like a jack-rabbit, he jumped up and announced that he could sing the lead. He knew all the words. Though he knew the lyrics, there is some dispute about whether or not he had a hand in writing the song. Instead, it seems that Frankie, like a creative jazz musician, improvised some of the wording and altered the melody to fit his talent. It took more than twenty takes to get the song the exact way Goldner wanted it. He was finally satisfied, convinced he had produced a hit record. He also understood that Frankie could be promoted to being a major star of rock and roll. It is not surprising then to learn that Goldner and his partner, Joe Kolsy, decided to manage their young singer's career. And because of the tight relationship that Goldner had with Morris Levy, backer of Alan Freed, the record got star billing on Freed's radio program. It played so often, it seemed to saturate the airwaves. Surprisingly, none of the usual sharks took credit for writing the song, so Frankie, Jimmy, and Herman received full credit. Disappointments and litigation would follow.

"Why Do Fools Fall in Love" was embraced by disc jockeys and listeners. It became Gee's first hit single in January 1956. It sprinted up the charts, landing at number six on the *Billboard* pop singles chart, then continued its ascent to the top of the *Billboard* R&B singles chart, where it was the winner for five weeks. Frankie and the Teenagers had become stars, and—at least on paper—rich ones.

They were one of the hottest teenage groups at time when groups all over the city were banging on the doors of record companies to record hit songs. Among the most successful ones to emerge during the 1950s were Dion and the Belmonts, the Cadillacs, the Cleftones, the Coasters, Bill Haley and the Comets, Danny and the Juniors, Jan and Dean, the Del-Satins, the Del-Vikings, the Diamonds, the Drifters, the Flamingos, the Five Satins, Johnny and the Hurricanes, the Impalas, Little Anthony and the Imperials, the Isley Brothers, the Mello-Kings, the Monotones, the Moonglows, the Penguins, the Platters, the Valentines, Billy Ward and His Dominoes, the Wrens, and dozens more. Many of them were one-hit wonders. But Goldner was determined that Frankie Lymon and the Teenagers would have a string of hits. They recorded "I Want You to Be My Girl," which gave the group its second hit, reaching number 13 on the national *Billboard* Hot 100 chart. Along came four additional top ten R&B singles, including "I Want You to Be My Girl," "I Promise to Remember," "Who Can Explain?" (the B side of "I Promise to Remember," which ascended the charts on its own), "The ABC's of Love," and "I'm Not a Juvenile Delinquent." To add to the popularity of the group and to augment his own considerable profits, Goldner produced a compilation of their hit singles in an album titled *The Teenagers Featuring Frankie Lymon.*

The spotlight on Frankie grew brighter and the other Teenagers seemed to fade into the surrounding shadows. Frankie was deeply impressed by himself. In addition to being a hit singer with thousands of adoring fans, some of whom wanted to mother him, he was a lover of women who wanted to initiate him into the pleasures of sex as if he were a virgin boy on the threshold of giving up his innocence. Little did his fans know that Frankie had a ravenously insatiable love for older women. He often dated women who were twice his age, and in public he would pass each one off as his mother. Of course, if reporters saw him in different cities with different mothers, they quickly realized Frankie's game. No matter how protean, a boy could only have one biological mother. Of course, he could have referred to them as stepmothers or foster mothers, thus explaining the confusing array of mothers. However, a wink and sly comment were usually all that was necessary, for most reporters shied away from noting Frankie's many lovers. After all, he was such a youngster and exposure of his many lovers would have been unseemly during the discreet 1950s. He was lucky that no reporter portrayed him as a victim of statutory rape. One reporter, upon learning of Frankie's first marriage, predicted that where there are numerous lovers, there will surely be numerous wives.

It is not surprising that solipsism and narcissism produce yearnings to be the sole target of a celebratory spotlight. Across the musical spectrum those who shared a spotlight with a partner or group often chose to become solo acts. Lymon was no different. In 1957, while on tour with the Teenagers in Europe, he chose to be the sole occupant of the rocket that was shooting him into the farthest reaches of celebrity. To show fans that Lymon could perform without his group and be as good or better than he had been with them, Goldner gave Frankie one solo spot after another. The audiences still cheered and stamped their feet and applauded loudly after Lymon finished a set. Because there was another recording about to be released, and still capitalizing on the Frankie and the Teenagers brand, Goldner did nothing to delete the presence of the Teenagers. He figured that he would not roil the retail waters of success, so the song "Goody Goody" was released as recorded by Frankie Lymon and the Teenagers. In fact, it used prerecorded backup tapes as well as backing by anonymous session singers. Shortly thereafter, an album titled *Frankie Lymon and the Teenagers at the London Palladium* was released. Frankie officially departed from the group by September 1957.

Without Frankie, the Teenagers used a series of substitute lead singers. None lasted long. The first to join the group was Billy Lobrano. There was also Howard Kenny Bobo, who sang lead on "Tonight's the Night" with the Teenagers; and then came Johnny Houston, who sang the lead on two other Teenager songs. Morris Levy had bought up Goldner's musical empire and he didn't want to be stuck with an unprofitable investment. Having recorded the Teenagers on Goldner's old label, End Records, Levy decided the group was a sinking fund. He untethered the Teenagers without an anchor and set them adrift. Frankie's position was far more secure, but he too would also be cut loose.

Morris Levy, always an opportunist, knew weakness when he spotted it and would pounce like a lion on a wounded gazelle. Goldner presented him with the perfect opportunity, for Goldner was a compulsive gambler and could not stop betting no matter how much money he lost. His compulsive behavior resulting in lost money was as predictable as a deciduous tree losing its leaves. But while a tree grows new leaves every spring, Goldner had exhausted his resources. To sweep away his mountain of debts that had begun to elicit threats from mob loan sharks, he sold off his properties to his good friend, Morris Levy, whose motto could have been a friend in need is a friend indeed, as well as in deed. With Goldner's musical empire now deeded to Levy, the godfather of rock and roll became one of the most intimidating men in the music business. Levy quickly moved to take over control of Frankie's career. He thought Frankie's records would stuff the coffers of unpaid royalties. Frankie's next solo record was "My Girl," but it didn't strike the same compelling doo wop notes as did his earlier recordings. He was now in harness to the unsatisfied president of Roulette Records. He was disappointed in the record's lack of success. It was not in keeping with his belief in himself. He was growing more and more restless. Was it possible that he would never enjoy the highs of his earlier successes? It was a frightening consideration. The early hits had inflated Frankie's ego, and he figured the pattern would continue. But nothing is preordained in show business. Stars can produce hits, then flop; careers can rise and fall. All stars, past their profitability, are endlessly replaceable. In fact, there are assembly lines of aspiring stars, each waiting for that one chance that will change their lives.

It takes considerable self-awareness to realize that one's career has begun a slow, downward slide. The heady days of the past are too vivid to be easily tossed aside. One gets older, one's audience gets older, and tastes change. It is the self-aware artist, perhaps with the help of a sagacious manager, who can adapt to new cultural tastes. The zeitgeist can be a whirlwind that blows apart houses of cards. And by 1960, Frankie was yesterday's darling. His recording of "Little Bitty Pretty One" anemically rose to number 58 on the Hot 100 pop chart. To maintain his Sunset Boulevard–like illusions he relied more and more on heroin, which he had been injecting since the age of fifteen. That was it for Levy. He didn't want a no-hit drug addict on his label. He cut Frankie loose, and the desperate singer, with no place to go, signed up for drug rehabilitation.

With or without drugs, fate would slap down Frankie. On July 19, 1957, in an episode of Alan Freed's popular TV program *The Big Beat*, a simple act of youthful exuberance would result in racist outcries. As the show was coming to a close and credits would soon start rolling, Freed told his teenage audience to take to the dance floor. Frankie, who had just finished singing, leapt from the stage and grabbed a cute white girl. The two joyously danced to the closing music, their faces aglow with joy. The screen went dark and so would the show. Stations from all over the South said they would cancel *The Big Beat* because it broadcast a white girl dancing with a black boy. In the South, black boys had been lynched for less. Not only was the show canceled in the South, but ABC pulled the plug nationwide.

The next few years were no kinder to Frankie. He had short-lived relationships with Columbia Records and 20th Century Fox Records. But without hits, his value had sunk: he was singing in clubs for fees in the mid to high two to three digits. (He sang at my high school graduation for $50.) While he couldn't generate hits and found himself in a constant state of disappointment, he did find solace in the arms of Elizabeth Mickey Waters, whom he married in 1964. She gave birth to Frankie's only child, Francine, who, rather than being a bundle of joy, was a reason for Frankie to escape deeper into the world of heroin. Francie died two days after being born. It's not surprising that the marriage went downhill, but a final termination was not necessary, for Waters was still married to her first husband when she said "I do" to Frankie. Perhaps a change of scene would breathe new life into his dying career.

"Go west, young man" was a slogan that had driven millions of unhappy people west. And so Frankie moved to the City of Angels, a place where stars are born, often achieve stratospheric success, but just as often flicker, fade, and die in bitter obscurity, though some are memorialized by media sentimentalists and nostalgia buffs.

For Frankie, the move to LA resulted in just the kind of publicity he thought his career needed. Newspapers and fan magazines announced that he had found the love of his life with Zola Taylor, an original member of the famous singing group the Platters. In addition to photos of her and Frankie that appeared in print, photos of Zola in the rock and roll movie *Rock Around the Clock* were printed. When asked by reporters where she and Frankie had married, Zola said she married Frankie in Mexicali, Mexico, in 1965. The marriage was not long lasting. Reporters now asked why the marriage had ended. Zola said it was because of Frankie's drug use. Many now thought the marriage had been a publicity stunt, and that was ultimately confirmed by Frankie. But it was not until after Frankie's death, when his various alleged widows were fighting over the rights to his song "Why Do Fools Fall in Love," that Zola's claim that she and Frankie had actually married vaporized, for no marriage license could be produced. Reporters were sent to Mexico to dig up the evidence of a marriage and found nothing. Zola finally came clean, and in a gossip column written by Major Robinson Taylor, she said the marriage had indeed been a joke. Joke or not, the marriage had not spurred new interest in Frankie's sinking career.

But because singing was all he knew, and because it was what had produced his memorable successes, he continued to plug along. Perhaps he would enjoy good fortune again. He even took up tap dancing, which he added to his performance at the Apollo Theater. Though the audience appreciated his performance and gave him an enthusiastic round of applause, it did not bestow stardom on him. He was fast heading to being a nostalgia singer, many of whom are often found on PBS fund-raising programs, performing on cruise ships, or in retirement villages. And he was only in his twenties. What would he do if he could make it into his thirties and forties? He had appeared on numerous television programs, such as *American Bandstand, The Ed Sullivan Show*, and *Hollywood a Go-Go*, where he lip-synced "Why Do Fools Fall in Love" and other early hits. He was twenty-two years old and lip-syncing a song that had been a hit when he was thirteen. His voice was no longer that of an angelic choir boy. His face and body had matured. The charm of an energetic, talented thirteen-year-old was no longer in evidence. He tried new songs, but past hits were all that audiences wanted to hear. After that, it was thank you very much, goodbye, we'll see you again.

His sadness could only be relieved by a short-lived euphoric shot of heroin. In the 1950s and 1960s, addicts were looked upon as potential dangers to society, for they would commit crimes, sometimes violent ones, to get money to buy their next fix. Or they might, as parents warned their children, hang around school yards, trying to get kids hooked on the drug, and then force them into lives of degrading crime. Rather than treating addicts, the culture insisted that they be taken off the streets and incarcerated. It is not surprising, then, that Frankie would eventually be arrested. Such an arrest would generate good publicity for the arresting officers and the prosecutors. On June 21, 1966, cops slapped cuffs on Frankie. When he came to trial, he was given a choice: go to prison and become a victim of prison rapes, or go into the Army and serve your country. He was told, as were so many other young men, that the Army will make a man of you. The choice was an easy one. The young soldier reported as ordered to Fort Gordon in Georgia for basic training. It was not to Frankie's liking, but he felt that he was a lot better off than being a convict. In addition, he got leaves to go into nearby Augusta and enjoy himself. While on leave, he met a young woman named Emira Eagle, a school teacher at Hornsby Elementary School. The two fell in love and married in June 1967. Though happy in his marriage, Frankie's experiences in the Army proved a disappointment, not just to him but also to the Army. He felt he was still a celebrity, not someone who should have to clean latrines, mop floors, and wash pots, pans, and dishes. Resentful, restless, and yearning to rekindle recognition for his talent as a singer, he often went AWOL so that he could be signed for small singing gigs in and around Augusta. The Army was not impressed with Frankie's ambition to be a star again. It awarded Frankie with a dishonorable discharge. Honorable or dishonorable, it made no difference to Frankie, for he was now free to pursue his career goals. Though he had moved into his wife's house and continued singing at small local clubs, he heard the siren call of New York, where his career had originally taken off. In 1968, thinking he was following his destiny that would lead to an exciting comeback, he traveled to New York. Once in the Big Apple, Frankie signed a contract with Big Apple Records. At the same time, Morris Levy thought the time opportune to release Frankie's records in conjunction with Big Apple. Levy and Frankie's manager planned a huge promotion about the return to recording of one the historic figures of doo wop. Frankie could not have been happier. Everything was in place for him to ascend to the top of the charts again. Frankie settled into the home of his grandmother in Harlem. To celebrate his good fortune, he did not pop a cork from a bottle of champagne; instead he used a syringe to suck up a celebratory dose of heroin. He had been clean since entering the Army, but he was finished with that life. He was back where he belonged. The heroin entered his body like a bolt of lightning. It went straight to his brain and shut down his respiratory system.

(An explanation of what happens: When heroin enters the body, it travels via the bloodstream to the brain, where it is quickly converted to morphine. Morphine is then available for binding at what are called mu-opioid receptors in the brain. Mu-opioid receptors are located throughout the brain and in the brain stem. Those located in the brain stem inhibit the workings of the respiratory centers found there, leading to a condition known as respiratory depression. During a heroin overdose, a relatively large amount of morphine becomes available to the brain. When this large amount of morphine binds to mu-opioid receptors in the brain stem, profound respiratory depression results and the victim of a heroin overdose eventually stops breathing. When this occurs, oxygen supply to the brain and heart plunges, and the victim dies from cardiac arrest secondary to respiratory arrest.[2])

The body of twenty-five-year-old Frankie Lymon lay on the floor of his grandmother's bathroom, a needle stuck in his arm, his cold lips slightly parted. The body was all that remained of what had been an ingratiating and charming young singer who loved dancing, singing, and being the center of attention. His body was buried at Saint Raymond's Cemetery in the Throgs Neck section of the Bronx, in New York City. The grave of Frankie Lymon was as alone as those of all forgotten celebrities, whose fame had faded into anonymity. No fans came and laid flowers at his headstone. In fact, no one took care of it. It was as abandoned as Frankie's career. It stood there, derelict, weather beaten, and unmarked, no better than a grave in a potter's field.

Finally, Emira Eagle had arranged for a new headstone to be installed. Its inscription reads, "In Loving Memory of My Husband Frank J. Lymon Sept. 30, 1942–Feb. 27, 1968." Opportunistic as ever, the labels that owned some of Frankie's songs figured that his death would drive fans to purchase his records. It didn't happen. Though his style had influenced Michael Jackson, fans did not perceive Frankie as the prototype of a moonwalking thriller. His recording of "I'm Sorry" and "Seabreeze" were released in 1969, and neither one had the verve and energy of his greatest hits.

Years passed. Many new singers became media darlings, earning millions of dollars, filling stadiums, and wearing their glitz like medals. Frankie, however, was—at best—a footnote in the history of rock and roll. But a few people thought that fate unfairly treated the young singer. Twenty-four years after his death, Frankie was honored by being inducted into the Rock and Roll Hall of Fame. Five years later, his life was resurrected in the bio movie *Why Do Fools Fall in Love*. Though the movie was a tribute to Frankie, it was disappointing. It didn't succeed in making Frankie into a household name.

Roger Ebert, the popular appraiser of movies, wrote that he was disappointed in the screenplay and in the direction of the film: "There are several angles this material might have been approached from, and director Gregory Nava tries several without hitting on one that works. By the end of the film, we're not even left with anyone to root for; we realize with a little astonishment, waiting for the court verdict, that we don't care who wins."[3]

If Frankie had any posthumous influence, it was in the repertoire of other singers. Diana Ross, for example, was able to turn "Why Do Fools Fall in Love" into a major hit, reminiscent of the days when Frankie and the Teenagers's recording of the song rocketed to the top of the charts. Ross's album, containing the hit, was the first to be produced by Ross herself, and it became her second certified platinum album. It was also certified gold in the United Kingdom and Canada. But its success would also launch a series of lawsuits that generated tabloid ink across the country.

Diana Ross wasn't the only one who found Frankie's material worth singing. At doo wop festivals, a reformed Teenagers group was always met with great enthusiasm after they sang the songs that Frankie had popularized. Not only were his songs in vogue among nostalgia fans, but Frankie's death had become a warning necrology that pointed to a succession of singers, all of whom died of drug overdoses. The long list included Jimi Hendrix, Janis Joplin, Whitney Houston, Keith Moon, Jim Morrison, Sid Vicious, Tom Petty, and Michael Jackson, among others. Those lives that had been defined by the triad of sex, drugs, and rock and roll could not withstand the temptation to lose themselves in the euphoria that only drugs could provide.

But it was not drugs that launched lawsuits regarding Frankie's estate; it was the reborn success of "Why Do Fools Fall in Love," which had been given new life by Diana Ross. It was started by three women, each of whom claimed to be Frankie's widow. Through their lawyers, they contacted Morris Levy about the copyrights to Frankie's songs. Each claimed entitlement to the copyrights. Their claims made for an interesting tangle of contradictions that would require the wisdom of Solomon to sort it all out. There they were Zola Taylor, Elizabeth Waters, and Elmira Eagle. Each solemnly claimed to be Frankie's heir. Levy was no doubt annoyed by the claimants, for it was against his nature to part with valuable properties. You want the copyrights, then sue me. He had the deep pockets to keep a lawsuit active for however long it took for the others to back off. He would stand firm, and they would fade. But the litigation continued, for millions of dollars were at stake, as were lawyers' fees.

To begin, there were questions about the legality of the alleged marriages, for Frankie had not divorced any of the widows. Each of the claimants presented similar problems. Waters was married when she tied the knot with Frankie. She went on to divorce her previous husband, but not until 1965, which was after she and Frankie had become husband and wife. Then there was Taylor, who claimed that she and Frankie had married in Mexico in 1965; however, she could not produce a marriage license or any other document that would have confirmed such a marriage had taken place. Frankie's marriage to Eagle, however, was documented. It took place in the Beulah Grove Baptist Church in Augusta, Georgia, in 1967. Frankie, unfortunately, wasn't free to marry her, because he had failed to divorce his earlier wives. The contortions of legal reasoning are a maze that few people can navigate. The first court decision awarded Frankie's estate to Waters. As expected, Eagle challenged that ruling and the Appellate Division of the New York State Supreme Court chose Eagle as the legitimate heir. She would receive a windfall of royalties, especially after the success of Diana Ross's recording of "Why Do Fools Fall in Love."

That, however, was not the end of it. An important question arose: was Morris Levy entitled to half a songwriting credit for "Why Do Fool Fall in Love"? The original recording listed Frankie, Herman Santiago, and Jimmy Merchant as creators of the song. Later releases, however, were without the names of Santiago and Merchant, and Frankie was listed as cowriter of the song with George Goldner. To complicate matters, it was established that Goldner had sold his companies to Levy in 1959. Goldner's name vanished and was replaced by Levy's as a cowriter of the song.

During the labyrinth of testimony, it was learned that neither Goldner nor Levy had paid Frankie his songwriting royalties. The legitimate heir, Emira Eagle, would now be entitled to those royalties. Not so fast, said lawyers for Merchant and Santiago: in 1987, Merchant and Santiago sued Morris Levy's estate to reestablish that the original recording had accurately listed them as cowriters of the song. The US District Court for the Southern District decided that Santiago and Merchant were, indeed, two of the original songwriters of "Why Do Fools Fall in Love." While Santiago and Merchant awaited payment, they would soon be disappointed. In 1996 that ruling (surprise, surprise) was reversed by the US Court of Appeals for the Second Circuit on the basis of the statute of limitations: copyright cases must be brought before a court within three years of the alleged civil violation, while Merchant and Santiago's lawsuit was not filed until thirty years later. Goodbye, Merchant and Santiago.[4]

Though dead, Levy and Frankie came out on top: the court ruled that they were the owners of "Why Do Fools Fall in Love," and the song currently remains in the names of Frankie Lymon and Morris Levy.

Though Frankie and the Teenagers were doo wop trendsetters, they did not succeed in earning anywhere near what today's megastars earn, especially those who perform at sold-out concerts and have sold their catalogs for hundreds of millions of dollars. Poor Frankie. As Emira told Don Rhodes, the music columnist at the *Augusta Chronicle*, in 2019: "I caught Frankie at a good time in his life. I often tell people that Frankie didn't end up living a glorified life. His in the end was a wasted life ruined by drugs. He was used and misused, and he used others also. His was a wasted life, and he was so talented."[5]

Had Frankie lived, he would have been part of the nostalgia craze. On the twenty-fifth anniversary of their first hit, the reformed Teenagers performed to a cheering, sold-out crowd of fans. The updated Teenagers included two originals, Jimmy Merchant and Herman Santiago, who were joined by Eric Ward (of the group Second Verse) and Pearl McKinnon. As long as doo wop fans from the 1950s want to immerse themselves in the warm glow of nostalgia, the Teenagers and other groups from the 1950s will continue to attract audiences happy to relive old memories. And the estates of Frankie and Levy will continue to be paid.

Sal "the Swindler" Pisello

The Great Cutout Swindle

SAL "THE SWINDLER" PISELLO FOUND HIS GREATEST OPPORTU-
nity to perform a major swindle in the record business. He had
made his mark in the food service business, but the record business
offered him a possibility for the biggest payoff of his career.

As with others in this book, he too was associated with Morris
Levy, whose tentacles seemed to have reached into every aspect
of the record business. In addition to doing business with Levy,
Pisello was an alleged member of the Gambino crime family and
had profitable associations with the Genovese and DeCavalcante
crime families as well.

While investigating MCA, the large movie production and
record company, the Justice Department came across Pisello,
who somehow managed to finesse his way into an office at MCA
headquarters. What was an alleged member of organized crime
doing as an ostensible executive at one of the biggest entertainment
companies in America? According to the FBI documents, Pisello
was suspected of involvement in a number of fraud and embezzle-
ment schemes that earned him a reputation as a con artist. His
clever scams had been focused on restaurants and food service
companies that he controlled as well as several meat companies. In

addition, the IRS had discovered that Pisello had filed only four income tax returns between 1965 and 1982, paying a mere $2,500 in federal taxes. It was also noted that the Italian National Police regarded Pisello as an international swindler because he had supposedly defrauded a jeweler out of $102,000 at the Hotel Di Paris in Monte Carlo. However, there was insufficient evidence to bring an indictment.

For the Justice Department, Pisello's reputation was sufficient to launch a major investigation. It went on for two years and was a significant embarrassment for MCA. So much so that two of MCA's most prestigious board members, former senator Howard Baker and esteemed New York investment banker and philanthropist Felix Rohatyn, argued that MCA should cease its dealings with Pisello. Others, however, were reluctant to cut ties with Pisello because he was a potential source for millions of dollars in profits. Hence, Pisello remained in place.

Pisello was constantly presenting deals to MCA, each of which promised to be a bonanza, but few came to fruition. For example, he was supposed to design a mat for break dancing, for which MCA paid him $100,000. In another deal, Pisello was supposed to market and promote a new Latin music label, and for that MCA paid him an additional $30,000. The Justice Department attempted to get several senior executives to testify about Pisello's activities. But they were adamant in their refusals. After all, who wants to sacrifice their life by testifying against someone who was speculated to be a member of the Mafia? Because none of them wanted to be threatened by the mob and knew very little about Pisello, they had neither interest nor incentive in trading their testimony for immunity for nonexistent indictments. Nevertheless, a prosecutor continued to offer them immunity, just in case someone changed their mind. One nervous executive finally said he would testify in exchange for immunity, but nothing came of the potential deal. The others who were offered immunity said that if called to testify, they would cite their Fifth Amendment rights against self-incrimination.

One employee, who knew nothing of Pisello's criminal activity and had not been offered a deal, nevertheless commented:

> *Pisello was comical in a way—always elegantly attired in hand-tailored suits . . . but still carrying the unmistakable cachet of a hustler up from the mean streets of Brooklyn. He wore a diamond ring so large that the standing joke around the office was, "Do you shake Sal's hand or kiss it?" He drove a bronze Cadillac Eldorado convertible with a special gold trim and gold wire wheels. There was nothing remotely like it in MCA's parking lot. Pisello just plain stuck out. You couldn't miss him. Everyone knew who Sal was, they just didn't know exactly what he did.*[1]

What people at MCA had heard was that Pisello had moved to Los Angeles from New York in the early 1970s. They didn't know why he moved, but some discovered that he had opened a restaurant shortly after his arrival. He began using it as a place to meet with people in the music business and propose numerous quick-money deals. He told stories about himself as an international bon vivant, a man who enjoyed the best of everything: whether in Europe or the United States, he stayed in elegant suites in five-star hotels and patronized only the trendiest restaurants; in Hollywood, he ate at the restaurants where celebrities and powerbrokers ate; he was a fashion plate whose wardrobe and jewelry was in the finest John Gotti tradition. And like a hot shot film producer, out to attract young aspiring actresses, he could be seen driving up and down Sunset Boulevard in flashy cars. When paying a check in a restaurant, he was sure to pull out a thick roll of hundred dollar bills. In private, Pisello offered his guests the charm of a professional con artist; it seemed to ooze out of him. His charm warmed all those who he entertained in his luxurious home, where he took pride in being a superb cook. His charm, as might be expected, had a purpose: he was often proposing great money-making deals to his affluent guests.

A charming bon vivant was not who the Justice Department was interested in. They wanted to know what an alleged member of the Gambino crime family was doing striding the halls of MCA, a man whose name appeared in numerous investigations over a period of twenty years. Tipped off to shine a flashlight into some shadowy deals, the FBI thought that Sal Pisello had been involved. But he was like a cat in a dark alley, leaping over walls, escaping clutching hands. It was not only the Justice Department that investigated Pisello. He had been investigated by the FBI, the Internal Revenue Service, the Drug Enforcement Agency, and police on the East and West Coasts. And in Milan and Rome, Pisello was shadowed by the police who also tapped his phone. They had suspected him of being an international drug dealer and a jewel thief. But suspicions are not proof, and so Pisello was not bothered. In America, law enforcement officials thought Pisello imported large quantities of heroin into the country from Mexico. Again, there was no proof. Though a target of investigators, Pisello had the ability and skills to skate slickly over the surface of insufficient or circumstantial evidence to render himself free from indictments. For example, in one of his deals, Pisello formed a group of affluent doctors and businessmen and got them to invest nearly $500,000 in a restaurant that he owned, Roma di Notte on La Cienega Boulevard. The restaurant was later destroyed in a fire, along with its financial records. Fire investigators later listed the blaze as suspected arson, and the case has never been solved. In another case, Pisello was the subject of a tax evasion investigation as a result of his alleged attempt to set up a drug-smuggling operation in the Fulton Fish Market in West Los Angeles. (Alleged seems to have been an adjective that defined most of the criminal allegations against

Pisello.) In a DEA report, it is noted that Pisello went to Rome and checked into a five-star hotel. There he made reservations for two high-ranking Sicilian members of the Mafia. According to the DEA, the three met to set up a smuggling operation that would have brought heroin from Turkey into France and Italy and then smuggled it into the United States. Pisello's connection in the deal was the Gambino capo Aniello Dellacroce (mentor to John Gotti). Yet Pisello again skated away from possible prosecution. One would have thought that the Justice Department would have given up on a man who slipped out of more traps than Houdini.

Finally, the Justice Department thought they might be onto something of value. The Justice Department uncovered records that showed that MCA had paid large sums of money to World Records, a company owned by Pisello, Rocco "the Butcher" Mussachia, and Frederico Giovanelli. The latter two were alleged members of the Genovese crime family. When MCA executives were shown the records and asked what Pisello did at MCA, those executives—for all their interest in cooperating—might just as well have shrugged their shoulders. When asked why Pisello had an office at MCA, again no one knew the reason. When asked what services he performed, still again no one knew. Justice Department executives, however, were able to get one executive to comment that "[Pisello] knew nothing about the record business. I couldn't understand why he was there."[2]

No wall of silence or ignorance was about to prevent the Justice Department's bulldog prosecutor Marvin Rudnick from giving up. He wanted to know how Pisello had swum through the nets of the human resources department to arrive at MCA. Rudnick learned that Pisello's first contact with the company came in late 1983, when he claimed to be a representative of Englewood, New Jersey–based Sugar Hill Records. He supposedly arranged a deal for MCA to distribute the company's small amount of inventory. Even to Sugar Hill, Pisello was a mystery. The company's lawyer said he had negotiated a deal with MCA but had no idea how Pisello got involved. Pisello would later claim that he simply walked into MCA and made an appointment to see the vice president in charge of the record division. Thereafter, he talked the guy into making a deal. To many it was a doubtful explanation. Yet Pisello moved on and was subsequently instrumental in negotiating MCA's purchase of the Checker/Chess/Cadet record catalog of master recordings of classic rock and roll songs from Sugar Hill. For his assistance in affecting the outcome of the deal, Pisello was forgiven a debt: he did not have to pay back $130,000 of advances that MCA had paid him.

In addition, as part of the purchase deal, MCA canceled Sugar Hill's $1.7-million debt and lent Sugar Hill another $1.3 million to assist them with their current cash flow problems, according to a May 1985 report by MCA internal auditors. In November of that year, Sugar Hill filed for protection under Chapter 11 of the US Bankruptcy Code. According to MCA auditors, $300,000 of a $1.3-million Sugar Hill loan went to pay off a priority interest in Checker/Chess held by Morris Levy, who was then a target of three federal grand jury investigations. Wherever there was a big deal in the record business, Morris Levy seemed to be either directly involved or operating surreptitiously in the shadows. He was a man who would not be denied.

Regardless of how Pisello made his way into MCA, the Sugar Hill deal justified his presence at MCA. Rudnick, however, continued to doubt Pisello's explanation of how he arrived at MCA. While continuing his investigations, Rudnick heard various stories. One that was never confirmed was that a senior executive gave an order that Pisello was to be given free rein and no one was to bother him. There were whispers that Pisello had performed an important favor for a senior MCA executive that saved his career; the price for that favor was Pisello's unexplained position at MCA. Though he didn't have a title and there was no record of a regular salary, Pisello was nevertheless put in charge of MCA's cutout division: a multimillion-dollar source of business for MCA. (Cutouts are so called because one corner of an album cover has been cut off to indicate that the recording is a remainder or part of an overstock in inventory and can be sold to deep discount distributors from ten cents to one dollar.) All cutouts are deleted from a record company's catalog. (Numerous insiders have compared the cutout business to the used car business, where dealers bid to buy used cars and then attempt to sell them at huge markups.) When Pisello emerged as if from a magician's trick at MCA, the company had ten million cutouts in its warehouse. The potential profits from selling those cutouts to distributors generated a fever of greed in opportunistic dealmakers.

To get rid of inventories of cutouts, which take up an enormous amount of warehouse space, record companies ask interested discount buyers to submit sealed bids. The company that bids the highest dollar amount gets to buy the entire inventory of cutouts and sell them at a considerable profit. However, that was not the procedure embraced by Pisello. He had no intention of operating in a competitive marketplace. If there were sharks in the water circling that huge body of cutouts, Pisello would be the alpha shark. And MCA had no objections.

At the time, Rudnick was getting too close to the inner workings of MCA. He would have to be put on a tight leash. MCA would need to keep Rudnick from sniffing around areas that should be off limits. The head of MCA, Lew Wasserman, for years had been Ronald Reagan's agent, friend, and confidant. When Reagan was president of the Screen Actors Guild, he passed a regulation permitting MCA not only to be a theatrical agency but also to be a producer of movies and television programs. The ruling added millions of dollars to MCA's coffers. Thereafter, MCA returned the favor, making sure that Reagan would star in TV shows that it produced and become a multimillionaire.

According to Dan E. Moldea in his book *Dark Victory: Ronald Reagan, MCA, and the Mob*, "Lew Wasserman immediately wanted to get MCA into the television production business on a large scale. In order to gain authorization for this dual status, MCA had convinced SAG to approve an exclusive 'blanket waiver' of its rules. . . . In July 1952, there were meetings between certain members of the SAG board and MCA, including Wasserman, Schreiber, Beilenson, and Kramer. No record of these private meetings was kept."

> *At the conclusion of these talks, Reagan and SAG national executive secretary John Dales—working in concert with Beilenson—managed to engineer a "special arrangement" between the union and the giant talent agency. However, a Justice Department document stated that "Wasserman and Schreiber could sell SAG anything" because of their relationship with Reagan.*
>
> *The unprecedented deal granted MCA permission to operate in the profitable field of television production with its talent agency, MCA Artists, and its new television production company, Revue Productions, headed by MCA executive Taft Schreiber. Nothing like it had ever been approved by the SAG board before.*[3]

It's not surprising that when running for governor and president, Reagan could depend on support from Wasserman and many of his associates. After Reagan was elected president, MCA's lawyers asked the president's Justice Department to yank Rudnick's leash. While circumscribing Rudnick's area of investigation, MCA was willing to sacrifice Pisello, if it meant that no one at MCA was to be incriminated. And so the Justice Department yanked Rudnick's leash, scolded him, and attempted to limit his authority. The Justice Department hoped that by limiting Rudnick's investigation of Pisello that MCA would emerge as an innocent bystander. Rudnick, however, was a man with a mission and not easily dissuaded from doing his job, especially when he was right.

It was not so easy. Rudnick was a brilliant prosecutor who scared the top brass at MCA. He was digging up much dirt for a possible prosecution that could embarrass the top brass at MCA. The justice department called Rudnick to Washington, again gave him a dressing down, and told him to lay off MCA. Refusing to abide by Justice Department directives, Rudnick was eventually diverted from looking into certain of MCA's activities; however, he continued arming himself for a prosecution of Pisello. He would ultimately win a conviction that resulted in Pisello serving two years in prison.

It was Pisello's cutout deal with a small-time cutout dealer named John LaMonte that led to Pisello's eventual downfall. A plot to earn millions of dollars was uncovered by Rudnick. He found out that LaMonte, who not only sold cutouts but had also sold counterfeit hit records, had served a term in prison for his counterfeiting activities. Having served his time, LaMonte was hot for a big score to get back on his feet, and MCA's cutouts would be his golden road to wealth. Or so he thought.

Normally LaMonte bought his cutouts from one of several small companies that specialized in selling them. He was a minor player who had never gotten an opportunity to deal directly with a major label. But a deal with Pisello and MCA would elevate LaMonte to being a major player. The eager LaMonte struck a deal with Pisello to purchase MCA's 4.2 million cutout albums and cassettes for $1.3 million. The resale profits would be several times the purchase price. LaMonte could barely contain his enthusiasm at the prospect of making millions of dollars. He figured that as the owner of the House of Sounds, he had a successful track record of buying and selling discount records. He not only dealt with the cut-corner album covers, but he had also cut so many corners when wheeling and dealing that he had attracted the attention of law enforcement. Though he had been convicted after a 135-count indictment for racketeering, wire fraud, and copyright infringement, he was not a chastened man. One would have thought that an eighteen-month prison sentence would have made him cautious about dealing with criminals. It was not to be. He started a new company called Out of the Past and continued to sell his oldies and cutouts. Seven years after his release, he was again riding high, but not quite high enough. He was on the lookout for a deal that could augment his profits. Serendipitously, a call from Sonny Brocco with whom he had partnered told him of a large volume of MCA cutouts that were available for purchase. This was just what LaMonte had been looking for. If successful, he could become the go-to merchant for cutout sales from all the major labels. If he could buy the full inventory of MCA cutouts and resell the load, he would make millions of dollars and have a reputation as a reliable and resourceful deal maker. It was a mouth-watering prospect, an opportunity that rarely came along. Brocco then arranged for LaMonte and Pisello to meet. At the meeting, LaMonte was supposed to learn the details of the deal that Pisello would put together. LaMonte was initially impressed by Pisello, who had been his smoothly charming self, an easy-to-like entrepreneur. But shortly thereafter and much to LaMonte's annoyance, Pisello brought Morris Levy into the deal. It was not what LaMonte wanted. From experience, LaMonte was well acquainted with Levy's methods of using strong arm tactics and his connections to the mob. LaMonte had dealt with Levy several years earlier. At that time, La Monte had been counterfeiting and selling Motown records, which Levy had also been doing. Levy threatened LaMonte and demanded a $25,000 payment and a cessation of the selling of Motown counterfeits. LaMonte complied. He didn't want to antagonize Levy and then have to deal with some of his Mafia associates such as Tommy Eboli, Johnny Dio, Anthony "Fat Tony" Salerno, Vincent "the Chin" Gigante, and Sonny Franzese, among various others. Only a fool would fail to comply. But now the potential profits of the MCA deal that were like dancing dollar signs in LaMonte's eyes were all that mattered. If he had to deal with Levy, he thought he could handle him, especially if Pisello and Brocco represented his interests.

The fear of mob violence would not surface until the deal went off track. Before that happened LaMonte accepted the four million MCA cutouts. But while examining the inventory he saw that the most profitable albums from famous individual singers and groups had been removed. Where were they? Had they been sold to another company? LaMonte was furious. How could he realize his dream of a multimillion-dollar profit if the most profitable albums had vanished? He angrily let Pisello know that he was not going to pay more than a million dollars for albums he hadn't received. LaMonte called Sam Passamano, a high-ranking executive at MCA, and told him: "So I just want you to know that your guys are creaming my load of cutouts and I ain't ever going to pay for this stuff unless they put the sweeteners back in." After promising to look into the matter, Passamano called LaMonte and said, "John, if it ever comes up I'll deny that this conversation took place, but you're right, you're getting screwed."[4]

Six hundred thousand albums by famous singers and groups had been sold to another distributor. LaMonte had no place to turn but to Levy and his Mafia partners. He figured that after he explained what happened that they would understand and demand that MCA include the creamed albums or significantly lower the purchase price. It didn't quite work out that way. A year later, LaMonte commented, "I musta been sittin' on my brain or something not to see what was coming."[5]

Even before the delivery of the cutouts, LaMonte was so intensely focused on the enormous profit he anticipated that he had ignored possible signs of trouble when Pisello demanded off-the-book cash payments and double billings that would secretly net Pisello three to five cents per album. LaMonte also ignored the possibility of ensuing problems when he learned that Levy would be the deal's guarantor. He had already ignored his own experiences and Levy's reputation at Roulette Records of cheating singers out of their royalties and threatening those who objected. He also knew that Levy sold counterfeit records, often to a chain of record stores that he owned, and then went to the major labels and negotiated deals for him and others to cease selling counterfeits. After the record companies paid Levy thousands of dollars to stop the sale of counterfeit records, he would use another of his record labels to continue selling counterfeit records. LaMonte knew who he was dealing with, but like many others who lived to regret their relationship with Levy, LaMonte would continue to work on a deal for the pot of gold that he believed awaited him. He just kept his eyes focused on the prize. His narrow vision made him a perfect sucker for a con artist's scam. After he had seen sixty tractor trailers arrive at his warehouse and deliver all those MCA cutouts, the world seemed his oyster. What could possibly go wrong?

After LaMonte discovered that 600,000 of the most profitable albums had been sold to other distributors, Levy came calling. It was not a friendly talk. In his most intimidating manner, Levy demanded 100 percent payment for the full contents of all sixty tractor trailers. LaMonte emphatically refused. In so doing, LaMonte had initiated a war not just with Levy but also with the Genovese crime family and its boss, Vincent Gigante.

Neither Pisello nor LaMonte knew that at this time Marvin Rudnick was assembling a two-count income tax indictment and a prosecution of Pisello that dated to the 1970s. Rudick discovered that Pisello had received $250,000 of loans and advances for a number of MCA projects. Most of those projects, even if they had come to fruition, which they didn't, would not have benefitted MCA. To prove that all the money Pisello received were loans,

Rudnick showed that there were repayment checks, some of which had been signed, some of which were unsigned. Of all the checks, the ones that had been signed bounced, and MCA never tried to collect. The company simply wrote off the amounts as unpaid. Some loan!

Meanwhile, Levy was becoming angrier and angrier that LaMonte had refused to pay for the cutouts and was ignoring his threats. This was no mere contretemps but a potential battle royale. Into the developing storm came Gaetano "Corky" Vastola. He was a big tough man, who had little patience for fools and those who were his perceived enemies. Hoping to calm the storm, LaMonte went to visit his Mafia partners. Vastola was also present. Being confronted with no escape, LaMonte said he would pay for what he owed but would never do business with these guys again.

As LaMonte was speaking, he didn't notice Vastola walk up beside him. Suddenly, it happened. Vastola hit him with a roundhouse right, his ham-sized fist slamming squarely against LaMonte's left temple, shattering bone, pulverizing blood vessels. The concussion was tremendous, sending LaMonte reeling in a wide arc, knocked senseless, his legs turned to rubber but somehow managing to keep him upright. Blood spurted from his nose, mouth, ears, and left eye.[6]

Brocco drove him home, but the next day, LaMonte was in so much pain, he was taken to a nearby hospital. Photographs of him in a hospital bed show a man with bandages on his face, his left eye swollen shut and bruised, tubes going into his nose and mouth. If profound pain can be implied in a photograph, the one of LaMonte's battered face speaks with shocking clarity.

It was too late for LaMonte to regret his decisions about dealing with Pisello and Levy. As he said, he must have been sitting on his brains. Nothing would now repave his dream of a golden road that led to millions of dollars in cutout profits. His fantasy was as shattered as his face. But at least he could gain revenge of a sort by testifying against those who wanted him dead. He became an undercover government witness, later entering the witness protection program.

Levy and Gaetano went on trial for extortion and conspiracy in the MCA cutout deal. As soon as the media began looking into the scandal, MCA finally fired Pisello. Odd, though, that a man who was not an employee could be fired by a company that insisted that Pisello had never been an employee. Senior executives threw off any personal responsibility for Pisello and his actions as if discarding the contents of a wastepaper basket. They portrayed themselves as victims (what else is new?) of deceitful criminals and prosecutorial harassment.

Pisello was sentenced to a two-year prison term for tax evasion. Prosecutors in the case asked the judge to have Pisello jailed immediately. But Pisello appealed his conviction and was briefly free on $15,000 bail. In response to the granting of bail, the Los Angeles office of the Justice Department's Organized Crime Strike Force stated that since Pisello's sentencing, new evidence had been secured that showed that Pisello had received about $700,000 in unreported income from record industry transactions in the last few years. With that new evidence, there was a possibility that new charges would be filed against Pisello, who might attempt to flee the country in order to avoid incarceration. At the time of his sentencing, Pisello was described in court documents as an alleged international heroin trafficker and high-ranking soldier in the Gambino crime family of New York who, in 1983 and 1984, engaged in a series of record business deals with Los Angeles–based MCA Records.

Interviewed outside the courtroom, an angry Pisello denied all of the government's allegations against him, including the tax charges. "I'm not a member of organized crime and never have been—I'll go to prison for 20 years if anyone can prove that. I go to church every Sunday and the only organization I ever belonged to was the Holy Name Society." He added with a rueful laugh, "I'm in the record business for one year and I'm supposed to have destroyed the industry?" He called MCA "the nicest corporation in the world. There was nothing wrong in this on MCA's part. We're the victims here—me, MCA, Roulette and Levy."[7] He continued: "I'm a victim. Mr. Rudnick has made me a victim. Me MCA, Roulette, and Levy—all victims here. . . . Mr. Rudnick says I'm organized crime. I don't know what it's all about to this day. I look in the mirror in the morning and say, 'Who the hell am I?'"[8] *The Los Angeles Times* ran an article on the front page of its business section saying that MCA was "more deeply involved with reputed mobster Salvatore Pisello than was previously revealed in court."

Though he won a conviction of Pisello, Rudnick's level of responsibility as a prosecutor had been circumscribed and he was finally fired in 1989 for insubordination and failure to follow orders. Pisello served two years of a four-year sentence on tax evasion. Following his release, he returned to Hollywood, where he attempted to sell a pair of scripts, one for a comedy and one for a drama, each about the Mafia.

Morris Levy, found guilty of the extortion of John LaMonte, sold his music business holdings in 1990 for a reported $70 million and died before he could begin his ten-year sentence. Gaetano Vastola was serving a seventeen-year sentence (at the time). He is now ninety-five years old and living in New Jersey. LaMonte is hidden away in the Witness Protection Program. No MCA executives were ever charged with wrongdoing. MCA, Inc. was sold in 1990 to Japan's Matsushita conglomerate for $6.1 billion. Lew Wasserman made $300 million on the sale and remained as chairman of the company. He died a very rich man. Marvin Rudnick went into private practice in Los Angeles, where his sterling reputation for brilliance and integrity led to a successful career.

"Politics is written all over this; the whole thing stinks," said former strike force attorney Waltz. "If you ask me, it's not Marvin Rudnick's competency or handling of the Pisello case that should be the issue here, but rather the Justice Department's apparent muzzling of a prosecutor following pressures placed on them as a result of him poking around."[9] Of all those involved, Marvin Rudnick emerged as a heroic figure devoted to finding the truth by steadfastly investigating the bad guys.

The shabby treatment of Rudnick and the actions by the Justice Department to stifle him created a sea of negative publicity for the Justice Department. A controversy arose and played out in the media about whether it was right for the government to rein in a determined prosecutor under pressure from MCA. News stories pointed out that MCA had many high-level political connections to President Reagan and those in the White House and Justice Department. MCA's board of directors had proven that they were an army of powerful and influential men, many of whom were Washington power brokers, representing both parties. They served the company like loyal determined soldiers, all engaged in defeating one honest man.

CHAPTER 8

Drugs, Music, and the Mafia

DOES HEROIN INSPIRE CREATIVITY? DOES A SHOT IN A VEIN HELP to generate hits? One musician told me when I was doing publicity for him that the great poet Samuel Taylor Coleridge was an opium addict and look at what he accomplished! It was the musician's rationale for shooting up heroin, though he never wrote anything as good as "Kubla Khan" or *The Rime of the Ancient Mariner*. It didn't matter to my client when I told him that Coleridge's opium addiction caused his wife to flee and alienated his close friend, the Romantic poet William Wordsworth. Coleridge's opium addiction left him continually beset by irritability, advancing into anger. His large intestine was so blocked it felt as if cement had hardened there. To gain some relief, Coleridge became dependent on enemas. But it wasn't only his physical and emotional well-being that suffered: the longer he remained addicted to opium, the less mental clarity he possessed. It was a terrible loss for so brilliant a poet and critic.

Unlike my musician client, the Mafia found no inspiration from Coleridge. For them, heroin was an ever-flowing river of money, following the dried-up riverbed that resulted from prohibition's end. As speakeasies became legitimate bars and nightclubs, former bootleggers turned to the sale of drugs, and heroin was the priciest and most profitable. Poor neighborhoods and black ghettos were prime targets for the sale of heroin. But it was not only desperate poor people looking to escape the harsh economies of the Great Depression; it was an entire culture centered on jazz. For jazz musicians the euphoria from heroin opened their souls to improvising exciting riffs, some of which were brilliant flights of musical virtuosity; others were tedious repetitions, as if a record had gotten stuck. The most brilliant and seminal jazz musicians whose lover was heroin were Charlie Parker, Sonny Rollins, Bud Powell, Lee Morgan, Stan Getz, Fats Navarro, Charlie Parker, John Coltrane, Billie Holiday, Dexter Gordon, Miles Davis, Gerry Mulligan, and Chet Baker, among lesser-known musicians.

Maxim W. Furek writes that "during the Harlem Renaissance (1918 until the mid-1930s), this predominately black area was an epicenter of musical creativity and heroin. Although some have blamed the jazz culture for heroin addiction, a more rational argument points to the Italian Mafia [the Mafia supplied the heroin, but no one forced musicians to inject it]. Heroin trade proliferated during the jazz-fueled Harlem Renaissance and into the 1960's and 1970's. In 1977 Nicky Barnes, believed to be Harlem's biggest drug dealer, was the leader of a crime syndicate known as 'The Council.'"

Even before the French Connection, the jazz-heroin connection was graphically made in Nelson Algren's 1949 novel, The Man with the Golden Arm. *The controversial best seller rejected the oft-used "dope fiend" label, common in pulp fiction, and depicted heroin [addiction] as a serious literary topic.* The Man with the Golden Arm, *a gritty black-and-white film adaptation, was the first of its kind to tackle the issue of illicit drug use.*

In his autobiography, Miles Davis discussed the prevalence of heroin. He wrote: "There was a lot of dope around the music scene and a lot of musicians were deep into drugs, especially heroin. People—musicians—were considered hip in some circles if they shot smack. Some of the younger guys like Dexter Gordon, Tadd Dameron, Art Blakey, J. J. Johnson, Sonny Rollins, Jackie McLean, and myself—all of us—started getting heavily into heroin around the same time. Despite the fact that Freddie Webster had died from some bad stuff. Besides Bird (Charlie Parker), Sonny Stitt, Bud Powell, Fats Navarro, Gene Ammons were all using heroin, not to mention Joe Guy and Billie Holiday, too. There were a lot of white musicians—Stan Getz, Gerry Mulligan, Red Rodney, and Chet Baker—who were also heavily into shooting drugs. "[1]

And because the Mafia owned many of the jazz clubs, it had a ready-made store for selling the stuff, which the mob called babania and the musicians called smack. Though some Mafia bosses forbade low-level soldiers from engaging in drug trafficking, the bosses did not adhere to their own prohibitions. They had not forbidden their soldiers and associates from participating in drug trafficking because of any moral qualms. Rather, it was a fear of legal penalties. The penalties could be so draconian that the bosses feared that any soldier or associate who faced prosecution would flip and testify against his higher-ups. Nevertheless, the profits from the sale of heroin continued to flow at a spectacular pace; mobsters used the rivers of heroin money to invest in legitimate businesses. What wasn't laundered was reinvested in bigger and bigger drug deals. The profit growth turned into a tsunami.

The profits were a temptation too inviting to be ignored by many mobsters. They may have feared being whacked by their bosses, but it was a chance many took. When Gambino capo Gene Gotti was indicted for selling drugs, the Gambino boss, Paul Castellano, would have ordered him killed; however, Gotti avoided execution when his nemesis was gunned down in front of Sparks Steak Houses at 210 East 46th Street in Manhattan. Though Gotti avoided being killed, he was sentenced to fifty years in prison, serving a total of twenty-nine years in the Federal Correctional Institution in Pollock, Louisiana. A true adherent to the code of omerta, Gotti never flipped. What happened to Gotti did not discourage other gangsters from dealing drugs: in 2008, eighty members of the Gambino crime family were arrested for drug trafficking as well as murder.

The most preeminent mafioso who built an empire on heroin, but who had been convicted only of pimping, was Lucky Luciano, boss of the National Crime Syndicate. Luciano had begun dealing drugs as a young man and continued even after his deportation to Italy after World War II. He insisted that the Mafia kept heroin out of Italian neighborhoods. But it was an absurd claim. Not only was it available in Italian neighborhoods, but mafioso who lived in those neighborhoods continued to sell the drug to their friends and neighbors, including teenagers who quickly became addicted. Nevertheless, the Mafia continued to push the myth that it never dealt drugs. They did so not only because of severe laws but also because they would have lost their political protection if it became widely known that the Mafia was getting young people addicted to heroin. The politicos protected them against prosecution for victimless crimes, such as those of gambling and prostitution. If, however, it became widely known that judges, cops, and prosecutors sold protection to drug-dealing mobsters, the newspapers and the public would have turned against them. So everyone paid lip service to a flouted prohibition. Yet the public bought into the myth, which was given widespread credence by the movie *The Godfather*.

In an attempt to explode the myth that the Mafia didn't deal drugs, the Federal Bureau of Narcotics, which came into existence around 1930, a year before Luciano helped to create New York's five families, made a point of noting the Mafia's involvement in the importation and distribution of heroin. Initially, the heroin was made into tablets and distributed much as oxycodone and Oxycontin are. The tablets were sold on the streets. Unfortunately, many of the labs that created the tablets blew up, drawing the attention of law enforcement. They operated like modern meth labs. When illegal labs blew up, action had to be taken. In 1935, New York police claimed to have seized more than $300,000 worth of tablets from illegal street vendors. That is more than $4.5 million in today's money. Yet a year earlier, police discovered that vast quantities of morphine were being shipped from Corsica to Marseille and then sent by ocean liners to New York. And because the mob controlled the docks of New York, it was easy for them to get the drugs into circulation. The police, either by design or ineptitude, were not able to stem much of the flow of drugs into New York. Indeed, during the 1930s, many police were paid to look the other way; the incentive provided by payoffs was accepted by many cops, for their salaries were pitifully low. During World War II, as warfare waged on the Atlantic and Pacific Oceans, the flow of heroin into the United States dramatically slowed to a trickle; however, by the end of the war, the importation of heroin increased by more than 80 percent. It continued to be controlled by the Mafia and the Unione Corse, the Corsican version of the Sicilian Mafia.

During his testimony about the workings of the Mafia, turncoat Joe Valachi revealed the long history of the Mafia's dealings in drugs. Valachi said that the Mafia was all about money. And if vast sums of money could be made from the sale of drugs, then the Mafia would be into it big time. Senators learned that from the early years of the twentieth century, immigrants from Sicily preyed upon other Italians, either threatening them with protection rackets or enlisting them to sell drugs. When immigrants became truck drivers, for example, they were threatened into becoming drug couriers. Men who worked the railroads were also forced to transport quantities of drugs disguised as baggage. The mob arranged for trucks to meet liners from France docking in New York. The trucks, with or without the knowledge of drivers, would be loaded with boxes or other containers of drugs. If the drivers were unaware of what they were carrying, their trucks would be hijacked and the drugs removed. If the drivers were in on it, they were paid for their services and warned to keep their mouths shut.

Learning of the vast sums of money being made by the bosses from drugs, many Mafia soldiers and associates were furious that they were prohibited from dealing drugs. The hypocrisy of the bosses infuriated street hoods. They knew, for example, that Mafia boss Paul Castellano was making a fortune from the drug trade. So the street guys went out on their own, pushing drugs and hiring others to sell the drugs for them. They took obvious chances of being arrested or killed. They believed, with some justification, that if they focused their sales on black neighborhoods no one would care.

Though the Mafia was raking in fortunes from gambling, loan-sharking, pornography, protection rackets, construction rackets, and labor unions, drug profits for bosses as well as for soldiers were too tantalizing to ignore. For an investment of a thousand dollars, one could realize a $100,000 profit. But with the cornucopia of money coming in from all rackets, why invest a paltry $1,000 when one could invest $100,000 or one million dollars. The returns were irresistible.

So great were the profits to be made in the drug trade that various battles broke out between different Mafia families for the control of drugs. Soldiers from one family would offer to defect to another family if they would be permitted to either engage or enlarge their drug-trafficking operations. If their existing families found out about their prospective defections, they would be killed. One killing would lead to another killing, but the drug trade would continue to flourish. In addition, as heroin addiction spread in inner-city neighborhoods, crime increased, and so politicians reacted by calling for ever more severe penalties. It resulted in thousands of low-level dealers and even addicts being sentenced to long-term prison sentences.

Yet families such as the Bonannos continued to profit from drugs. In fact, due to its deep involvement in the drug trade, the family was referred to as the Heroin Family by prosecutors and investigators. Though it was one of the smaller of the five New York Mafia families, it was extremely cohesive: its top leadership all came from the small Sicilian town of Castellammare del Golfo. Its initial base of operations was Williamsburg, Brooklyn. Like all Mafia bosses, Joe Bonanno—in his self-serving biography *Man of Honor*—claimed that his family had nothing to do with narcotics trafficking. He seemed to be modeling his public persona on the Don Corleone character in *The Godfather*.

However, the Bonanno family's involvement in the drug trade became irrefutable due to the activities of Carmine "Lilo" Galante, aka "the Cigar," for—except when eating—he always seemed to have a cigar clenched between his teeth. Galante had risen to become the boss of the Bonanno family in the 1970s. His viciousness, ruthlessness, and fiery temper made him one of the most feared gangsters in the Mafia. He wanted to make the Bonanno family the biggest and most feared of the five families. In addition, he wanted to control the entire trafficking of drugs on the East Coast. In pursuit of his goals, he had some of his shooters kill eight members of the Genovese family. Afterward, he stated that there was no one who could stand up against him and vowed to make Carlo Gambino shit in Times Square. The other bosses, including the semiretired Joe Bonanno, regarded Galante as not only a loose cannon but also a man so unhinged that he was threat to everyone. They agreed that Galante should have a grave destiny. On July 12, 1979, Galante decided to have lunch at his cousin's restaurant, Joe and Mary's, in the Bushwick section of Brooklyn. One of his bodyguards left early, complaining that he wasn't feeling well.

Another was preoccupied with making phone calls from a booth in the restaurant. After Galante forked in the last mouthfuls of a huge lunch, he lit up his cigar. He did not see the three masked gunmen rush into the restaurant; he did not see them as they neared his table. He did not hear their excited, heavy breathing. By the time the gunmen blasted away at Galante, he didn't need to see or hear them. A shotgun blast blew him out of his seat. He fell to the ground, his cigar still clenched between his teeth. Photos of his bloody end were on the front pages of tabloids, a bonanza for their publishers and news dealers.

It wasn't only the Cigar who was deeply involved in the drug trade: the Lucchese crime family and its boss were as deeply into it as the Bonanno family. In the 1940s, Tony "Ducks" Corallo (known as Ducks for his facility in avoiding indictments) was a protégé of Lucchese and a future leader of the crime family. He was heavy into dealing heroin. In 1941, he was caught with a large cache of heroin that had a value of $150,000. At trial he was sentenced to a mere six months in jail. Yet he was still called Ducks. But by 1986, it was all over for the Duck: he was sentenced under the RICO statute to one hundred years in prison for being a member of the Mafia's governing commission.

He wasn't the only Lucchese member to deal drugs. Underboss Salvatore "Tom Mix" Santoro earned millions of dollars from heroin trafficking for decades. Lucchese further put the lie to the mythical Mafia prohibition against drug dealing by promoting Santoro to be a capo. In March 1951, Santoro was indicted on charges of conspiracy to import opium and convert it into heroin. Santoro went into hiding and allegedly spent time in Europe before returning to Oyster Bay, New York. On September 24, 1951, he surrendered to federal authorities in New York City, and on January 7, 1952, after pleading guilty to narcotics charges, he was sentenced to four years in prison. Prior to announcing the sentence, the judge told the court that Santoro was a "bad fellow." And like the Duck, he was later found guilty of being a member of the Mafia commission and sentenced to one hundred years in prison.

Regardless of arrests and punishments, the sale of heroin in Harlem continued to thrive. Several black gangsters succeeded in making millions of dollars from the Harlem drug trade. They were Bumpy Johnson, Frank Lucas, and Nicky Barnes. So successful were they in making heroin part of the culture that east Harlem was considered an open air drug market. It was in such a market that a young Frankie Lymon got hooked on heroin.

And though years later, the general moviegoing public was led to believe that a devastating blow had been delivered to the heroin market by the detectives of the *French Connection*, it was not so. The vast amount of heroin that was seized was subsequently stolen by corrupt NYPD cops working for the Lucchese family. It all wound up back on the streets. It had been a pointless investigation, though an exciting movie.

Former organized crime detective Ralph Salerno told me that those who believed the myth of a Mafia prohibition against the sale of drugs often cite Carlo Gambino's 1957 decree that no family member should sell drugs. He added that pissed-off members of the Gambino family cursed Gambino behind his back for enacting a double standard, for they all knew that the boss and his cohorts were making millions of dollars from the sale of drugs. In fact, Joe "Piney" (known as Piney for extorting Christmas tree vendors) Armone, who was deeply involved in payola in the record business and in the sale of counterfeit records, was also a heroin entrepreneur. He had been appointed overseer of the Gambino family's heroin operations by Joseph Biondo, who had controlled the family's part in the French Connection heroin smuggling network. Though Armone was a cautious and wary man, he was nevertheless arrested on a narcotics charge and sent to prison. Following his release, he was again put in charge of the Gambino family's heroin operations.

According to the Federal Bureau of Narcotics (FBN), Armone frequented De Robertis Pasticceria and Lulu's Bar at 207 Second Avenue and headed a drug ring that operated in the area of East 14th Street and First Avenue. On October 1960, a French drug smuggler and the Guatemalan ambassador to Belgium and the Netherlands were arrested by the FBN as they delivered one hundred pounds of pure heroin to an associate of Armone, a longshoreman named Nicholas Calamaris. Another one hundred pounds of the drug were seized during subsequent raids on stash houses throughout New York City, making it the FBN's largest heroin seizure at the time. Armone was arrested after he ordered an informant to make a drug delivery to an associate on 116th Street in east Harlem. The FBN also identified several French nationals who had negotiated the price of heroin with Joe Biondo, who had financed the drug deal. Though the FBN wanted to nail the French financier who had partnered with Biondo, they never learned his name. And Armone refused to give the FBN any information.

Armone was safer in prison than on the street. In January 1964, while enjoying himself in the Reno Bar in Manhattan, he was shot five times. He survived, and his associate and friend Biondo visited him in hospital every day for three months. It was not a good year for Armone: on October 1, 1964, he and eleven other mobsters were indicted in the French Connection case. They were accused of transporting $20 million worth of heroin from 1956 to 1965, using sailors, businessmen, and a diplomat as drug couriers. During the trial, one of the jurors was approached outside the courthouse by Patricia DeAlesandro, a former *Playboy* bunny and a friend of Armone. DeAlesandro tried to bribe the juror, but he reported the incident to law enforcement. DeAlesandro was later convicted of bribery and sentenced to five years in prison. In 1965, Armone was convicted and was sentenced to fifteen years in prison. With the help of powerful friends, Armone gained his release after serving two-thirds of his sentence. A free man, he was promoted by Paul Castellano to be a capo in the Gambino family. His years of being involved in the drug trade were further evidence that the Mafia dealt in drugs.

> *Piney was convicted of heroin dealing in the early 60s but faced no repercussions for it upon his release, in fact he was promoted by Gambino's successor Paul Castellano. Carlo Gambino also allowed his relatives from Sicily, brothers Rosario, Giuseppe and Giovanni Gambino to [set up] shop in America. They were part of a huge drug trafficking network linking the States to the old country which was run by the Sicilian Mafia. The Gambino brothers operated in Cherry Hill, New Jersey, and were among the biggest heroin dealers on the East Coast. Rosario Gambino was eventually brought down in the Pizza Connection case in 1985 and was finally deported to Italy in 2009 to face outstanding charges there. His brother Giovanni, known as John, would later on rise high in the Gambino crime family.[2]*

No longer being investigated as a drug dealer, Armone was being surveilled by the FBI in 1986, according to Brian Ross of NBC News, for his participation in a new wave of payola, the bribery of disc jockeys to play particular songs, thus making those songs into hits. Armone, Ross said, was operating out of an Italian bakery on the Lower East Side of Manhattan. He was shown attending a celebrity music industry dinner at the Waldorf Astoria, where thirty men, all known as independent record promoters, were seen mingling with record producers. The independent promoters were receiving millions of dollars a year to make sure that certain songs became hits. If anyone could be said to be representative of the link between heroin and the music industry, it was Armone.

And finally there was the Genovese family, once a target for Carmine Galante. But the Genovese family was too big and powerful to be wiped out by the Bonannos, and it continued dealing drugs. In fact, its boss, Vito Genovese, was convicted of dealing heroin and sentenced to fifteen years in prison, where he died. His absence permitted the elevation of Vincent "the Chin" Gigante into the role of boss. And as noted in an earlier chapter, Gigante was not only a friend since boyhood of Morris Levy, but he was also his partner at Roulette Records. Drugs and rock and roll went together like lox and cream cheese on a bagel, or like clams and linguine.

Levy and Gigante made millions from the deaths of their rock singers. While stars who died of drug overdoses generated millions of dollars in sales while alive, their deaths brought many more millions to those who owned their copyrights, catalogs, and master recordings. In other words, a dead megastar was worth more to a record company than a live one. And Levy and Gigante were the beneficiaries.

When one contemplates the list of rock stars who died from drug overdoses, one is stunned by such a huge waste of talent. In addition to Frankie Lymon of the Teenagers, there were Jimi Hendrix, Jim Morrison, Janis Joplin, Brian Jones, Sid Vicious, Tim Hardin, Paul Butterfield, Whitney Houston, Tom Petty, Dee Dee Ramone, and Prince. And, of course, there were the even bigger headline grabbers: Elvis Presley, the King; and the other king, Michael Jackson, whom Elizabeth Taylor called the King of Pop.

Within this group, there is another group known as the 27 Club, consisting of musicians and an artist who overdosed or committed suicide at age twenty-seven. Members are Brian Jones, Jimi Hendrix, Janis Joplin, Jim Morrison, Jean-Michel Basquiat, Kurt Cobain (who, though a heroin addict, killed himself with a shotgun), and Amy Winehouse (whose official cause of death was alcohol poisoning). Though death by drug overdose or gunshot is not something to celebrate, the 27 Club has been the morbid subject of numerous songs, many of which celebrate the victims, and some even seem jealous of the deceased. The list includes "27" by Fall

Out Boy; John Craigie's song "28," which appeared on his 2009 album *Montana Tale* and live album *Opening for Steinbeck*; the song "27 Club" by Ivy Levan; and Magenta's 2013 studio album *The Twenty Seven Club*. Letlive featured a song named "27 Club" on its 2013 album *The Blackest Beautiful*. "Long Live Rock & Roll" from the album *Baptized* contains the lyric that "they're forever 27—Jimmy, Janis, Brian Jones." Rapper Watsky's song "All You Can Do" contains the lyric, "I tried to join the 27 Club." Black Ben Carson includes the song "The 27 Club." Adore Delano released a song called "27 Club" on her 2017 studio album. In 2017, the MonaLisa Twins released "Club 27." The Pretty Reckless released a song titled "Rock and Roll Heaven." The list goes on and on.

The four rock stars whose deaths by needle received legendary status were Brian Jones, Janis Joplin, Jimi Hendrix, and Jim Morrison.

BRIAN JONES. FEBRUARY 28, 1942–JULY 3, 1969.

If he had nothing else to recommend him, his founding of the Rolling Stones alone would have given him a star in rock and roll heaven. As a musician, songwriter, and record producer, Brian Jones combined it all to create a vision for what hyperbolically came to be called the Greatest Rock and Roll Band Ever. He brought together Keith Richards and Mick Jagger, who—if the present is any indicator of the future—will probably keep touring until hauled off to assisted living facilities. Jones, however, died while still in his twenties. He joined the aforementioned club of the damned, the 27 Club, of those who took their own lives at the age of twenty-seven.

As a member of the Rolling Stones, he played numerous instruments, including the rhythm guitar, and sang backup vocals. As talented as he was, however, Jones could not help being drawn to the temptations that destroy talent: alcohol and drugs. As his talent waned and his personality became increasingly obnoxious, he alienated his band members. The other Stones maneuvered him out of the spotlight and replaced him with Mick Taylor. From there, Jones had a quick slide into oblivion. He was found dead in his swimming pool at Cotchford Farm in East Sussex (the former home of A. A. Milne, creator of Winnie the Pooh) by his girlfriend, Anna Wohlin, who was convinced Jones was alive when he was taken out of the pool. She insisted that his heart was still beating. Attending doctors, however, said Jones was dead. A coroner's report noted that the cause of death was drowning by misadventure and that the deceased's liver and heart were enlarged from drugs and alcohol.

His death seemed inevitable, for he had been arrested for drugs and warned by a kindly judge, "For goodness sake, don't get into trouble again or it really *will* be serious."[3] Kindness, however, would not temper Jones's need for drugs. He was a self-guided missile aimed at his own grave ending. His addiction to drugs was so destructive that writer Gary Herman noted that Jones was "literally incapable of making music; when he tried to play the harmonica his mouth started bleeding."[4] Though he was no longer of value to the Stones, he was denied the opportunity to go on a North American tour with the band because of his status as a convicted druggie. On June 8, 1969, Jagger and Richards informed, he was out of the picture.

As with all members of the 27 Club, Jones was eulogized in songs and poems. Pete Townshend expressed his poetic talents in "A Normal Day for Brian, A Man Who Died Every Day." And Jim Morrison expressed his own poetic talents in "Ode to L.A. While Thinking of Brian Jones, Deceased." At a Stones concert following Jones's death, Jagger read Percy Bysshe Shelley's poem "Adonais" about John Keats. As soon as Jagger finished, stage hands released hundreds of white butterflies into the air.

Because Jones, like other celebrity martyrs to death's early calling, would be an emblem of youth's promises cut short, he was buried ten feet below ground level. Fans, without their own sense of self-esteem, would not be able to grab trophies of necrophilia.

JANIS JOPLIN. JANUARY 19, 1943–OCTOBER 4, 1970.

Joplin was a force of nature, a hurricane of talent that seemed to blow all others out of her path. Seeing her perform was like seeing a woman drenched in the sweat of self-realization as she belted out her songs with such personal feeling, she seemed to have excavated her soul. It was either 1969 or 1970 that I saw her perform at Bill Graham's Fillmore East on the Lower East Side of Manhattan. Her energy, her vibrancy was a kind of yelling at the moon. She was a woman on fire. When pressed to slow down or she might end up like the self-destructive Billie Holiday, Joplin responded: "I'm here to have a party, man, as best I can while I'm on Earth. . . . If that's what I gotta do to stick around for another forty years, you can have it."[5]

Though there are numerous instances of Joplin being stoned on heroin, her performance at Woodstock serves as an example of her dependency. Joplin appeared on stage at Woodstock at approximately 2:00 a.m., on Sunday, August 17, 1969. She had informed her band that they would be performing at the concert as if it were just another gig. On Saturday afternoon, she and her band were flown via helicopter with a pregnant Joan Baez from a nearby motel to the festival. Joplin was stunned to see such an enormous crowd. This was not what she was used to. The site of thousands of music fans made her nervously giddy. After the helicopter landed, a group of reporters rushed toward Joplin. She couldn't coherently answer their questions. She asked her friend and lover, Peggy Caserta, to answer all questions.

Eventually her nervousness dissipated and she was now excited at the prospect of performing in front of so many fans. However, the time of her performance was delayed and delayed for nearly ten hours, because other musicians were required to perform before her time came. With nothing else to do, Joplin spent much of that time shooting heroin. The movie *Woodstock* shows Joplin and Grace Slick standing near amplifiers that blasted the music of Canned Heat. That was 7:30 p.m., and Joplin did not go on stage until 2:00 a.m. During her performance, her voice became increasingly hoarse and at times she seemed to be wheezing. She was no longer a bundle of nerves but seemed wrecked by booze and heroin. She asked the audience if they had everything (drugs?) they needed.

Pete Townshend writes in his 2012 memoir: "She had been amazing at Monterey, but tonight she wasn't at her best, due, probably, to the long delay, and probably, too, to the amount of booze and heroin she'd consumed while she waited. But even Janis on an off-night was incredible."[6]

Her death did not occur as a public event; it happened in room 105 in the Landmark Hotel on Franklin Avenue in Hollywood. Howard Sounes writes: "It is not known what Janis did in her room for the next hour and a half, but around 1 a.m., she got her heroin works out and injected a vein in her left arm, which bore the marks of previous injections. Then she put away her works and went to the hotel lobby—a few strides down the corridor—to get change from the night clerk for the cigarette machine, returning to 105 with the pack. She closed the door and went to her bed, which was in the corner facing the window. She started to undress, stripping down to her blouse and underwear, and reached to put her cigarette packet on the nightstand. As she did so she keeled over, hitting her face on the table as she fell to the floor."[7] On Sunday, October 4, 1970, Joplin was found dead on the floor of her room by road manager and friend, John Byrne Cooke.

Bottles of alcohol, but no drug paraphernalia, were found in room 105; however, in a 1983 book by Joseph DiMona and Los Angeles corner Thomas Noguchi, they claimed a friend of Joplin's had removed evidence of heroin use, then put it back after being informed that an autopsy would be performed. The removal of drug evidence was typical in such cases, averred Noguchi, who had investigated many cases of death by drug overdose. The autopsy did reveal that Joplin died from an overdose of heroin, which was compounded by alcohol. The coroner's office stated that her death was accidental.

Like many other members of the 27 Club, Joplin's life and death were the subjects of numerous songs, including the Mamas & the Papas's "Pearl," Leonard Cohen's "Chelsea Hotel #2," Jerry Garcia's "Birdsong," Mimi Farina's "In the Quiet Morning," and Joan Baez's "Children of the Eighties."

JIMI HENDRIX. NOVEMBER 27, 1942–SEPTEMBER 18, 1970.

Jimi Hendrix may have been the most dazzling and blazingly original guitarists in the rock firmament. His popularity during the late 1960s and into the 1970s meant sold-out concerts wherever he performed. Though his performances were magnetic, he was more than a performer: he was an event.

Yet as electrically energetic as he could be in concert, offstage he could be almost comatose. One afternoon, in the PR office where I worked, I saw Jimi snoring, passed out on couch. If it weren't for his less-than-syncopated snoring, I might have thought he was dead. In fact, it wasn't long thereafter that he was dead. Alcohol and drugs may have fueled his performances, but the combination killed him. According to Hendrix biographer Charles Cross, "few stars at the time [of his death] were as closely associated with the drug culture as Jimi."[8] His friend Herbie Worthington said Hendrix just couldn't drink. "He simply turned into a bastard" when he drank.[9] According to friend Sharon Lawrence, liquor "set off a bottled-up anger, a destructive fury he almost never displayed otherwise."[10] Alcohol turned Jimi into a violent, paranoid, jealous man, who once accused his girlfriend Carmen Borrero of having an affair with Eric Burdon and then threw an empty bottle of vodka at her. It nearly took out one of her eyes. On May 3, 1969, Jimi was arrested while passing through customs at Toronto International Airport after heroin and hashish were found in his luggage. But he was a revered icon, and he could sail through storm-tossed waves in hurricanes and land surefooted on dry land. It was not surprising that at the conclusion of his trial, he was acquitted. He had stated that the drugs had been planted in his luggage. Who could challenge the statement? Who would want to disbelieve such an admired star? Who would want to see the magnificent Jimi Hendrix moping in a jail cell sans guitar?

Though no one wanted him to rot in jail, they couldn't send him to rehab. He, like Joplin, was cut out for wildness, for parties that never seemed to end. His, however, ended as quietly as a tomb. He breathed his last in London, where an ambulance transported him to St. Mary Abbots Hospital where Dr. John Bannister pronounced him dead at 12:45 p.m. on September 18. He had apparently taken nine Vesparax sleeping pills. Charles Cross writes,

> *The nine pills he swallowed would have been almost twenty times the recommended dose for a man of Jimi's frame and weight and would have made him lose consciousness quickly. Some time during the early morning hours, the combination of the Vesparax, the alcohol in his system, and the other drugs he'd used that night caused Jimi to heave up the contents of his stomach. What he spit up—most wine and undigested food—was then aspirated into his lungs, causing him to stop breathing. A person who was not inebriated would have had a gag reflex and coughed out the material, but Jimi was well beyond that.*[11]

Following an autopsy and coroner's analysis, it was concluded that Jimi had aspirated his own vomit and died of asphyxia while intoxicated with barbiturates. The nine Vesparax sleeping pills were eighteen times the recommended dosage.

The Rock and Roll Hall of Fame concluded that "Jimi Hendrix was the most gifted instrumentalist of all time, a self-taught electric guitarist whose fluid, immersive style was perfectly suited to embrace—and then revolutionize—the late '60s psychedelic rock movement."[12]

Jim Morrison. December 8, 1943–July 3, 1971.

For many of his fans, Jim Morrison was the Lord Byron of the world of music. He was handsome, sexy, prolific in his sexual conquests, and a fan of his own penis. He reportedly had an IQ of 149. He had immersed himself in the writings of Montaigne, Nietzsche, and Sartre. He wrote poetry, and unlike many other musicians who trespassed on the definition, Morrison was admired by professors and other poets. So highly regarded were the lyrics of the Doors (a name inspired by Aldous Huxley's *The Doors of Perception*, referring to LSD) that critics in normally staid newspapers devoted columns to serious analysis of those lyrics. They regarded Morrison as an authentic symbolist poet, comparing him to Arthur Rimbaud. Morrison's lyrics railed against authority, self-imposed limitations, as well as rules and laws that bound one to strict conduct. One of their songs, "Break on Through (To the Other Side)," clearly expressed such values. And more portentously: "No One Here Gets Out Alive."

Morrison had the mind of a revolutionary anarchist on a mission to explode civilization. Perhaps the most emphatic gesture that expressed his contempt for the strictures of society occurred when he was accused of exposing himself before an audience in Florida on March 1, 1969. Though he vehemently denied the allegation, he was arrested and charged with dropping his pants before some twelve thousand fans at a Doors concert. He rejected a plea bargain and so following a sixteen-day trial he was found guilty of indecent exposure and profanity by a six-person jury. He was sentenced to jail and had to pay a fine. At the sentencing, Judge Murray Goodman told Morrison that he was a "person graced with a talent,"[13] admired by peers, fans, and everyone in the popular music business.

Following the news of Morrison's arrest and conviction, the popularity of the Doors fell off a cliff. Various outraged groups held decency rallies in response to Morrison's indecent act. Morrison grew increasingly angry, fulminated against an assortment of enemies, and increased his intake of alcohol, and his often unhinged behavior kept many out of his orbit. As if fleeing from himself, he escaped to Paris but still continued to self-destruct.

Was he simply on a death trip? An acquaintance of Morrison suggested as much in an *Esquire* article several years ago: "'He died for the simplest reason, that he couldn't stand living.' But Hopkins and Sugarman deny that accusation, claiming Morrison just wanted to shake everything he could out of life. Perhaps. But in this account, he was seduced by the dark side of the force."[14]

Morrison's death in Paris had the elements of many celebrity deaths. Claims of coverups and secret payoffs proliferated. Numerous friends and acquaintances, including Marianne Faithfull, said his death resulted from an accidental heroin overdose. But because there was no autopsy, who knew?

Jim Morrison's death has been the subject of endless debate. This was primarily the fault of Pamela Courson, and those who helped her conceal that she and Jim were heroin users. . . . It was only years later, when Alain Ronay revealed in Paris Match *that Pamela had confessed to him that she and Jim had been snorting heroin the night before he died, that it became apparent he had probably overdosed or had a heart attack while under the influence of heroin.*[15]

The author added that "[Courson] readily confessed that she and Jim had been using heroin the night before"[16] Morrison's death. Courson, who claimed to be the common-law wife of Morrison, adopted his surname after his death and as if paying tribute to her lost love died of a heroin overdose on April 25, 1974.

Yet before Morrison's death became widely known, the movie director Agnes Varda, a friend of Morrison, said she had been the one who misled reporters by telling them that Morrison was alive and resting in seclusion. She was only one of four people to attend his funeral. He was buried at the famous Père Lachaise Cemetery in Paris, the resting place of Oscar Wilde, Edith Piaf, Chopin, Marcel Proust, Gertrude Stein, Olivia DeHavilland, Sarah Bernhardt, Georges Bizet, and many other luminaries.

Morrison's death occurred two years to the day after the death of Brian Jones and nine months after the deaths of Jimi Hendrix and Janis Joplin.

Though one would not necessarily associate the members of the 27 Club with Israel, there is in Tel Aviv an outdoor painting of the 27 Club members. Unlike the other subjects of the painting, Kurt Cobain and Amy Winehouse did not die of drug overdoses. Nevertheless, because of their popularity as singers and because they died at age twenty-seven, they are included. Cobain, though a heroin addict, shot himself; Winehouse drank herself to death. The Tel Aviv painting, executed by John Kiss, who was assisted by Itai Froumin and Roman Kozhokin, was completed on Rosh Hashanah, the day of judgment and the celebration of the Jewish new year. The painting does not judge its subjects nor does it lament those whose lives blazed across the firmament of popular culture like shooting stars before being extinguished.

CHAPTER 9

The Return of Payola

FOLLOWING THE SACRIFICE OF JEWISH DISC JOCKEY ALAN FREED to the clamorous mob who wanted him nailed to a cross of purity, just to prove that the record and broadcast industries were as innocent as angels, payola hibernated. While Freed had been paid hundreds of dollars here, thousands of dollars there, a new brand of payola was born in the 1970s. It was no longer small potatoes: independent promoters were making millions of dollars. (Some of them were accused of being Mafia connected, though no evidence was ever produced to confirm those accusations. However, alleged Mafia member Joseph Armone acted as the Gambino family liaison with some promoters.) The new independent promoters could make tens of millions of dollars by promoting often unknown recordings and—presto!—turning them into hits. Sometimes hundreds of thousands of dollars were spent to make a single record a hit. The money would be spread around to popular, influential disc jockeys in markets that had huge audiences. It got to the point that record companies were spending millions of dollars to make a handful of records into top hits. The spent millions reduced record company profits, and in some cases meant that once strong bottom lines had become tentative pale lines. Was it worth spending millions to promote records that were played almost endlessly on air but never made it to the Top 40 or even the Hot 100? Such records were called turntable hits. Fred Dannen writes,

Consider Carly Simon's hit single "Jesse," on Warner Bros. Records. Said an executive at a competing label, "Jesse" is legendary as one of the most expensive singles of all time in the amount of indie promotion money spent on it. I don't know the actual number, but if you told me $300,000, I wouldn't blink. The amusing thing is, it was top ten, it got a lot of airplay, but they didn't sell any albums. It was perceived a hit record. But the album was a stiff. So was it a successful project? Not for anybody. Except for the independent promoters. You can't blame them for taking the money.[1]

So who were those independent promoters (aka the Network)? They were men whose names do not register in the public's imagination. However, Fred Dannen prints a list of names that originally appeared in a 1980 edition of *Billboard*. Those named were Joseph Isgro of Los Angeles; Fred DiSipio of Cherry Hill, New Jersey; Gary Bird of Cleveland; Dennis Lavinthal of Los Angeles; Jerry Brenner of Boston; and Jerry Meyers of Buffalo. (One of them, Joseph Isgro, like Alan Freed, was sacrificed by the record companies to the gods of hypocrisy; though indicted for payola, his case was dismissed by the presiding judge.)

The scandal of a new wave of payola began following a story by Brian Ross, whose NBC News report ignited a fire of indignation. Ross had been waiting in the lobby of the Helmsley Palace Hotel to see who showed up for a meeting of independent record producers. William Knoedelseder writes,

At approximately 4:45, as he made his third or fourth casual stroll around the perimeter of the Helmsley's palatial first floor,

Ross stopped short. He saw John Gotti stride into the lobby from the parking garage, flanked by his underboss, Frank DeCicco, and Gambino family consiglieri Joseph N. Gallo. Transfixed, Ross watched the trio walk up to an older man sitting on a tufted leather banquette near the center of the room and begin talking.[2]

That older man was Joseph "Piney" Armone. The Gambinos were there to meet with Armone and discuss with him the doings of the Network.

Later that evening, the promoters and record company executives arrived at the Waldorf Astoria, where a convention was about to burst into song in celebration of rock's biggest stars. Tuxedo-clad record industry hot shots and gorgeous babes in slinky low-cut gowns were entertained by Chuck Berry, Keith Richards, Ron Wood, Neil Young, Billy Joel, and Chubby Checker, among various other luminaries of rock music.

Ross's news segment, rather than celebratory, arrived like an earthquake. Stunned executives and indignant independent promoters acted like politicians caught accepting bribes. In a voiceover, Ross narrated what was seen on the screen:

This block on First Avenue on the Lower East Side of New York is a stronghold of the Gambino Mafia family. According to FBI and New York police, the Mafia capo who runs things on this block, and in places far from this block, is Joseph Armone, the man with the glasses, a convicted heroin trafficker who on most days can be found conducting mob business at a back table in the pastry shop.

For months now, the activities of Armone and other have been watched closely by the FBI and police as far away as Los Angeles, as part of an investigation of corrupt practices in the rock music business, and what appears to be the reemergence of payola at rock music stations.

The video then went to the celebration at the Waldorf Astoria. Ross continued:

Among the guests, two of the most powerful and feared men in the rock music business: Joseph Isgro, who authorities say has described Mafia capo Armone as his partner; and Isgro's close associate, Fred DiSipio, who rarely does business without his associate, Mike, by his side. [There was no evidence to suggest that Isgro was feared or that Armone was his partner. In fact, no one could prove anything more than Isgro's family was friends with Armone.] DiSipio and Isgro, each with this own company, are top men in what is called the Network, about thirty men, many at this dinner, all known as independent record promoters, who industry executives say are getting millions of dollars a year from record companies to make sure that certain songs become hits on certain rock music radio stations. And how some independent promoters go about their business, how they get records on the air, is now the scandal of the industry. [Why was payola in the record business a scandal when businesses across America provide favors for customers and clients as a means of facilitating commerce?]

Ross went on to state:

Just how important the rock music business is to the Mafia became clear last month at this New York City Hotel. . . . Joseph Armone, the man from the pastry shop, arranged an unusual meeting with the top three men in the Gambino Mafia family, including Gambino family boss John Gotti—in the view of the FBI, a mob summit meeting.[3]

Ross's report sounded like a fire alarm that caused Warner Communications, RCA/Ariola Records, MCA, and Capitol Records to sever ties with independent record promoters. An investigation into allegations of payola in the music industry soon took off. (Fear of a repetition of the Alan Freed payola investigation caused record company executives to flee into rounds of indignation and hypocrisy: "We had no idea! We're innocent! Absolutely innocent!")

When questioned by Justice Department attorney Marvin Rudnick, Isgro admitted to knowing Joseph Armone but said he was his uncle's best friend, had known him for years, and regarded him as a family member. He added: "I call him Uncle Joe and I have a linguine dinner with him every time I go to New York."[4] He emphasized that he never did business with Armone or any members of the Mafia. Isgro insisted that he did nothing wrong. Yes, he accepted huge sums of money from record companies, but he didn't pay off disc jockeys to play records. He had relationships that went back years. He was an expert at record promotions and was successful in delivering results: all legal! Rudnick found Isgro credible and believed that he may have been a fall guy. Yet other investigators couldn't wait to get their hooks into Isgro.

The following article by Desson Howe, "Payola Probe Deepens," appeared in the *Washington Post* on March 4, 1986:

Warner Communications and RCA/Ariola Records joined the ranks of MCA and Capitol Records yesterday in dropping ties with independent record promoters as investigation deepened into allegations of payola in the music industry.

The Recording Industry Association of America, which represents all major record companies, was subpoenaed, meanwhile, by a federal grand jury in New York to disclose all documents relating to "the role of independent promoters in the record industry."

The association, which must appear before the court Thursday, yesterday reiterated that it has "no knowledge" that any promoters are involved in any "illegal activity."

In addition to the grand jury investigations, an "NBC Nightly News" series last week reported allegations of connections between certain independent promoters and organized crime.

Warner had decided it was "the appropriate time" to drop the independent promoters, according to Warner Communications Vice President Geoffrey Holmes. He denied the recent investigations of payola—a practice in which promoters pay to have their clients given air play—were the main reason for Warner's decision. But he said there was "no question" that the decision was influenced by "the events of last week . . . This obviously was the catalyst."

RCA/Ariola, the parent company for RCA and Arista Records, said its statement—made later yesterday, after Warner's statement—was "similar" to Warner's. "We know of no wrongdoing in the activities of the independent promotion firms we retained," said Robbin Ahrold, vice president of communications for RCA/Ariola.

"However, as a major distributor of recorded music, we are concerned about the perception of our industry by the public."

Neither RCA nor Warner knew of subpoenas submitted to them for the grand jury, their spokesmen said.

Officials from both Polygram Records and CBS Records said yesterday they are watching the situation before making any decisions on their respective independent promoters.

Capitol Industries-EMI and MCA Records had announced last week that they were dropping at least some independent promoters.

Ghasker Mennen, chairman and chief executive officer of Capitol-EMI, said his label was dropping all independent promoters to ensure that the company doesn't "unwittingly contribute to any problems that may exist."

The Recording Industry Association of America in its Friday statement declared "immediate and decisive corrective action" would be taken if law enforcement agencies informed the group of illegal acts.

"Until such time, we find it unjustified and distressing that the recording industry is so indiscriminately maligned by insidious innuendo," the statement said.

"The dropping of independent promoters in favor of in-house promoters," said Holmes, "has been something Warner has always welcomed." He pointed to 1981 when "we publicly disclosed and dropped independent promoters as an exclusive deal. We were the only ones that did it."

Holmes said Warner's sales and profitability went down after that action and "no one else in the industry was willing to go along with us."[5]

Though the major record companies disavowed the value of the independent promoters and put them at arm's length, the companies never forgot how the Network had turned records into million-dollar hits. The companies were patiently waiting for the investigators to pack up their files, turn off the lights, lock their doors, and go home. Three years later, many of the record companies resumed doing business with independent promoters. They had not been investigative targets. They were free and safe to return to the old ways of promoting records. It may have been costly to promote records into becoming hits, but the profits from hit records and ancillary items more than justified the expense. By 1989, major labels were spending as much as $70,000 to make a single album a success. It was an excellent investment, for as a comparatively small amount of money flowed out, an avalanche of money often poured in.

Nevertheless, the independent promoters had to be careful. Ever since 1960, when payola became a federal crime punishable by a $10,000 fine and a one-year prison sentence, promoters sought legal ways of influencing deejays. Instead of handing envelopes of money to deejays, promoters worked with radio stations on joint marketing promotions, setting up contests, raffles, prizes, events, etc., none of which is illegal. The result of clever marketing promotions is that radio stations increase their listenership, and record companies get more air play for their records. As long as the station is completely transparent and there is no quid quo pro, the station is on safe ground. Of course, why would a station participate if there weren't a quid quo pro? But such arrangements are difficult to prove. A bigger challenge to promoters was the advent of MTV, which diminished the role of the promoters. Yet as long as record companies need to generate hits, they will get promoters to use their magical skills.

There is one story of a promoter who arranged to have the credit card bills and other expenses of a deejay paid by a third party, whose business had nothing to do with records or broadcasting. In still another case, the story goes that money was funneled through a shell company to a deejay's offshore bank account, which was registered in the name of another shell company. That shell company was a subsidiary of yet another shell company. And at stations where the program director may decide what records are played, there are many variations on the theme of payola.

Isgro, however, was not involved in any of those machinations. And though the media had little to go on, it kept making life difficult for him. It kept trying to prove there was a connection between Armone and Isgro. It heated up after John Gotti's underboss Frank DeCicco was blasted into thousands of pieces by the ignition of a carefully planted bomb. Gotti, thereafter, promoted Armone to the newly vacant position. Armone now had a target on his back, and the feds soon indicted him for his well-known racket of drug dealing. Following a trial, he was found guilty and sentenced to fifteen years in prison. An NBC News reporter subsequently asked

Isgro what his relationship was with Armone. For the umpteenth time, Isgro explained that Armone had been a family friend. He complained that the media was treating him as if he were Don Vito Corleone. It's true that the media seems to love Mafia stories and being able to pin the tail on a soldier, capo, or Mafia associate results in a gotcha story.

And guilt by association has been a follow-the-numbers clue not only for law enforcement and reporters hot on the trail of a gotcha story but also for ambitious senators and congressional representatives who want to generate media attention and stir up voters. Senator Joseph McCarthy, for example, had made a career out of accusing often innocent people of being communists just for associating with party members, joining left-wing organizations, or lending their names to petitions perpetrated by such organizations. For fervent anticommunists, McCarthy became a soothsayer and then a martyr. No one with the slightest association with communists was safe from trial by malign innuendo. Even the esteemed scientist J. Robert Oppenheimer, whose atom bomb brought Japan to its knees and forced it to accept unconditional surrender at the end of World War II, was accused of being a communist based on his close relationships with those who were members of the Communist Party. It was not unusual in the 1950s, as I well remember, for mothers to warn their children not to associate with bad kids; otherwise, adults would think you were of same ilk as your pals. "People will judge you by the friends you keep." I must admit here that as an adult I was nearly victimized because I represented a PR/marketing client who was investigated by the FBI and then put out of business. An FBI agent had called me and aggressively wanted to know my connection to the client. When I said I did his marketing, there followed numerous questions about what I had specifically done and what did I know about my client's business. I finally convinced my interrogator of my ignorance and innocence, but it was slightly unnerving to be thought complicit in my client's illegal activities. By the way, I never discovered what illegal activities my client had been involved in. Once his business was shut down, I never heard from him again, though he did send me my final check.

Ross, though an honest and admired investigative reporter, had—unintentionally perhaps—gotten the guilt-by-association ball rolling by reporting,

> *Joseph Armone, the man from the pastry shop, arranged an unusual meeting with the top three men in the Gambino Mafia family, including Gambino family boss John Gotti—in the view of the FBI, a mob summit meeting.*
>
> *One hour after meeting the top people in the American Mafia, Isgro and DiSipio were at the Waldorf Astoria, taking their place among the top people in the American [m]usic business.*[6]

How does one prove a negative? How could Isgro prove he was not in bed with the Mafia? If Isgro had insisted "I'm not a member of the Mafia," how could he prove it? Would a reporter or prosecutor be persistent enough to say to him, "Prove it?" To which, of course, Isgro could have responded, "You prove it!" Fred Dannen reports that Isgro was furious about reports of him associating with Mafioso. He told one reporter: "I'm destroyed. My whole business was ruined by insidious innuendo." To a second reporter, he said, "Where was my crime?" He went on, noting that

> *I've worked twenty years. I started at the bottom of the fucking pile here. I got out of Vietnam [with several medals]. I fucking got into this business. I've worked hard all my life, never being arrested in my fucking life. I've acquired the American dream here. And by one guy coming on, not saying anything, he destroys my entire business. Absolutely devastates my fucking business.*[7]

Indeed, Isgro had worked himself up from the bottom. After leaving the Marines, having served honorably in Vietnam, he worked for Decca Records as a promotion man, earning $135 a week. That's not exactly the salary for a member of one of the most powerful Mafia families! Isgro next worked for Roulette Records, also as a promotion man. Though Roulette's president Morris Levy was an associate of the Genovese crime family, he didn't hire Mafioso as underlings. They would be his associates, and Isgro was simply an employee. Years later, Morris Levy commented: "He was a good kid. I don't think he was great, but he tried hard."[8] From Roulette, Isgro became a regional promotion director for Motown, operating out of Philadelphia. After nine years with Motown, he was promoted to national director of pop promotions. He left Motown, then worked for EMI for one year. He was finally sufficiently experienced and had made enough contacts to go out on his own. He became an independent promoter, operating out of Los Angeles. By 1981, he reached his peak, becoming one of the most successful promoters in the country. The energetic entrepreneur also started a management company and record company. As if that weren't enough to keep him busy, he became a successful real estate investor and developer and opened a popular restaurant in Los Angeles named Stefanino's. The restaurant was a popular destination for movie stars, including Frank Sinatra and those associated with his Rat Pack.

But by then Isgro had made such a name for himself that he became a target for investigators. Unfortunately for Isgro, concurrent with his being investigated, MCA was being investigated because of its dealings with Sal Pisello and the sale of cutouts. MCA wanted to get the spotlight taken off of itself and shined on another. Isgro was the perfect target for the Justice Department. Or, as Rudnick speculated, a fall guy. If the investigators could begin a full-scale investigation into the practices of independent promoters, MCA and other record companies would be able to retreat into the shadows of innocence and also force jittery promoters to accept leaner contracts than they otherwise might have agreed to.

To make sure that MCA would emerge from investigations as clean as an Eagle Scout, MCA's president, Lew Wasserman, called in political favors. He knew he could count on President Reagan's help. Reagan's White House door was always open to Wasserman, his friend, agent, and advisor. It cannot have come as other than expected that Wasserman was able to get Justice Department officials to muzzle federal prosecutor Marvin Rudnick. He was directed away from investigating MCA, though he could continue his investigation of Sal Pisello. But Pisello wasn't the only potential defendant in Rudnick's sites; he was also investigating Isgro. When Rudnick questioned Isgro about John Gotti and Armone, the promoter insisted that he had never met Gotti and had never done business with members of the Mafia, including Armone. For two hours, he candidly answered all questions put to him by Rudnick. He was not evasive, he was not vague, and he was not hesitant in his responses. In addition to answering all of Rudnick's questions, Isgro claimed that the record companies were trying to diminish the cost of promoting records by feeding negative information about him to Ross and the FBI. Rudnick did not respond to that assertion, but he was impressed by Isgro's apparent honesty and noted that Isgro may have been a fall guy.

Why a fall guy? Isgro had brought an antitrust suit against MCA and Warners, and the companies may have wanted the public to perceive Isgro as a mobster, which would help them undermine his credibility, thus helping to win their case. Isgro, indeed, seemed headed for a fall; his reputation was being smirched, and his business was decimated after the record companies divested themselves of his services. There must have been a level of schadenfreude among record company executives who had learned that Isgro, when at the top of the pyramid of independent promoters, was reportedly making $5 million a year, a sum far greater than the executives were earning. As great a sum as was the $5 million, the record companies had been spending about $50 million annually to promote their records. However, following Ross's revelations and the opening of investigations, that sum dropped to just under $15 million. The record companies were determined to prove they had clean hands. They found a way not to be directly complicit in payola: their money earmarked for promotions would go through middlemen, thus the record companies had inoculated themselves from being accused of continuing to employ the services of disgraced independent promoters.

Isgro was not so lucky as his former retainers. He was made to appear as if he was complicit in illegal actions. He was on the ropes, being battered but not counted out. Bookies would not have bet on a happy future for him. The near-knockout blow arrived on November 30, 1989, four years after the Brian Ross story had aired: a grand jury voted to indict Isgro on fifty-one counts of payola, drug trafficking, racketeering, obstruction of justice, and tax fraud. He was like George Armstrong Custer about to be scalped. If found guilty, Isgro could have been sentenced to as much as two hundred years in prison and fined $1.5 million. In addition to Isgro, named in the indictment were Raymond Anderson, a former executive at Columbia Records, and Jeffrey Monka, thirty-one, accused of laundering money. Isgro, who surrendered to US Marshals, was held on $500,000 bail. Monka was held on $100,000. Shortly after the indictment, Anderson was expected to surrender. The three were charged with making undisclosed payola payments to programmers at radio stations for adding records to their playlists from 1980 to 1986. The stations were not named as defendants in the indictment, and none of their employees was charged. Along with racketeering, the three were charged with conspiracy to obstruct and impede the Internal Revenue Service, conspiracy to defraud many record companies, obstructing justice, mail fraud, conspiracy to distribute cocaine, and filing false tax returns. Only a conviction on a single count of the indictment would have been enough to enclose Isgro in a small, damp cell.

The victims of the promoters, according to the indictment, who were allegedly defrauded were Columbia, MCA, Warner Bros., RCA, and Polygram Records. Isgro's lawyer, Donald Re, stated that his client's business interests were diverse and legitimate, and he emphatically denied any wrongdoing by his client. To counter Re's statement, prosecutors said they would put Isgro's bodyguard on the witness stand, and he would testify that his boss paid money to Armone and others as part of his payola operation. The bodyguard was given refuge in the Witness Protection Program.

Almost as if to justify the work of the independent promoters, numerous newspapers, covering the case, reported that in an average year more than five thousand records are released in the United States. Such a large volume of records requires that record companies must maintain large staffs to promote those records. If not, most of the records would never receive air play, and sales would plummet, causing some companies to cease operating. To complement the work of their promotional employees and even reduce the number of in-house employees, record companies, it was reported, had hired independent record promoters. Those independent promoters were said to be a cost-effective alternative to employing large staffs of promotion workers. It also saved employees from violating the antipayola laws. Independent promoters apparently were on their own.

As if the record companies were advising the prosecutors, the charges against Isgro did not include any accusations that his illegal activities had been carried out by orders from the record companies. It was a neat trick: here was a man taking large sums of money to benefit the record companies, but the record companies had never asked him to pay off deejays and program directors. The Recording Industry Association of America, a trade group that comprised all the major record labels, did what one would have expected it do: it condemned payola and emphasized that its members had required all independent promoters to sign contracts in which they attested that they would never resort to payola to get a client's records air play.

There are those in the radio and record industry who maintain, however, that such procedures are mere subterfuge. The program director at one radio station in a large eastern city, who asked not to have his name used, claimed that record companies knew what was going on, but to protect themselves, they added on layers of protection, following Isgro's indictment. They thus provided themselves with credible deniability.

One record company executive claimed a unique use of payola: it was not undertaken to produce hit records. Instead it was undertaken to prevent competitive record companies from developing hit records through their own use of payola. One might ask, "if you're paying money to prevent a competitor from achieving success, what's to stop a deejay or program director from using that money to generate airplay for one of your records?" As an afterthought, the executive said that if a record does not appeal to listeners, no amount of payola is going to make it a success. What he didn't say was that playing an unappealing record over and over again means that a potentially popular record may never be given an opportunity for sufficient air time to build a receptive audience. One can only wonder about the role of payola or the lack thereof in the initial popularity of such super groups as the Beatles, the Supremes, and the Rolling Stones back in the early 1960s.

When Isgro finally went to trial, record company executives, who had paid out millions to independent promoters, must have been grinning like wolves about to kill, then feast on a soon-to-be-dead deer. Their grins would be turned to grimaces.

The following article by Chuck Phillips, "Payola Probe with No Payoff," appeared in the *Los Angeles Times* on April 9, 1996:

Ten years ago, the government's probe of the music business seemed to have all the makings of a major scandal: sex, drugs, rock 'n' roll, and seedy Mafia-laundered payola.

But thanks to a bumbling series of government gaffes, the investigation turned out to be a bust—costing taxpayers more than $10 million without putting a single criminal behind bars.

The case, which spurred grand jury investigations in five cities, came to an end two weeks ago, when a Los Angeles judge accused prosecutors of violating the speedy trial act and dismissed a 57-count indictment against Burbank record promoter Joseph Isgro. "This thing has been nothing but a joke from start to finish," says Isgro, who seven years ago was indicted for payola, racketeering and conspiracy to distribute cocaine. "I'm probably the only guy whose case took seven years to get thrown out on a violation of the speedy trial act. I've pretty much put it all behind me by now, but I must admit, it still makes me mad."

Taxpayers might also be miffed if they realized how badly their tax dollars were mishandled in the prosecution of Isgro's case, which changed hands several times as a series of government officials were either fired, sanctioned for wrongdoing or forced out. The case was dismissed once before after a judge in 1990 rebuked a senior prosecutor for coaching perjured testimony from the government's key witness. Revived by the U.S. 9th Circuit Court of Appeals in 1992, the case was thrown out again last month. The latest setback is likely to be the last for the beleaguered payola probe. Officials at the Justice Department, sources say, have decided to throw in the towel.

"From the standpoint of the government," said one source in the Justice Department, "this case has been a snake pit from day one."

Isgro was indicted in November 1989 after the Justice Department abandoned its probe into alleged organized crime figure Salvatore James Pisello and his involvement in the sale of cut-out records at MCA Records. The allegations about Pisello's affiliation with MCA came at a time when the Universal City-based entertainment combine was being shopped for sale.

"The reason that the government had no chance of winning this case is because it had no case to begin with," said Donald M. Re, Isgro's defense attorney. "The primary purpose of Joe's indictment was to draw attention away from a previous government probe into possible illicit activities at MCA Records—and to that end, it was absolutely successful." Re isn't the only one who thinks Isgro's case was politically motivated. Marvin Rudnick, a former assistant U.S. attorney with the organized crime strike force in Los Angeles, says he was removed from the MCA case because of pressure on the government from top MCA officials.

After the Justice Department fired Rudnick, many news reports suggested that the government had mishandled the investigation because it implicated Hollywood friends of former President Ronald Reagan.

"The government spent so much money on this case they had to salvage it somehow," Isgro said. "All of a sudden they came after me."

Isgro was one of the most successful members of the Network, a loose affiliation of nine key independent record promoters who reportedly charged the record industry $60 million a year to ensure radio airplay for songs.

The case was based primarily on the testimony of radio programmers and former associates who plea-bargained with the Justice Department. Most of the charges were payola misdemeanors, but prosecutors broadened the case into a major rack-

eteering and obstruction of justice case based on the testimony of
Isgro's former accountant, Dennis DiRicco.

U.S. District Judge James M. Ideman abruptly dismissed
the charges against Isgro in September 1990, after learning that
lead prosecutor William S. Lynch concealed information that
contradicted DiRicco's testimony against Isgro. (DiRicco, a
former IRS agent, had been found guilty of laundering money
for a Colombian drug operation. Lynch failed to disclose that
DiRicco testified in that case that Isgro had done nothing wrong.
DiRicco cut a deal for his testimony against Isgro and never did
time.)

Lynch was formally reprimanded by the Justice Department
and resigned shortly thereafter. Another prosecutor, who re-
placed Lynch after the case was reinstated by an appellate court,
was removed from the case last year.

The case languished for four years and changed prosecutors
twice more before U.S. District Judge Consuelo B. Marshall
dismissed it.

Isgro, who was executive producer of Danny DeVito's 1992
film "Hoffa," says he still acts as consultant for several record
companies and recently moved his business to Encino.

"It bothers me when people say that the government bun-
gled the biggest payola case in history, because I think they did
an excellent job of trying to frame me," said Isgro, noting that
his career was derailed.

"I was wrongly accused," Isgro said, "and in the end, not
one person ever testified that I provided them with drugs or
payola or prostitutes or had any ties to organized crime. All
those scandalous allegations that you reporters got so much mile-
age out proved to have no substance whatsoever. The govern-
ment spent 10 million bucks for this?"[9]

Following the disposition of the Isgro case, many in the record industry said that, regardless of what the record companies and radio stations might claim, payola in one form or another continued. There were outstretched gloved hands that provided payola, whether it was artist managers, brokers, or sales reps. No one's fingerprints were on any transactions, which had become increasingly more sophisticated and devious. As long as record companies needed to sell albums and build audiences for those albums through repeated on-air plays, there would be inducements to make sure that certain songs were played until they echoed in the minds of listeners. And it wasn't just money that changed hands: there were drugs, dates with prostitutes, leased luxury cars, vacations, the clearing of gambling debts, and so on. And if a record couldn't make it onto the air, program directors and deejays could report to trade publications that certain songs were receiving an inordinate amount of air time. The ensuing publicity resulted in other radio stations playing those songs, just so they could remain in the sweet spot of popularity.

Though Isgro faced other legal problems (which had nothing to do with payola and so are not the focus of this chapter), he rose like a phoenix to thumb his nose at those who had happily predicted his demise. He was the executive producer of the hit movie *Hoffa* that starred Jack Nicholson, was directed by Danny DeVito, and was written by David Mamet. In the midst of all the hoopla, publicity, predictions, and celebrity interviews that surround movie awards ceremonies, *Hoffa* was nominated for six Academy and Golden Globe Awards; it won two.

According to his website, Isgro is a producer at Raging Bull Productions. In 2007, he bought the rights of the Lucky Luciano story, which is in preproduction. His other movie projects include the titles *Pablo Escobar* and *The Stone Pony*. In addition, he is the focus of an upcoming documentary titled *The Hit Man*, which explores his success as an independent producer and profiles those who wanted to end his career by accusing him of some of the most egregious and outlandish crimes.

And it's not just movies that Isgro is playing a vital role in: his experiences in the records business have given him valuable insights into helping artists achieve success. I quote from his website, https://joeisgro.com:

We offer a range of services to empower artists and help them thrive in the entertainment industry. Here's a bulleted list summarizing our key services:

- *Radio/Music Promotion*
- *TikTok Promotion*
- *Social Media Marketing*
- *Film and Television Production*
- *National Mix Show*
- *Digital Radio Promotion*
- *Distribution Deal*
- *Music Video Production and Promotion*
- *Advertising*
- *Branding/Sponsorships*
- *Song licensing*
- *Performance Coaching*
- Staging and Choreography

We provide the comprehensive support and expertise necessary for artists to establish themselves and succeed in entertainment.[10]

Successful entrepreneurs are like championship boxers who may be knocked down again and again, but they get up and fight until they win or lose. Some retire as winners, others as losers. Regardless, they demonstrate stamina and determination while the fight to win goes on. Isgro, for one, continues to be a brilliant creative force in contemporary entertainment.

Pop to Doo Wop to Hip Hop

WHILE LISTENERS TO MUSIC ARE OFTEN CARRIED AWAY BY THE lyrics, melody, and beat of what they're listening to, they do not get to see who actually controls the songs that beguile millions of listeners and generate millions of dollars in sales. The following eye-opening account appeared on *Cultursonar.com*:

> *There's a tale in the Hip-Hop world that tells of a night in the early 1990s when rap mogul Suge Knight dragged rapper Vanilla Ice to a 15th-story hotel balcony and dangled him by his ankles. He threatened to make Ice crack on the pavement below unless Vanilla agreed to sign over his royalties to the hit "Ice Ice Baby." Although Mr. Ice denied his legs were ever strong-armed, Suge's intimidation methods convinced him to hand over 25% of the rights to the record.*[1]

To those who work regular 9:00 to 5:00 jobs, such an extreme form of persuasion might seem a bit extravagant, if not entirely outlandish. One does not hear of CEOs hanging their vice presidents out of windows or off of balconies (though many may dream of doing so). However, in the music business anything may be possible. And if an artist, producer, or arranger works for a mob-owned record company or runs afoul of mobsters who have a financial interest in a company, such behavior, or the threat of it, may be commonplace. Certainly, the threat of such behavior was present at Roulette Records. And if a singer or group was managed by a guy with mob connections, violence and its ever-present threat may be implicit in the management contract. It kept performers in line; it prevented disenchanted and deceived performers from demanding an accounting of royalties. It prevented furious performers from breaking their contracts.

The power of gangsters in the music industry preceded rock, doo wop, hip hop, and rap. One example occurred in Chicago in the 1960s. Sam Giancana, head of the Chicago Outfit, had ordered a hit on his good friend Frank Sinatra. It was not the first time Giancana had ordered a hit on Sinatra. The first occurred after Sinatra belligerently antagonized the head of the Nevada Gaming Commission by repeatedly cursing at him, which led to an investigation and the rescinding of the gambling license of Giancana's Cal Neva Lodge. Giancana owned 50 percent of the Lodge, and Sinatra was fronting as owner for him; the other half of the Lodge was owned by Joseph Kennedy Sr., who also employed a front man. While Kennedy wanted to avoid being known as a gambling tycoon, Giancana was not only not permitted to own a casino because of his notorious reputation as a gangster and felon, but he was also prohibited from even setting foot in a Nevada casino. It was bad enough that Sinatra's "big mouth" (as Giancana ranted) had caused the loss of the license, it was even worse that Sinatra refused to pay Giancana the $400,000-plus that the gangster had paid for his 50 percent share of the Lodge. The second issue that caused Giancana to order a hit on Sinatra resulted in the singer promising the gangster that he was in so deep with the Kennedys that he could stop Attorney General Robert Kennedy from going after Giancana. Instead the attorney general had Giancana closely shadowed by FBI men twenty-four hours a day, seven days a week. Giancana hated Kennedy and was furious: he cursed Kennedy as that "little bastard," cursed Sinatra for not delivering on his promises, and finally cursed the FBI. Giancana considered Sinatra a phony with a big ego and an even bigger mouth, all of which were dangerous to the mob. Giancana wanted his blood. When Sinatra learned there was a contract on his life, he had no doubt that Giancana would have him killed; he called back East and begged Meyer Lansky and Frank Costello to intervene. Lansky came to Sinatra's rescue and the singer was saved. On the occasion of a second contract on Sinatra's life, the singer Phyllis McQuire, who was Giancana's mistress, cooed during love making that if Sinatra was killed she would feel terrible listening to his love songs. It was those songs that Giancana and McQuire listened to during their love making. Giancana relented, and Sinatra's life was again saved.

Gus Russo in his book *The Outfit* writes:

In the fall of 1962, Mooney (i.e., Giancana) was ready to exact his pound of flesh from Frank Sinatra, the man who had sold him a bill of goods regarding the Kennedy "deal." Throughout 1962, Mooney had overseen a massive remodeling of his Villa Venice Restaurant, and according to some of his cronies, the entire undertaking was aimed at making a onetime killing with Sinatra's Rat Pack as bait.

Starting on November 26, and for the better part of a month, Dean Martin, Frank Sinatra, Eddie Fisher, Sammy Davis, Jr. and Jimmy Durante appeared for free at the Villa Venice. During the sold-out run, there were lavish parties and receptions in Mooney's suite while the suckers were being ferried to the Quonset Hut [nearby the Villa] to be relieved of their money at the craps, blackjack, and roulette tables.[2]

Giancana netted more than three million dollars from the event. A month later, the Villa burnt to the ground, and one can only assume that the insurance payment was significant.

The FBI knew what happened (how could they have missed?) and cornered Sammy Davis Jr. with a few highly dangerous and provocative questions. Davis sensibly responded, saying, "I can't talk about it. Baby, I got one eye, and that eye sees a lot of things that my brain says I shouldn't talk about. Because my brain says that if do, my one eye might not see anything for a while."[3]

Sinatra's turn at the Villa Venice was not surprising, not only because it was Sinatra's salvation and redemption but also because it was in keeping with Sinatra's role as a gofer and court jester for Giancana. Throughout his long association with Giancana, Sinatra gave concerts when the gangster ordered him to do so. And Giancana as well as other mobsters profited handsomely from Sinatra's concerts, for they often scalped tickets to his concerts and then skimmed proceeds from the sale of box office tickets. Even when Sinatra and other Rat Packers had previous engagements, a command to sing for the mob could not be denied. For example, when Giancana demanded that Eddie Fisher sing at the Villa Venice, Fisher had to bow out of an engagement at the Desert Inn to satisfy Giancana. Following those arrangements Giancana decided that he wanted Fisher for an additional three weeks. Fisher complained to Sinatra, who assured Fisher that he would smooth things out with Moe Dalitz, the owner of the Desert Inn.

Sinatra may not have been the ideal front man for Giancana, for his name was like a flapping red flag in FBI wiretaps. The agents, in one example, had tapped the phone of Tom Marson, a friend and neighbor of Sinatra and a member of the Gambino crime family. The two are in a famous photo of Sinatra with members of the Gambino family taken backstage at the Westchester Premier Theater. Sinatra has one arm around Marson and his other arm around Gregory DePalma. Federal agents tapped the phone of Marson and recorded a conversation between Marson and DePalma in which they discussed skimming cash from an upcoming Sinatra concert at the Westchester Premier Theater. The tapped information resulted in ten indictments handed down by a New York grand jury in June 1978. The investigation also revealed that Sinatra was paid $50,000 under the table for his first performance. Sinatra's connections to the mob became so evident that an FBI agent attempted to turn the singer into confidential informant, but FBI director J. Edgar Hoover nixed the plan. Nevertheless, as J. D. Chandler wrote in *Crime Magazine*,

> *[Hoover] thought Ol' Blue Eyes was a murderer and a Mafioso with a golden voice. Despite Hoover's FBI amassing the largest file on Sinatra of any entertainer in U.S. history, none of the damning information there ever made it to a grand jury. Numerous times the government got close to indicting Sinatra, but it never did. Sinatra had friends in the highest places, first President Kennedy and then President Nixon and finally President Reagan. Each, in different ways and to varying degrees, came to his aid when he most needed them, enabling him to front for the mob with impunity.*[4]

By the late 1960s Sinatra's public persona was that of a mob associate, a romantic rogue rather than a killer or bruiser. One could see him on the Johnny Carson show, where Don Rickles made jokes about Sinatra being a mobster and nearly kissing his ring, if not the hem of his pants. Sinatra was so popular with mobsters that they attended all of his concerts as if command performances. Dean Martin commented that if one dropped a bomb on one of those concerts, half of organized crime would be wiped out. Though Sinatra was never accused of being a made man, even by loyal sidekick Rickles, Sinatra had certainly been made by the mob, going back to his early days in New Jersey under the protection of Mafia boss Willie Moretti.

It wasn't just Sinatra and the Rat Packers who had to deal with the mob. In fact, anyone who performed in a Las Vegas casino in the 1950s, 1960s, and 1970s had to deal with the mob. They were the casino owners, whether out front or in the shadows.

By the time the rock and roll tsunami swept away the popularity of many of the so-called saloon singers and crooners of the Sinatra era, the mob held dominion over much of the music business. They were sharks posing as lifeguards: they stole royalties but pretended to protect performers who had signed contracts that made them slightly better off than indentured servants. For mobsters, the advent of rock and roll was a vast opportunity to cash in, almost as rewarding as prohibition had been. For a generation of teenagers ignorant of the Mafia's control, rock and roll signaled the birth of a new era of sex, drugs, and rebellion. Rock and roll throbbed with excitement; its sexuality came with a thumping beat; it was blunt, not subtle. Elvis, Jerry Lee Lewis, Little Richard, and Chuck Berry were celebrants of rock's sexuality. Rock inspired teenagers to thumb their noses at the squares, at their parents, at the sentimental love songs of their parents' generation. The hit parade was replaced by the Hot 100. Rock mocked pomposity. And it integrated the races. Rhythm and blues concerts drew white and black kids, who mingled and often danced as equals.

Into this ocean of eager teenagers swam opportunistic managers, startup record companies, and newly minted agents; they were like a shiver of sharks. Record companies, such as Roulette, signed young, naïve boys who wanted to be stars. They were paid a few thousand dollars up front or given a car, but they never received all the royalties owed to them. They were cheated not only out of the royalties but also out of the copyrights for songs they had written. The young singers were chained to companies that would sooner break their arms than let them break contracts. Managers, who were well versed in the art of temptation, had cooed unfulfillable promises, then seductively pushed contracts that were Faustian bargains. Following the seduction and the signed contract came the unexpected expenses for recordings, for studio time, for backup singers, for musicians, for producers, for advertising, printing album covers, marketing, and promotion; it was a series of never-ending indebtedness that couldn't be offset with royalties. Accountants were the magicians of the record business, as they are of the movie business: they can make royalties disappear behind a curtain of phony figures. Singers who thought they would receive big checks instead received invoices for money owed.

To add an element of control, many managers provided their charges with drugs. A 1973 congressional investigation blew the whistle on the practice that sent not only managers scurrying into the shadows but also top record company executives, some of whom were fired. The ensuing turmoil and vast PR efforts to restore good reputations by record executives did nothing to help such victims as Frankie Lymon. Doo wop had provided young singers, such as Lymon, with a genre that shot them into stardom. But it also provided a devastating shot in the arm.

An interesting case was that of Dominic Montiglio, who moved from being a doo wop singer to being a soldier in Vietnam to being a member of a murderous Mafia crew. He worked for the Gambino crime family and earned $250,000 a week, far more than he earned singing doo wop. However, it all crashed in 1983, when Montiglio was arrested for racketeering and chose to cooperate with the FBI. The mob supposedly put out a million dollar contract on his life, but he survived to help the government sentence fifty-six mobsters to prison, many of whom had financial interests in the music business. He is the subject of an engaging documentary titled *Lynchpin of Bensonhurst: The Dominic Montiglio Story*. Montiglio died at age seventy-three on June 27, 2021, in Albuquerque, New Mexico. Though his story is a cautionary tale, his testimony did not end or slow the flow of money in the music industry. Doo wop remained popular until it was pushed aside by more diverting genres. Nevertheless, doo wop was the predominant sound of popular music in the 1950s. Its popularity flowed out of rhythm and blues. While rhythm and blues was originally considered "race" music, doo wop became an accepted genre that appealed to whites and blacks.

Doo wop originated among African Americans in the 1940s. It was a big city sound, where groups of four, five, or six singers gathered to create distinctive harmonies. It had a simple rhythmic beat and engaging melodies. It was an apt genre for poor kids who could gather on street corners, in subway stations, under scaffolding, in high school bathrooms, under bridges, and in recessed storefronts, all of which added an acoustic smoothness to their harmonizing. No instruments were required: no guitars, no drums. The lyrics were often about love, requited or unrequited. The appeal, obviously, was to teenage romantic angst. The songs had one lead singer and background vocals. In many songs there were sentimental recitatives addressed about girls who had found love with another and about boys having found the perfect girl. Because the singing often contained nonsense words, most commonly doo wop, those words became the name of the music. But the name did not emerge during the height of the doo wop popularity; instead it was editorially used for the first time in 1961 in the *Chicago Defender*, when the popularity of doo wop was decreasing. The expression had been used in a song titled "Blue Moon" sung by the Marvels. The words can also be heard in a 1945 record titled "Just A-Sittin and A-Rockin." The phrase "do wop de wadda" was heard in the song "Mary Lee" sung by the Rainbows. The same phrase was heard in the 1956 hit "In the Still of the Night" sung by the Five Satins. It quickly gained currency in such hits as "Sincerely" sung by the Moonglows, "Earth Angel" sung by the Penguins, "Gloria" sung by the Cadillacs, "Daddy's Home" sung by Shep and the Limelights, "I Only Have Eyes for You" sung by the Flamingos, and "My True Story" sung by the Jive Five. Though those songs were sung by young black men, Italian American teenagers also took to the music and formed doo wop groups. Both ethnicities lived in poor neighborhoods and found the music a way to entertain themselves. Among the well-known Italian American groups were Dion and the Belmonts, the Capris, Randy and the Rainbows, the Earls, the Chimes, the Mystics, Johnny Maestro and the Crests, the Regents, and the Duprees. Perhaps the best known was Dion and the Belmonts, a group that emerged out of a poor neighborhood in the Bronx like the one in the movie *A Bronx Tale*, which ends with a doo wop group harmonizing on a street corner.

There were also racially mixed groups such as Frankie Lymon and the Teenagers, whose original lead singer, Herman Santiago, was of Puerto Rican descent. Other racially mixed groups included the Del-Viking whose hits included "Come Go with Me" and "Whispering Bells." There was also the Crests, which included Chico Torres and Johnny Mastrangelo (aka Johnny Maestro). Their big hit was titled "16 Candles" and can be heard in several movies about the 1950s and early 1960s. There were few female doo wop singers; however, two women, Lillian Leach of the Mellows and Margo Sylvia of the Tune Weavers, created hit songs.

Numerous members of doo wop groups were also members of local gangs, which were considered public menaces, not only in the boroughs of New York City but also in cities across the country. In Baltimore, for example, many of the teenage gangs had their own territories, where their doo wop members sang. If one gang attempted to invade another gang's territory, warfare would erupt: chains, switch blades, the heavy buckles on garrison belts, and zip guns were the weapons of the era. Pennsylvania Avenue in Baltimore was one such territorial dividing line, and if one gang crossed that line into another gang's territory, knives flashed, chains swung, bullets flew, and swinging heavy belt buckles gashed cheeks.

Though doo wop singers could be heard in dozens of cities, New York City had the largest number of groups and was known as the home of doo wop. Go up to Harlem in the 1950s, and one could hear doo wop singers performing on corners only blocks apart, under the elevated Metro North railway that ran above Park Avenue, in the Lexington Avenue and 125th Street subway station, and in the Broadway and Eighth Avenue subway stations. Noted Harlem doo wop groups comprised the Ravens, the Wrens, the Crows, the Sparrows, and the Larks, known collectively as the Bird Groups.

The cornucopia of doo wop singers and other groups presented an irresistible harvesting opportunity for the Mafia and other crime organizations, and not just in New York. In Philadelphia, for example, "the Godfather of the Philly Sound, Philly Groove founder John (Stan the Man) Watson utilized muscle provided by the notoriously-brutal Black Mafia in Philadelphia to grow and sustain his label through intimidation tactics. It was in response to Berry Gordy and his famed Motown Sound that 'Stan the Man' Watson started Philly Groove Records in 1967 and created the Philadelphia Soul Sound, a similarly-styled brand of R&B on the east coast."

While if Gordy did indeed maintain ties to the mob they were relatively marginal. Watson's connections to the underworld were more direct. The federal government considered Stan the Man a highly-placed associate of the Philly Black Mafia. Watson's signature act on Philly Groove was The Delfonics, a four-man singing group born and raised in West Philadelphia known as the original pioneers of the Philly Soul Sound. Their 1968 ballad "La La (Means I Love You)" was a smash hit and sold over a million copies. The Philly Black Mafia was founded around the same time as Watson's record label by a group of murderous thugs, racketeers, extortionists and drug peddlers led by Sam Christian and trying to veil their illegal activities under the guise of religion (the Nation of Islam) and community outreach. When Christian was locked up for killing a pair of rivals in an Atlantic City nightclub, Eugene (Bo) Baynes assumed the PBM throne. Baynes was close friends with Watson and Watson employed him as a road manager, promoter and all-around fixit man. Informants told the FBI that Watson would send Baynes into radio stations to strong arm disc jockeys into playing Philly Groove records. He worked mostly with the Delfonics. According to one federal document, when the group discussed possibly leaving Philly Groove and beginning to collect and book for their own shows in the early 1970s, Baynes stepped in and intimidated Delfonics members into staying and still allowing him and Watson to collect and book on their behalf.[5]

And then there was New Jersey. The state was known not only for its corrupt politicians but also for its Mafia-run nightclubs. With the help of organized crime in New Jersey, individual singers and groups could rise to become stars. One need only look at the early career of Frank Sinatra who was boosted to fame through the efforts of his godfather, Willie Moretti. And once the mob created stars, the mob's hooks went deep. Their stars were valuable assets like annuities that could pay off year after year, if successfully managed. Not surprisingly, the mob protected their assets with threats and violence.

Bob Gaudio of the Four Seasons noted that the Jersey Boys were pressured by guys from Brooklyn, who attempted to extort money from the group after they had dumped their manager. Enter Angelo "Gyp" DeCarlo, a capo in the Genovese crime family, who represented the family's interests in New Jersey. He stepped forward as if he were the group's protective uncle, so much so that he is portrayed in the musical drama as a kind-hearted, savvy counselor whose interest is the welfare of the group; he only wants to help them solve their problems. One problem occurs when a singer cannot pay the extortionate vigorish on his debt to Norm the Bag. Gyp takes care of the problem. Such behavior, as one might suspect, was not characteristic of Gyp, a man who loved being a gangster and who committed multiple murders. Having settled the vigorish problem not exactly in the style of State Department diplomats, he emerged as an important presence in the group's ongoing success.

Gyp was a good friend of other entertainers too, one of whom was Frank Sinatra. The singer was also a friend of Vice President Spiro Agnew. And when Gyp was imprisoned, he asked Sinatra if there was a way the singer could help get him a pardon. Sinatra asked Agnew to speak with President Nixon about the unfortunate case of Gyp, who was suffering from cancer. Nixon had his attorney general arrange for Gyp to be pardoned, and his release came forthwith.

Here, according to an FBI file, is what transpired:

> *In 1972 while DeCarlo was incarcerated in Atlanta, Frankie Valli and The Four Seasons performed for the prisoners. De-Carlo asked Valli to get in touch with his [DeCarlo's] old friend, Frank Sinatra, and ask him for help. By this time Sinatra was very close to both President Nixon and Vice-President Agnew. Nixon, of course, was in need of money for his re-election campaign. According to the FBI files, Sinatra made a $100,000 cash contribution to Maurice Stans. Peter Malatesta, a member of Agnew's staff and a close friend of Sinatra, contacted John Dean and asked for a presidential pardon for DeCarlo. Sinatra made another payment of $50,000 in December 1972, and two days later DeCarlo was pardoned. The grounds for the pardon were that DeCarlo was*

terminally ill, but according to Newsweek and the FBI file, DeCarlo was soon "back at his old rackets, boasting that his connections with Sinatra freed him." He died the following year of cancer.

The FBI dismissed the allegations against Sinatra, but Senator Henry Jackson of Washington, chair of the Senate Permanent Committee on Investigations, charged that the pardon "bypassed normal procedures and safeguards." Jackson's investigation led to serious charges against President Nixon, the U.S. Marshall Service and the IRS, but action was pre-empted by Agnew's resignation and the Watergate scandal. No charges were ever brought against Sinatra.[6]

It was apparent to the FBI that Gyp's sphere of influence ran wide and deep. He was a corrupting force in New Jersey, where businessmen, cops, judges, and various political figures were indebted to him. Between 1961 and 1963, federal agents wiretapped conversations between Gyp and his mob associates. The taps revealed the extent and depth of corruption among law enforcement officials, respected businessmen, and prominent politicians, including Newark mayor Hugh Addonizio and Hudson County wheeler-dealer and power broker John J. Kenny. The information on the taps was a death sentence to the career of Addonizio and to the career of Kenny. But even more shocking was Gyp's talk about his expertise in killing people. He said that the most humane way of doing so was to shoot someone in the heart.

DeCarlo speaks on the taps: "Let me hit you clean. . . . So the guy went for it. . . . We took the guy out in the woods and I said, 'Now listen. . . . You gotta go. Why not let me hit you right in the heart, and you won't feel a thing.' He said, 'I'm innocent . . . but if you gotta do it. . . .' So I hit him in the heart, and it went right through him."[7] According to FBI files, Gyp was referred to as a methodical gangland executioner.

Further evidence against him turned up in testimony from Mafia defector Gerald Zelmanowitz. In September 1968, Zelmanowitz visited Gyp's office, where he saw Louis Saperstein lying on the floor; he had been badly beaten. His face was bloodied and covered with spit. His swollen tongue protruded through swollen bloody lips. Saperstein was beaten because he owed $400,000 to the Genovese crime family and had not been paying the weekly vig of $5,000. While Zelmanowitz stood in shock, he watched as two mobsters kicked the motionless body of Saperstein. Then they picked him up, placed him on a chair, and continued pummeling him. Saperstein slid off the chair and was hauled up again, dumped on the chair and pummeled some more. That routine went on again and again until Gyp ordered the men to cease beating their victim. Afterward, Gyp told a semiconscious Saperstein to repay the entire loan by December 13, 1968, or he would be a dead man. Saperstein didn't pay the debt; instead he died on November 26, 1968. Foreseeing his fate, Saperstein wrote a letter to the FBI explaining what had happened to him and the threats made by Gyp. The letter resulted in an autopsy being ordered, and the pathologist found a large quantity of arsenic in Saperstein's body. In March 1970, Gyp was convicted of conspiracy to commit murder and was sentenced to twelve years in prison. In December 1972, he was released from prison and died from cancer on October 20, 1973. The court had fined him $20,000 and given him until October 25, 1973, to pay the fine. Gyp's death five days before the deadline saved his estate $20,000. He was buried in Gate of Heaven Cemetery in Hawthorne, New York. The public had been notified that the funeral would happen in the afternoon. Instead his family arranged for a morning burial to avoid publicity.

There is no record of whether Sinatra attended the funeral, but it was apparent to mobsters that the singer had a magic touch with politicians and a Teflon relationship with law enforcement. What happened with Gyp was in keeping with Sinatra's connections with the mob throughout his life. It began in his youth. His uncle, Baba Gavarante, was a wheelman for a gang of thieves and was an associate of Mafia boss Willie Moretti. In 1921, Gavarante was sentenced to fifteen years in prison after being convicted as an accessory to murder for driving a getaway car following a robbery. It was Willie Moretti who arranged for many of Sinatra's early club dates and who threatened Tommy Dorsey to release Sinatra from a contract. Moretti admitted to an FBI informant that he had an association with Sinatra and that the singer kicked back into him, meaning that Moretti was regularly paid by Sinatra. By the 1940s, Sinatra had become friends with Charles Fischetti, aka Trigger Happy Fischetti. Sinatra was also friends with Trigger's brother, Joseph Fischetti, who had an ownership position in the Fontainbleu Hotel in Miami, where Sinatra often performed. Fischetti bragged that he also had a financial interest in Sinatra and acted as his agent in the early 1950s, setting up singing engagements for him in Chicago and Miami.

Sinatra and Moretti were not singular; instead they were representative of the symbiotic relationship of the mob and performers. The Crystals, for example, were another group that benefitted from mob support, in particular, from Joe Scandore, who was connected to the Genovese family. In addition to the Crystals, he managed and/or promoted the career of Don Rickles. "In 1961, Joe didn't appreciate how producer Phil Spector was treating the [Crystals] lead singer. Delores 'La La' Brooks recalled that Scandore had phoned Phil 'trying to tell him that The Crystals have to have a record out.' When Phil ignored his requests, Scandore swiftly flew an associate from New York to Los Angeles who 'ran Phil around the fucking desk,' and assured Spector if he didn't put a record out, he would 'kill his mother and break his arms.'"[8]

In addition to running producers around desks, mobsters ran record companies with the same disregard for civilized discourse. Sonny Franzese, an underboss in the Colombo crime family, for example, was a silent partner in Buddah Records, which released a number of hits by the Lemon Pipers, the Shangri-Las, and the Isley Brothers. When Morris Levy attempted to shake down the company for royalties on the Shangri-Las's hit "Walking in the Sand," Buddah's Art Kass and Neil Bogart turned to Franzese. Though tight with Vincent Gigante and the Genovese crime family, Levy backed off.

Sonny Franzese, who socialized with movie stars and famous singers and whose handsome face and charming manner were a magnet for women who were attracted by danger, was an especially tough gangster who was relentless in fulfilling his ambitions. If he wanted to own part of a record company, no one would stand in his way. In 1967, he gained a financial interest in Buddah Records (later known as Buddha Records), which was a new kid in the record business. As a part owner who used the company to launder money, he was not about to let anyone rip off the company. Besides, he could use the company's money to bribe deejays into playing Buddah's records. Like any entrepreneurial shark, he was always looking for his next prospect. Calla Records, of which Levy owned a piece, became a target for Franzese. It was not as profitable as Buddah, and its president, Nate McCalla, wasn't as smart as the owners of Buddah. McCalla, a tough guy in his own right, was also muscle for Levy; often with a baseball bat he went after those who counterfeited their records and those who owed them money. Nevertheless, McCalla betrayed his mob associates by skimming concert money; he paid the price of not reimbursing the mob with his life in 1980. His death was a lesson to others: no one steals from the mob and lives.

Franzese, though not involved in the execution of McCalla, was a prolific killer in his own right, and a notorious bank robber, who was in and out of prison much of his life. In 2006, he discussed techniques for committing murders with Gaetano "Guy" Fatato, a Colombo associate, who was also a government informant. He taped Franzese claiming that he had killed a lot of men and by a lot he meant more than ten.

Jerry Capeci, former mob reporter for the *New York Daily News* and operator of the website gangland.com, wrote:

Prosecutors want jurors to listen to tapes where Franzese, who celebrated his 93d birthday two weeks ago, talks to a pal about his prowess as a mob hitman who was suspected in many gangland-style slayings by authorities over the years but "never caught." Since murder is a favored wiseguy tool, the feds say Sonny's skill at it would tend to prove that he was part of the racketeering conspiracy during the years—2002 to 2006—that he is charged with several loansharking and extortion scams.

Franzese noted that he had committed numerous murders in connection with his membership in the Colombo crime family," prosecutors Elizabeth Geddes, James Gatta and Rachel Nash say in court filings.

At the time he was speaking, Franzese thought he was talking to an up and coming mob recruit who was going to be "made." Actually, Gaetano (Guy) Fatato, whose status as a mob turncoat was disclosed by Gang Land in 2007, was working for the feds and wired for sound. One reason he never got caught, Franzese told Fatato, was "that he used to wear nail polish on his fingertips during murders to avoid leaving fingerprints," the prosecutors say in the papers filed in Brooklyn Federal Court. On October 13, 2006, while discussing the then-pending case against acting boss Alphonse Persico for the 1999 murder of William (Wild Bill) Cutolo, whose body had not yet been recovered, Franzese stressed the importance of disposing of murder victims. "Today, you can't have a body no more. . . . It's better to take that half-an-hour, an hour, to get rid of the body than it is to leave the body on the street," he said, according to the prosecutors. A few months later, on December

4, 2006, the prosecutors wrote, Franzese told Fatato that he had done "a lot of work" back in the 1950s and 1960s for the Colombo family: "I killed a lot of guys . . . you're not talking about four, five, six, ten."

He spoke glowingly of two "tough bastards" who, like him and current family boss Carmine (Junior) Persico, were involved in the shooting war that raged those years between loyalists of then-boss Joe Profaci and rebels aligned with the upstart Gallo brothers led by Crazy Joe Gallo.

Interestingly, the tough wiseguys he singled out for praise— Joseph (Joe Jelly) Gioelli and Salvatore (Sally D) D'Ambrosio— were each killed the way Sonny believes murder victims should be whacked today: their bodies were never found.

D'Ambrosio, who disappeared in December 1969, is said to have been killed in a Bensonhurst social club—his bloodstained shirt was found there later—on orders from boss Joe Colombo.

Franzese, whose mob star shone until he was convicted of a bank robbery conspiracy in 1967 and he was hit with a 50-year sentence, was so feared back then, he boasted to Fatato, that "a newspaper had once reported that he was responsible for hundreds of murders."

If Fatato were called on to take part in a hit, Sonny said "he should wear a hairnet to avoid leaving DNA evidence," the prosecutors wrote. He also offered grisly cooking lessons. Disposal of a body, Franzese advised Fatato, could be accomplished "by dismembering the corpse in a kiddie pool and drying the severed body parts in a microwave before stuffing the parts in a commercial-grade garbage disposal," wrote Geddes, Gatta and Nash.[9]

Not satisfied with being an important player in the music business, Franzese branched out into producing numerous successful movies. He was an associate producer of the 2003 movie *This Thing of Ours*, starring James Caan. He was also an investor in the 1972 porno movie *Deep Throat*, one of the most profitable movies of the seventies, having generated $50 million. Another movie that earned millions in which Franzese invested was *The Texas Chain Saw Massacre*, a gruesome slasher story that generated more than $30 million on an investment that topped out at $140,000. Franzese, though spending much time in prison for parole violations, had a long run: he died on February 24, 2020, at age 103. And like many mobsters who preceded him, he is buried in St. John Roman Catholic Cemetery in Middle Village, Queens County, New York. A New York City detective told the author that if Sonny Franzese had been a straight guy who only produced movies and records, he could have been a giant in those industries.

He outlived Morris Levy, who never gave up his crooked ways. In what has been called a threaten-and-settle scam, Levy claimed that John Lennon had infringed the copyright of the song "You Can't Catch Me" in his song "Come Together." Though the former was written by Chuck Berry, it was published by Levy, who claimed that there was not only a melodic similarity between "You Can't Catch Me" and the 1969 song "Come Together" but that the Lennon song used some lyrics from Berry's song (for example, "here come old flat-top"). Lennon settled out of court and agreed to record three of Levy's copyrighted songs for his upcoming *Rock & Roll* album. In his typical swindling fashion, Levy released a rough mix of the songs on an album not authorized by Lennon titled *Roots*. The angered Beatle sued and proved himself a credible and convincing witness in court. Lennon was awarded more than $400,000 in damages in August 1976. It was a minor slap on the wrist for Levy, who faced minor setbacks with revitalized efforts to make more deals. It's unlikely that he was discouraged from his modus operandi of adding his name as writer to the names of his songwriting artists. In many cases, Levy got off without having to pay his artists an additional penny. As noted in an earlier chapter, his refusal to pay royalties to a member of the Teenagers was perhaps his most notorious act of theft. And when one of the singers of "Why Do Fools Fall in Love" continued to demand payment, Levy threatened to kill the singer. And that was twenty years after the first royalty payment was due. One would think that the recording of a hit song that sold more than three million records would generate a sufficient quantity of money for Levy to have at least made a small payment. But even that was too much for his greed.

Levy, though he sat on vast sums of money like a sultan on a throne, moved with the celerity of a cheetah when it came to cashing in on new styles of music. In 1979, he became a key financial backer of Sugar Hill Records, a rap music label. Levy had plunged into the zeitgeist once again. That same year the label released a hit rap single titled "Rapper's Delight."

Levy's ability to rule his fiefdom like a medieval lord may have inspired others to follow in his footsteps. He could have been an uncredited role model for a new record owner, one who also plunged into the world of rap music. He was Suge Knight, who cofounded his own company, Death Row Records, along with D.O.C., Dr. Dre, and Dick Griffey. In the early 1990s, the company released a series of top-selling songs by money-making rappers whose hits generated more than $100 million a year in earnings. By the late 1990s, however, the label began to decline after the death of its star artist, 2Pac, the imprisonment of Suge Knight, and the departures of Dr. Dre and hit maker Snoop Dogg. Although Death Row was still financially successful, it was embroiled in a host of controversies, lawsuits, and violent acts by its artists and associates.

Before digging into the life of Suge Knight, some words about the most controversial form of rap known as gangsta rap or more conventionally gangster rap. It is a subgenre of hip hop, which is not just about music but about a lifestyle that includes drawing, dancing, fashion, and even politics. Years ago, working with Bianca Jagger, I set up a press conference with the Hip Hop Caucus in Congress regarding the remediation of mold in multiple dwellings. The Hip Hop Caucus promotes political equality, health care, economics, social justice, and education.

Gangsta rap erupted from hip hop like lava from a volcano. It was shocking, enthralling, bitter, appalling, cynical, engaging, disturbing, and amazingly popular. It focused on the values of street gangs and hustlers. By the early 1990s, gangsta rap had gone mainstream with the popularity of Dr. Dre, Snoop Dogg, and G-funk. Its popularity, however, brought on an onslaught of negative criticism that accused its singers and producers of promoting criminality and hateful behavior toward women, for the lyrics often dealt with drug dealing, misogyny, promiscuity, and murder. While the songs generated outrage among many in law enforcement, politics, and the media, others defended the music, claiming it depicted what was actually happening on the streets of inner-city neighborhoods throughout the country. It was true to life, not a fig leaf covering reality.

Among the early celebrities of gangsta rap were Run-DMC and LL Cool J, who had begun their careers before the advent of gangsta rap. The hip hop group the Beastie Boys also played a generative role as an early influence in the development of gangsta rap. The Beastie Boys had begun as a hardcore punk band, but they reinvented themselves as a hip hop group. The 1986 Beastie Boys album *Licensed to Ill* contains references to guns, drugs, meaningless sex, and other topics that were the essence of much gangsta rap.

The first big gangsta rap hit was the album *Straight Outta Compton* by N.W.A. in 1988. While earlier gangsta rap recordings had led to considerable handwringing by clergy and educators, *Straight Outta Compton* caused a major outcry due to its song "Fuck the Police," which resulted in strong condemnation from the FBI. Many critics said that the lyrics of the song were typical of gangsta rap and resulted in violent behavior and increased drug use. Such sentiments were backed up by a study conducted by the Prevention Research Center of the Pacific Institute for Research and Evaluation in Berkeley, California. Its study found that young people who listened to such songs were more likely to consume excessive amounts of alcohol and commit acts of violence. The study resulted in even greater criticism of the genre. Well-known celebrities, such as Spike Lee and Bill Cosby, and community leaders, such as Reverend Calvin Butts, condemned the music. One of Butts's sermons in which he preached against gangsta rap was referenced in the song "Thuggish Ruggish Bone" by the group Bone Thugs-n-Harmony. Nevertheless, gangsta rap continued to have its defenders, who claimed that poverty and lack of opportunity were the primary causes of inner-city violence and drug use. They cited the World Development Report of 2011, which noted that members of street gangs said that unemployment, lack of opportunities, and dire poverty drove them to join gangs and commit the crimes for which they had been accused. There is even a mockingly satirical song about it titled "Gangsta Rap Made Me Do It." Regardless of one's attitude, one cannot but be dispirited by the long list of rappers who were shot to death: from 1987 to 2023, sixty-seven performers were snuffed out by gunfire.

And that brings me back to the life and career of Suge Knight, a brilliant entrepreneur and talented athlete who wound up incarcerated. He was tough and determined, perhaps a little too much of both, and was possessed of an ambition that had the force of a hurricane.

The following appeared in an article about gangsta rap on www .culturesonar.com:

Following the Vanilla Ice incident, Suge used lead pipes and baseball bats to threaten music manager Jerry Heller and legendary gangsta' rapper Eazy-E in order to terminate the contracts of Dr. Dre, The D.O.C., and Michel'le. Suge's gang-ster tactics prevailed and along with Dre and The D.O.C, Suge founded Death Row Records in 1991. Over the next five years, he ran the label in a John Gotti-like fashion, violently suppressing anybody who stood in his way with the help of his MOB Piru/Blood associates. From pistol-whipping and strip-ping rappers George and Lynwood Stanley after they used a studio telephone without permission, to forcing a member of the rival Bad Boy Record Label to drink urine for not giving up information on P. Diddy, Suge's "mafioso" tactics made him a feared man in the industry. But like Levy, Suge's gangster ways eventually caught up to him. After multiple prison bids, lawsuits, and a trail of violence connected to his label, Death Row Records fell apart, along with the last gangster (to our knowledge) to dominate the record industry.[10]

Marion Hugh "Suge" Knight Jr. remains a fascinating char-acter worthy of a movie treatment. He was born April 19, 1965. In high school, he was a track and football star. He then went on to play college football as a defensive end for the University of Nevada Las Vegas (UNLV). During the NFL players strike in 1987, he was a replacement player for the Los Angeles Rams. As a young man, he also worked as a bodyguard for celebrities and as a concert promoter. It did not take the ambitious young man long to break into the music business by forming his own music publishing company. He hit it big when Vanilla Ice signed over royalties from the hit song "Ice Ice Baby," which was the result of the song including material allegedly written by Mario Johnson, one of Knight's clients. Rumors quickly spread that Knight had dangled Vanilla Ice by the ankles from a hotel balcony. However, Vanilla Ice has said that never actually happened, only that Knight threatened to throw him off the balcony; the claim was eventually resolved in court.

The following appeared in an article by Ben Westhoff in *L. A. Weekly* in an article titled "Did Suge Knight Really Dangle Vanilla Ice Off a Balcony":

> *VANILLA ICE: I went to my hotel room and Suge was in there with several people. He let me know he wanted to get some points off the record "Ice Ice Baby." Suge took me out on the balcony, started talking to me personally. He had me look over the edge, showing me how high I was up there. I needed to wear a diaper that day. I was an "investor" in Death Row Records with no return on my money.*
>
> *MARIO JOHNSON: When we went to the hotel that day, it was strictly for conversation. Nobody got pushed—nobody argued, no shoving—nothing. . . . When we got there everything was peaceful. Attorney David Kenner showed up, took a statement, and we got all our paperwork together. We didn't make [Vanilla Ice] sign papers. Our attorneys, through Sony, fought my case against Vanilla Ice.*
>
> *VANILLA ICE: He didn't hang me off from any balcony, okay? The story's been kind of blown out of proportion and I want to clarify that Suge and I have no bad feelings towards each other.*[11]

Meanwhile, stories, whether true or not, circulated about Suge's use of violence or intimidation in his business dealings. From the late 1990s into the early 2000s, he spent a few years incarcerated for assault and violations of probation and parole. In September 2018, Knight pled no contest to voluntary manslaughter in a fatal 2015 hit and run. As a result, he was sentenced to twenty-eight years in prison.

According to an article in *The Wrap*, "Disgraced former rap mogul Marion 'Suge' Knight is expected to be sentenced to 28 years in state prison, after reaching a plea agreement in the 2015 death of Terry Carter. Knight pleaded no contest to one count of voluntary manslaughter, the Los Angeles County District Attorney's Office said Thursday. He had faced charges of murder and attempted murder."

Knight pleaded no contest to one count of voluntary manslaughter, the Los Angeles County District Attorney's Office said Thursday. He had "Under the sentencing guidelines, Knight would receive the high term of 11 years in prison for the voluntary manslaughter count, which would double because he has a prior conviction under California's three strikes law," the DA's office said. "He also would receive an additional five years because the conviction was for a serious and violent felony and a year for the deadly weapon allegation."

A trial was scheduled to begin shortly, with jury selection beginning early next week.

In all, former Death Row Records boss Knight was scheduled to stand trial for one count of murder, one count of attempted murder and one count of hit-and-run stemming from a January 2015 incident in Compton, California, that left one man dead and another injured.

Knight was accused of intentionally running over Cle "Bone" Sloan and Terry Carter, 55, killing Carter and injuring Sloan. He had faced life in prison if found guilty, due to prior convictions.

Knight was ordered to stand trial in 2015. Since that time, his case has seen many turns, including multiple changes of lawyers and a number of instances during which the former rap mogul, 53, was hospitalized.

"By entering his plea, Knight also will resolve two other pending criminal cases. Knight was indicted for making criminal threats in August 2014. He also was charged for allegedly stealing a camera from a woman in September 2014,"

the DA's office added Thursday. "Those charges would be dis-
missed by a judge at sentencing."[12]

In June 2008, Death Row Records was auctioned in bank-ruptcy court. Global Music lost out to Wideawake Entertain-ment. Then, on January 25, 2009, an auction was held of all the company's belongings, including an electric guitar, which sold for $2,500.

After Suge pleaded no contest to voluntary manslaughter in September, the judge sentenced him to twenty-eight years in prison. Twenty-two years of the sentence were for running over his victim, and six years were because Suge had met California's three strikes law.

CBS News reported: "Knight's numerous defense lawyers had contended he was acting in self defense, but the Death Row Records co-founder pleaded no contest to voluntary manslaugh-ter last month, averting a trial on murder and attempted murder charges."

The prison sentence represents the low point of a long decline
for Knight, one of the most important figures in the history of
hip-hop. At his pinnacle in the mid-1990s, he was putting out
wildly popular records that are now considered classics from Dr.
Dre, Snoop Dogg and Tupac Shakur.[13]

Suge was incarcerated at RJ Donovan Correctional Facility in San Diego and will be eligible for parole in October 2034. One can only imagine how his incarceration will inspire him to produce more hit records, following his release.

As long as popular music is a reflection of reality, composers and singers will create lyrics that will upset those who see the world through rose-colored glasses. Gangsta rap has been the inevitable manifestation of a creative rebellion and even an outcry against the poverty and hopelessness that inspired it. It is also a brief, intense look at neighborhoods in need of help.

According to the Foundations of Music there are more than eighty popular songs about gangsters. That may be because gangsters, who invariably emerge from poverty, are known for thumbing their noses at authority and making their own rules. Those at the bottom of an economic pyramid may admire those gangsters who brazenly refused to be stifled by poverty and a lack of opportunity in the world of corporate America. Songs about gangsters (like movies about gangsters) not only generate hits but may also be inspirations for many to act like gangsters.

During the 1950s and 1960s, various branches of the military used to broadcast brief movies designed to recruit young men into signing up for military careers. By the 1970s, a few gangsters said that *Godfather I* and *Godfather II* were their recruitment movies, and several authorities on organized crime agreed.

CHAPTER 11

Scalping and Skimming

Tom Marson of the Gambino crime family phoned Frank Sinatra and told him that he should come to the Westchester Premier Theater. Sinatra said he couldn't make it: he was fulfilling another singing engagement. "You better get your ass here tomorrow," Marson yelled. Sinatra was there the next day.

Marson had invested $1.4 million in the theater. Though the Gambino crime family already had its tentacles in the record business, it deepened and expanded its dominant position by taking over a theater that would be a venue for concerts by big name performers. The Westchester Premier Theater, a solid-sounding name in a wealthy suburban county, provided an enticing opportunity for the mob to scalp tickets, skim money from legitimate ticket sales, sell tickets that were not on the books, and sell inflated stock in the theater. To keep the river of cash flowing, it needed a succession of sold-out concerts. Hence Frank Sintra, who performed numerous times at the theater. He could fill every seat in the theater for high-priced tickets. In addition, lines at the box office would impress investors and make stock in the theater a hot commodity.

Though he had no choice but to show up, Sinatra may have ultimately regretted it, for his presence resulted in a photo of him and the Gambino mob backstage that caused a storm of derisive editorial comments and cartoons and served to breathe new life into allegations that Sinatra was mob connected. It also was a primary piece of evidence in trial. Before the infamous photo was taken backstage, Sinatra had embraced Carlo Gambino, kissing him Mafia style on both cheeks. Sinatra and the mobsters then assembled for their group photo, everyone grinning or smiling at the camera. The photo, which was taken on April 11, 1976, shows Ol' Blue Eyes with his arms dangling over the shoulders of mobsters Gregory DePalma and Thomas Marson, the unnamed principal owners of the theater. Others in the photo are Mafia boss Carlo Gambino, his successor Paul Castellano, Jimmy "the Weasel" Fratianno, Richard "Nerves" Fusco, Salvatore Spatola, and Joseph Gambino. Fratianno, who served briefly as a mob boss in Los Angeles and was later demoted to being a soldier in the Dragna crime family, was eventually flipped by the FBI. He testified against his Mafia family members and went into the Witness Protection Program. He had admitted to killing eleven people and died in 1993. Sinatra when asked about Fratianno said he was nothing but a rat. Paul Castellano, who succeeded Carlo Gambino as boss, was assassinated in 1985 in a plot hatched by John Gotti. Castellano died of multiple gunshots in front of Sparks Steak House on East 46th Street in Manhattan.

Sinatra was not happy about the opprobrium that was flung at him like mud pies, all the result of that infamous photo. He attempted to explain it away, but only his most devout fans believed that Sinatra was merely accommodating admirers who wanted their photo taken with him. By 1981, he was able to emerge cleansed of his notoriety, at least in Nevada. As part of his application for a gaming license, he testified to the Nevada Gaming Control Board that he had never in his life seen the eight members of the Gambino crime family who appeared with him in the photo. He said that he was always happy to accommodate fans, and when they came backstage to meet him, he graciously agreed to pose with them as he would with any other fans. The board accepted his explanation, and Sinatra was able to obtain a gambling license. He had more Teflon than the so-called Teflon don John Gotti.

Though Sinatra continued to live his charmed life, the theater went into bankruptcy in 1977, and ten men were charged with racketeering, stock fraud, bankruptcy fraud, and obstructing justice. They faced a twenty-four-count federal indictment. Among those named in the indictment were Eliot H. Weisman, Gregory J. DePalma, and Richard Fusco. The latter two were named as undisclosed principals, and Mr. Weisman as the president of the theater.

In a June 7, 1978, *New York Times* article headlined "Charged with Fraud in Inquiry on Bankrupt Westchester Theater," reporter James Feron wrote (section B, page 3):

> *The former president of the bankrupt Westchester Premier Theater and nine other men were charged today with racketeering, stock and bankruptcy fraud and obstructing justice in a 24-count Federal indictment.*
>
> *Robert B. Fiske Jr., United States Attorney for the Southern District of New York, said Eliot H. Weisman, 40 years old, former head of the Tarrytown Theater; Gregory J. DePalma, 46, and Richard Fusco, 42, all of Scarsdale, had formed the theater corporation in 1971, with Mr. DePalma and Mr. Fusco as "undisclosed principals."*
>
> *"It was really a three-phase operation," Mr. Fiske said at a news conference. "There was the initial stock fraud. Then there was the skimming operation, when the theater first opened in 1975, and the result of the skimming, among other things, was that the theater went into bankruptcy."*

Finally, he said, "during the bankruptcy itself, the skimming continued, and there were further frauds on the creditors and others."

Among other crimes, the three principals are charged with racketeering, which carries a "penalty of 20 years in jail, a fine of $25,000 and forfeiture of proceeds." Mr. Fiske said that the public had lost an estimated $1 million over the five-year period and that "hundreds of thousands of dollars" had been skimmed.

The indictments, handed up by a Manhattan grand jury, followed a yearlong Federal investigation.

The stock fraud began, the indictment charged, with a public offering of common stock in the theater between May 25 and June 14, 1973, at a price of $7.50 a share.

Mr. Fiske said that under the terms of the offering a minimum of 275,000 shares had to be sold to the public on or before June 14, 1973, or the money paid for the stock would have to be returned to the purchasers. In their attempt to sell the minimum offering, the indictment charged, the defendants filed with the Securities and Exchange Commission and distributed to the public a prospectus that fraudulently omitted the roles and financial interest of Mr. DePalma, Mr. Fusco and others.

When the defendants were unable to sell the 275,000 shares, the indictment said, "they used a variety of fraudulent means to make it appear as though the shares had been sold lawfully." They did this, according to the indictment, by giving secret cash bribes to individuals to induce them to buy the stock, by promising extra stock under the table with purchases and by placing stock in the names of individuals who had not actually purchased it.

The price of the stock plunged to $2.50 within a month after the offering ended, and the shares are worthless today.[1]

Investigators went back to 1974 when Gregory DePalma and Richard Fusco built the theater. The construction costs greatly exceeded original estimates, so DePalma and Fusco visited their boss, Carlo Gambino, and asked to borrow $100,000. Gambino lent the money on the condition that Sinatra be brought into the deal. As one of the most popular headliners in the county, Sinatra would be a magnet for attracting thousands of fans. Construction proceeded and was finally completed in 1975. Though Sinatra was not available at the time, the theater opened with a torrent of publicity as its first headliner Diana Ross was adulated in the media. One big name performer followed another, and a river of money poured into the theater. It was just what DePalma and Fusco had wanted. The money was an irresistible temptation for the two mobsters, and they skimmed thousands of dollars. The more they skimmed, the less money the theater had to cover its operations. Though the theater was headed to go off a cliff and plunge into bankruptcy, the two mobsters continued their skimming. They also continued hiring performers who attracted thousands of fans. As long as they could sell tickets, the skimmers figured that the flow of money would never dry up. They were fortunate that Sinatra and his pal, Dean Martin, often performed at the theater. Each time they performed, the theater not only sold tickets for all the seats, but it sold hundreds of tickets that were not reported on the theater's books for accounts receivables. The multiplicity of frauds was comparable to the way the mobs used to run Las Vegas casinos.

While skimming was a drain on the theater, DePalma and Fusco sought to keep the theater operating through funds garnered from the sale of stock. The two began selling inflated stock to celebrities such as Steve Lawrence, Eydie Gorme, and Alan King, among various others. And because celebrities attract other celebrities, there was a steady market for the stock that lasted for months. Many of the celebrity investors liked owning a piece of a theater in which they could perform, and if they had big enough names, they were welcomed by DePalma and Fusco. It was a win-win opportunity. Those celebrities who were initially hesitant to buy stocks were quickly offered discounts; it was a sufficient inducement to rack up more sales. However, when it came to selling stock to bottom line–oriented business executives, DePalma and Fusco offered handsome kickbacks. Cash under the table has always been an irresistible temptation for those who want to avoid taxes and government scrutiny. Though the stock sold well for a brief period, its price began to tumble as the number of buyers dwindled. Existing owners of the stock, like all members of a spooked herd, watched with dismay that turned to panic as the value of their shares nosedived. They stampeded to sell their shares at whatever the market was offering. Nothing the scammers could do now would stop the stock from going into a death spiral; it crashed to a dollar a share and lay there like a comatose body.

That alone would have been enough to arouse the SEC and FBI that something was amiss. But then Tom Marson, whose phone was tapped by the feds, blurted out information that would set law enforcement on his trail, which led directly to the theater.

Marson should have lived by the old naval wartime maxim that loose lips sink ships. Instead, in a taped conversation, Marson and DePalma discussed skimming money from a Sinatra performance at the theater. It was also noted that Sinatra was paid $50,000 under the table. The FBI couldn't have been happier; they had the beginning of a case that would lead to ten indictments. The ten indictees, unsurprisingly, did not include Sinatra.

Though Marson and Fusco were minor Mafioso, Gregory DePalma was an important player in the structure of the Gambino crime family. He was born in 1932 and rose to be a capo in the family. He was a big earner who could never resist the temptation to steal whatever was not glued down. In addition to scamming and thievery, of which he was proud, he was proud of his numerous friendships with celebrities and sought them out as golf partners.

He particularly enjoyed playing golf with Willie Mays (the Say Hey Kid), considered the greatest New York Giants outfielder, who made one of the most spectacular catches in baseball history in the 1954 World Series: a high fly ball had been hit to center field, and rather than facing the oncoming ball, Mays turned and raced to the back of center field. While running, he quickly looked over his shoulder, then continued running toward the center field wall where he was perfectly positioned to catch the ball as if it had magically dropped into his mitt. He quickly turned and fired the ball directly to second base. He prevented two runs from scoring. Amazed fans erupted with cheers and applause. He was just the kind of celebrated hero that DePalma loved being around.

Though a good golfer, DePalma was no Willie Mays. The other top performer who won the adoration of fans and was DePalma's friend was (surprise, surprise) Sinatra. DePalma's self-assurance seemed to blossom like a rose bush in spring when he was befriended by charismatic athletes and entertainers. There was a grinning Sinatra, and there was DePalma looking as happy as a kid meeting one of his heroes in the infamous backstage of photo of him with Sinatra's arm dangling over his shoulder. The gesture implied that they were buddies for all the world to see and perhaps envy. Though the photo memorialized DePalma's close-ness to Sinatra, criminal defense lawyers at DePalma's trial would have been happy if the judge had refused to let it be submitted as evidence against DePalma during his trial for fraud. Though DePalma was able to escape a guilty verdict due to a hung jury in 1979, he pleaded guilty to bankruptcy fraud just prior to a second trial and was sentenced to four years in prison. None of his famous friends visited him.

When DePalma died in 2009, Jerry Capeci wrote,

Good riddance, said Joaquin (Big Jack) Garcia, the former G-man who snared DePalma and 31 other Gambinos—including the family's acting boss and underboss—for racketeering and other charges after a 28-month-long sting operation in which he posed as a budding mobster.

"The world is a better place without Greg," said Garcia. DePalma, he said, was a consummate gangster who did anything and everything he could to make an illegal buck. Garcia recounted an incident in which he watched as DePalma stole two stuffed dolls from a sidewalk vendor after filching some expensive paintings from [Leroy] Neiman during a visit to the artist's Manhattan digs.

"I can't help myself," DePalma chortled when the man he knew as Big Jack Falcone questioned why the gangster would chance getting stopped for such a paltry crime when he had thousands of dollars in art work he had just stolen from Neiman's duplex apartment on the West Side in a tube that he was carrying. . . .

DePalma was found guilty of shaking down Liza Minnelli's manager in his 2006 trial. It was his second encounter with celebrity-linked crime: DePalma was convicted in 1979 of bankruptcy fraud in connection with the building and shutdown of the mob-run Westchester Premiere Theatre where a smiling DePalma stands next to Sinatra in the photo that was introduced into evidence at his trial.[2]

Of DePalma and Fusco, Jimmy "the Weasel" Fratianno, a Mafia turncoat, who would go into the Witness Protection Program, commented, "Once the theater was in operation," DePalma and associates began "skimming the shit out of the joint." Fratianno explained by relating a story he was told from investor Tommy Marson: "They're skimming from the cash concessions, two restaurants in the place, bars, parking, T-shirts and souvenirs, selling comped tickets, selling their own tickets, and selling tickets for sixty-one permanent seats and a hundred and thirty-six folding chairs that are not on the theater's seating chart."[3]

The initial trial, which received prominent coverage in the *New York Times*, local tabloids, the *Westchester Gannet Newspapers*, and on local TV news shows, generated a surprise ending when a deadlocked jury caused a mistrial. The deadlock occurred after seven days of jury deliberations, following a trial that had lasted three months and that included testimony from more than fifty witnesses and generated nine thousand pages of transcript. The deadlock was the result of one determined juror, out of twelve, who refused to go along with the other jurors, all of whom voted for conviction. The defendants were jubilant at the outcome and grateful to the juror who was their savior. All the defendants hugged their relatives and praised their attorneys. Smiles and handshakes and congratulations were passed around like Christmas ornaments. Had the relieved and happy defendants been found guilty, they could have been sentenced to up to twenty years in prison. Though relieved that the trial ended as it did, the defendants knew that a new trial might result in convictions for all of them. They would face that peril when the time came. The one object to their acquittal, they knew, would be the testimony of Jimmy "the Weasel" Fratianno, who could launch them on a journey to long prison sentences.

The defendants' concern about Fratianno proved correct. His testimony started as matter of factly as if filling out a credit card application. He stated that his birth name was Aladena, but said that he was also known as Dr. Schwartz. He said he grew up in Italy, then moved to Cleveland and became a professional killer. Thereafter, his testimony riveted the attention of jurors. He announced that he had taken part in nine murders from 1947 to 1953 and two murders in 1977. He said that he recently made a deal with the government to tell all that he knew about organized crime and in exchange would receive no more than five years in prison. He claimed that Tom Marson had invested $1.4 million in the theater. Criminal defense attorney Barry Slotnick aggressively cross-examined Fratianno, not cracking the witness's soft-spoken demeanor. Though a big target for the arrows of defense attorneys, Fratianno was a moving target. None of the defense attorneys was able to puncture his credibility. Fratianno had a facility of responding to their condemning oratorical flourishes with wiseguy humor that caused spectators to laugh. Nevertheless, defense attorneys continued to hammer away at him, repeatedly telling the court that Fratianno, a notorious murderer, had made a deal with the government for his testimony. The agreement meant that Fratianno would go into the Witness Protection Program. Fratianno was unperturbed by the characterizations of him as a heartless murderer and readily admitted under questioning to his life of crime. He maintained his cool, reporting almost nonchalantly that he had seen many of the defendants in the theater on numerous occasions, especially during Frank Sinatra's concerts. He added, as if he were a critic of popular music, that he wasn't impressed by Sinatra, though other people were. The unimpressed critic would hang out in the theater's lounge while Sinatra sang. He finally noted somewhat dismissively that "[Sinatra] didn't impress me."

More importantly for the prosecution, Fratianno noted his close relationship with Frank "Funzi" Tieri, of the Genovese crime family. He said that he had met privately with Tieri in Manhattan, because Tieri was looking for ways to protect Marson's investment in the theater. How could he help protect that investment when DePalma and his associates were skimming the profits of the theater? They were like kids who had broken into a candy store late at night and cleaned out the counters of every sweet they could carry.

The overall effect of Fratianno's testimony was just what the prosecutors had wanted. DePalma for one read his expected fate on the faces of jurors who had paid rapt attention to Fratianno. DePalma's lawyers effected a plea deal with prosecutors that would land him in prison for four and half years. He was, as mobsters say, a stand-up guy. He took his commitment to the family as an inviolable allegiance. A traditionalist, he was bound by the rule of omerta: he did not make a deal to betray any of his cohorts. He did his time without arousing anxiety in others against whom he could have testified. And following his release from prison, DePalma kept a low profile. As a reward, he was promoted to capo in the Gambino family.

It wasn't only DePalma who galloped out of the money; it was also the former president of the Westchester Premier Theater Eliot H. Weisman. He was convicted in Federal District Court in Manhattan for racketeering, stock and bankruptcy fraud, and obstructing justice. His conviction followed forty-four counts of a federal indictment. He had been one of the ten men who were charged with conspiracy and fraud, resulting in the Westchester Premier Theater going into bankruptcy. Two other men who were named in court documents as unindicted coconspirators, but not defendants, were Frank "Funzi" Jieri, who fronted as boss of the Genovese crime family, and Aladena J. Fratianno, the former Mafia boss of the Dragna crime family of Los Angeles. They were accused of stealing proceeds from the theater at the expense of the legitimate stockholders and creditors. Prosecutors noted that investors in the theater lost about one million dollars, none of which was recoverable.

Though Sinatra was frequently mentioned during the trial of Weisman and DePalma, he was not a defendant. However, the infamous photo of him with the Gambinos was introduced so often by prosecutors that one would have thought that the photo was on trial. It was certainly splashed across hundreds of newspapers. One almost expected to see it on police bulletin boards among photos of wanted criminals.

Poor Sinatra: three of his concerts were said to have been targets for skimming tens of thousands of dollars in 1976 and 1977. Though performers, such as Sinatra, were well paid to perform at the theater, it's unlikely that most of them were aware of how the mob was skimming money. As a result, no performers were ever charged with crimes related to the theater.

A jury of six men and six women had brought an end to a major investigation that resulted in an exciting trial of ten defendants, each accused of stock and bankruptcy fraud and of skimming hundreds of thousands of dollars from the theater's revenues before it collapsed into bankruptcy on April 10, 1978.

Following the trial, Fratianno became a bankable media star. He was a hot subject for newspaper editors, who assigned reporters to dig up information about his life

Stories began with the birth of Aladena James Fratianno on November 14, 1913, who when as a boy thief was so fleet of foot that he was said to run and escape capture with the speed and cunning of a weasel. He graduated from being a thief to being a killer, whose preferred method for eliminating victims was strangulation with a rope. In 1975, he was made coboss with Louis Dragna of the Los Angeles Dragna crime family, known as the Mickey Mouse Mafia, as a result of its general ineptitude. Louis Dragna was the nephew of the family's former boss, Jack Dragna. However, when the imprisoned boss of the family was released, Fratianno was demoted to being a soldier in the family, a position he accepted with bitter resentment. As a boss, he was paid tribute by capos and soldiers; now he would have to pay tribute to a new boss. It would be comparable to a corporate CEO being demoted to being a junior executive.

The fates were not looking favorably on Fratianno. He was subsequently arrested for participating in the murder of Cleveland gangster Danny Greene. While jailed, Fratianno received the bad news that the boss of the Cleveland crime family James Licavoli had issued a contract on his life. Could things get any worse? He hadn't chosen a life of crime to be humiliated and threatened by other criminals. The hell with them. He no longer owed them any loyalty, and, fearing for his life, Fratianno decided to become an informant against his former Mafia compatriots. In compensation for his testimony, he received a five-year prison sentence for his numerous murders. As part of his deal and as a reward for good behavior he served only twenty-one months of his sentence. Newspapers noted that two of his victims were Anthony Brancato and Anthony Trombino, known as the two jerks and two Tonys who had been stupid enough to rob a Mafia-run casino in Las Vegas. Though he was safe from assassination in the Witness Protection Program, it was no place for a hot Mafia celebrity, especially when the public was hungry for Mafia stories during the era of *Godfather* fascination. What was the point of being a celebrity if no one could see or hear him? He left the Witness Protection Program and accepted a publisher's fat advance to write his story. This is more like it. With coauthor Ovid Demaris, he wrote a surefire best-seller, *The Last Mafioso*. Then as a certified best-selling author, Fratianno published a second book, *Vengeance Is Mine*, having worked with writer Michael Zuckerman. Fratianno was bathed in celebrity and appeared in numerous TV interviews, including one on *60 Minutes*, which was seen by millions of TV viewers.

Fratianno was the dying breath of the Westchester Premier Theater. Before the 3,500 seat theater was torn down, it was briefly taken over by the TV host of *American Bandstand*, Dick Clark, in 1978. He renamed it the Dick Clark Westchester Theater. He was no machinating Mafioso. And though his theater hosted numerous rocks groups, the theater could not be revived. The glory days of the theater were history. No one saw it as a venue for future rock concerts. Those who remembered all of the crowd-pleasing concerts that had taken place at the theater could now buy individual seats from the theater for twenty-five dollars. The seats would look great in suburban finished basements in front of large-screen TVs. And if you wanted to make your milieu even more reminiscent of the vanished theater, you could buy its lighting system, carpets, sound systems, pianos, and even dishes and glasses from the lounge, and all for a song.

An obituary of the theater appeared in the *New York Times*:

"This was a very classy operation," said the theater manager, Bobby Schiffman. "We had an airy, comfortable auditorium with 3,500 seats and free parking for 1,700 cars. We had a potential audience of 800,000 in Westchester. We had 600,000 more in Rockland and we're only one minute from the bridge. There is 600,000 more in Connecticut and 800,000 in Bergen County. We're near all the parkways and the Thruway."

The $6.5 million theater opened in March 1975 as the Westchester Premier Theater. Johnny Carson, Tom Jones and Liza Minnelli appeared in the first year, and there were 10 appearances by Frank Sinatra. But in 1977, the theater was declared bankrupt, and in 1979, three of the principals were convicted on charges of fraud and racketeering, including skimming of profits from Mr. Sinatra's sellout performances. Several other persons pleaded guilty to related charges at the time.

It has had two managements since then. The Lincoln Savings Bank, which bought the bankrupt theater, chose Dick Clark to give the theater a new image and a new name, the Dick Clark Theater, but he stayed only two years.

Mr. Schiffman, his assistant, stayed on as manager and turned to rock concerts to fill the theater. He also tried to make ends meet by renting to I.B.M. for its annual Christmas party, to Mercy College and Pace University for graduation ceremonies and to producers of closed-circuit television boxing matches.

This year, the theater had only 31 shows, and it needed 250 to pay what Mr. Schiffman calls "a huge nut" of taxes, repairs, insurance and heating and lights in the all-electric building, designed before the energy crisis. "There's no way in God's green earth to do that," Mr. Schiffman said. "I could get the audi-

ences, but I couldn't get the performers. When the building was planned in the early 70's, artists made 80 percent of their revenue from personal appearances. Now they make only 20 percent from appearances and the rest from records, and they don't have to work as much," he said. "When they worked 40 weeks, they played every joint in the country, but when they work 15, they play only major cities, and that's not Tarrytown."

The last show, a rock concert by Billy Squires, was a sellout. Critics said that was one problem—too many rock concerts gave the theater the image of a teen-age hangout, and made it uninviting to adults, even when the theater provided what Mr. Schiffman calls middle-of-the-road entertainment.[4]

In addition to Billy Squires, there was a cornucopia of rock, pop, and folk performers who sang at the Westchester Premier Theater, including Diana Ross, James Taylor, the Kinks, Southside Johnny and the Asbury Jukes, Meat Loaf, Peter Paul & Mary, the Allman Brothers, Carly Simon, Jerry Lee Lewis, Fats Domino, Bo Didley, the Shirelles, Gary US Bonds, Frankie Valli and the Four Seasons, ZZ Top, Engelbert Humperdinck, Teddy Pendergrass, Paul Anka, Marvin Gaye, Johnny Cash, Johnny Mathis, Judy Collins, Linda Ronstadt, Kris Kristofferson, Tom Jones, Captain and Tennille, Billy Joel, New Riders of the Purple Sage, the Band, Hot Tuna, Patti Smith, Liza Minnelli, Bette Midler, Gladys Knight and the Pips, the Four Tops, Carl Perkins, Al Green, Dean Martin, Steve Lawrence, Eydie Gorme, and Frank Sinatra, who was the most frequent star attraction at the theater.

Without the gangsters, the rock music business continues to rock along. Performers in Las Vegas are making tens of millions of dollars. There are worldwide tours generating even more millions. And as singers age into senescence and settle into their golden years, putting their soft rubber-soled Nunn Bush loafers up on their BarcaLounger extensions, they can contemplate the hundreds of millions of dollars they have been paid for selling their song catalogs to multinational conglomerates. All those days and nights of touring, of taking uppers and downers, of exhaustive nights with voracious groupies have paid off. And paid off in sums their young selves had never dreamed of. Those sums, if known to the gangsters of the early days of rock and roll, would now cause them to spin in their graves. And not only the gangsters and their partners and associates but also those young singers, Frankie Lymon and Jimmie Rodgers, who were cheated out of their royalties and whose songs continue to make money. The mobsters, through excessive greed, put out a contract on their own golden goose.

List of Murdered Hip Hop Performers

Name	Date of death	Age at death	Place of death	Cause of death
Scott La Rock	August 27, 1987	25	South Bronx, New York City	Shooting
Paul C	July 17, 1989	24	Queens, New York City	Shooting
Danny "D-Boy" Rodriguez	October 6, 1990	22	Dallas, Texas	Shooting
Charizma	December 16, 1993	20	East Palo Alto, California	Shooting
Stretch	November 30, 1995	27	New York City	Shooting
Seagram	July 31, 1996	26	Oakland, California	Shooting
Tupac Shakur	September 13, 1996	25	Las Vegas, Nevada	Drive-by shooting
G-Slimm	October 13, 1996	21	New Orleans, Louisiana	Shooting
Yaki Kadafi	November 10, 1996	19	Orange, New Jersey	Shooting
The Notorious B.I.G.	March 9, 1997	24	Los Angeles, California	Drive-by shooting
Fat Pat	February 3, 1998	27	Houston, Texas	Shooting
Big L	February 15, 1999	24	New York City	Shooting
Freaky Tah	March 28, 1999	27	New York City	Shooting
DJ Uncle Al	September 10, 2001	32	Miami, Florida	Shooting
Jam Master Jay	October 30, 2002	37	New York City	Shooting
Sabotage	January 24, 2003	29	São Paulo, Brazil	Shooting

(*Continued*)

Name	Date of death	Age at death	Place of death	Cause of death
Camoflauge	May 19, 2003	21	Savannah, Georgia	Shooting
Soulja Slim	November 26, 2003	26	New Orleans, Louisiana	Shooting
Mac Dre	November 1, 2004	34	Kansas City, Missouri	Shooting
Blade Icewood	April 19, 2005	28	Detroit, Michigan	Shooting
Proof	April 11, 2006	32	Detroit, Michigan	Shooting
Big Hawk	May 1, 2006	36	Houston, Texas	Shooting
VL Mike	April 20, 2008	32	New Orleans, Louisiana	Shooting
Dolla	May 18, 2009	21	Los Angeles, California	Shooting
Lele	July 1, 2010	23	Trujillo Alto, Puerto Rico	Shooting
Messy Mya	November 14, 2010	22	New Orleans, Louisiana	Shooting
Magnolia Shorty	December 20, 2010	28	New Orleans, Louisiana	Shooting
Bad News Brown	February 11, 2011	33	Montreal, Quebec, Canada	Unspecified violence
Adán Zapata	June 1, 2012	21	San Nicolás de los Garza, Mexico	Shooting
Lil Phat	June 7, 2012	19	Sandy Springs, Georgia	Shooting
Lil Snupe	June 20, 2013	18	Winnfield, Louisiana	Shooting
MC Daleste	July 7, 2013	20	Paulínia, Brazil	Shooting
Pavlos Fyssas	September 18, 2013	34	Keratsini, Greece	Stabbing
Depzman	September 21, 2013	18	Birmingham, England	Stabbing
Doe B	December 28, 2013	22	Montgomery, Alabama	Shooting
The Jacka	February 2, 2015	37	Oakland, California	Shooting

(Continued)

Name	Date of death	Age at death	Place of death	Cause of death
Flabba	March 9, 2015	37	Alexandra, South Africa	Stabbing
Chinx	May 17, 2015	31	New York City	Shooting
Bankroll Fresh	March 4, 2016	28	Atlanta, Georgia	Shooting
Mr. 3-2	November 10, 2016	44	Houston, Texas	Shooting
XXXTentacion	June 18, 2018	20	Deerfield Beach, Florida	Shooting
Jimmy Wopo	June 18, 2018	21	Pittsburgh, Pennsylvania	Shooting
Smoke Dawg	June 30, 2018	21	Toronto, Ontario, Canada	Shooting
Young Greatness	October 29, 2018	34	New Orleans, Louisiana	Shooting
Feis	January 1, 2019	32	Rotterdam, Netherlands	Shooting
Kevin Fret	January 10, 2019	24	San Juan, Puerto Rico	Shooting
Nipsey Hussle	March 31, 2019	33	Los Angeles, California	Shooting
RS	September 3, 2019	18	Amsterdam, Netherlands	Stabbing
Pop Smoke	February 19, 2020	20	Los Angeles, California	Shooting during home invasion
Houdini	May 26, 2020	21	Toronto, Ontario, Canada	Shooting
Huey	June 25, 2020	31	Kinloch, Missouri	Shooting
King Von	November 6, 2020	26	Atlanta, Georgia	Shooting
MO3	November 11, 2020	28	Dallas, Texas	Shooting
Einár	October 21, 2021	19	Stockholm, Sweden	Shooting
Young Dolph	November 17, 2021	36	Memphis, Tennessee	Shooting
Drakeo the Ruler	December 19, 2021	28	Los Angeles, California	Stabbing
Snootie Wild	February 27, 2022	36	Houston, Texas	Shooting

(*Continued*)

Name	Date of death	Age at death	Place of death	Cause of death
Goonew	March 18, 2022	24	Prince George's County, Maryland	Shooting
Archie Eversole	April 5, 2022	37	Decatur, Georgia	Shooting
Sidhu Moose Wala	May 29, 2022	28	Mansa, Punjab, India	Shooting
Hypo	June 2, 2022	39	Woodford Green London, England	Stabbing
Trouble	June 5, 2022	34	Atlanta, Georgia	Shooting during home invasion
Zayar Thaw	July 23, 2022	41	Yangon, Myanmar	Executed by Myanmar military junta
JayDaYoungan	July 27, 2022	24	Bogalusa, Louisiana	Shooting
PnB Rock	September 12, 2022	30	Los Angeles, California	Shooting
Takeoff	November 1, 2022	28	Houston, Texas	Shooting
AKA	February 10, 2023	35	Durban, South Africa	Shooting
Pacho El Antifeka	June 1, 2023	42	Bayamón, Puerto Rico	Shooting
Bigidagoe	February 25, 2024	26	Amsterdam, Netherlands	Shooting

NOTES

INTRODUCTION

1. Nick Tosches, "Mafia a Go-Go: The . . . ," *Los Angeles Times*, April 25, 1993, https://www.latimes.com/archives/la-xpm-1993-04-25-bk-26800-story.html.

2. William K. Knoedelseder Jr. "Head of N.Y. Record Firm Charged with Extortion; 16 Others Arrested in Sweep," *Los Angeles Times*, September 24, 1986, https://www.latimes.com/archives/la-xpm-1986-09-24-fi-8772-story.html.

3. William K. Knoedelseder Jr., "Salvatore Pisello: A Shadowy Figure in Records Deals," *Los Angeles Times*, May 4, 1986, https://www.latimes.com/archives/la-xpm-1986-05-04-fi-3550-story.html.

4. Knoedelseder, "Salvatore Pisello."

5. Knoedelseder, "Salvatore Pisello."

6. Richard Harrington, "Making Music with the Mob," *Washington Post*, April 10, 1993, https://www.washingtonpost.com/archive/entertainment/books/1993/04/11/making-music-with-the-mob/615b947e-ef2c-40e7-b53d-9cfe0d56f42f/.

7. William K. Knoedelseder Jr., "MCA Audit Details Ties to Pisello: Points to Funds Paid by Record Unit to Alleged Crime Figure," *Los Angeles Times*, May 10, 1985, https://www.latimes.com/archives/la-xpm-1985-05-10-fi-18310-story.html.

8. William Knoedelseder, *Stiffed* (New York: Harper Collins Publishers, 1993), 98.

9. Andy Newman, "Gigante Pleads Guilty to Obstructing Justice," *New York Times*, April 7, 2003, https://www.nytimes.com/2003/04/07/nyregion/gigante-pleads-guilty-to-obstructing-justice.html.

10. John A. Jackson, *Big Beat Heat* (New York: Schirmer Books, 1991), 83.

11. Jackson, *Big Beat Heat*, 189.

12. Jackson, *Big Beat Heat*, 211.

CHAPTER 1

1. Fredric Danner, *Hit Men* (New York: Times Books, 1990), 31.

2. Robert Lacey, *Little Man* (Boston: Little, Brown and Company, 1991), 169.

3. *Newsday*, "Mob Near Full Control of Jukes, Probe Finds," Leonard Baker, April 1, 1960, page 5.

4. *Associated Press, New York Times*, "Teamster Local Branded a Leech," April 16, 1959, page 21.

5. *Newsday*, February 21, 1959, page 1.

6. Edmond Valin, "Fred 'Jukebox Smitty' Smith," *The American Mafia*, http://mafiahistory.us/rattrap/infsmitty.html (accessed May 1, 2023).

7. http://www.gangsterbb.net/threads/ubbthreads.php?ubb=showflat&Number=809657 (accessed May 2, 2023).

8. *New York Times*, "Mobster's Son Receives Life Sentence for Orchestrating Father's Murder," Colin Moynihan, April 15, 2023, page A17.

CHAPTER 2

1. Richard Carlin, *Godfather of the Music Business* (Jackson, MS: University Press of Mississippi, 2016), 5.

2. Kenneth T. Jackson, editor, *The Encyclopedia of New York City* (New Haven: Yale University Press, 1995), 110.

3. Carlin, *Godfather of the Music Business*, 33.

4. Bruce Eder, "George Goldner Biography," AllMusic.com, https://www.allmusic.com/artist/george-goldner-mn0000648075/biography.

5. Eder, "George Goldner Biography."

6. Murray Kempton, *Rebellions, Perversities, and Main Events* (New York: Times Books, 1994), 226.

7. Carl Sifakis, *The Mafia Encyclopedia* (New York: Checkmark Books, 1999), 157.

8. Carlin, *Godfather of the Music Industry*, 167.

9. William Bastone, "The Priest and The Mob," *Village Voice*, March 7, 1989, https://www.villagevoice.com/2020/12/15/the-priest-and-the-mob/.

10. George Anastasia, "Godfather of Rock and Roll," Jersey Man Magazine, July 1, 2022, https://jerseymanmagazine.com/godfather-of-rock-and-roll/.

11. William K. Knoedelseder Jr., "Head of N.Y. Record Firm Charged with Extortion; 16 Other Arrested in Sweep," *Los Angeles Times*, September 24, 1986, https://www.latimes.com/archives/la-xpm-1986-09-24-fi-8772-story.html.

12. "Morris Levy Interview," YouTube, https://www.youtube.com/watch?v=qj6zKt9r2BQ.

13. Anastasia, "Godfather of Rock and Roll."

CHAPTER 3

1. Alan Dent, *Mrs. Patrick Campbell* (London: Museum Press, 1961), 78.

2. John A. Jackson, *Big Beat Heat* (New York: Shirmer Books, 1991), 88.

3. Chuck Berry, 1972, interview by Charles Osgood, rebroadcast *CBS Sunday Morning*, September 25, 2016.

4. "Chuck Berry," Rock & Roll Hall of Fame, https://www.rockhall.com/inductees/chuck-berry.

5. Hank Bordowitz, *Turning Points in Rock and Roll* (New York: Citadel Press, 2004), 64.

6. Jackson, *Big Beat Heat*, 92.

7. Marc Myers, "Moondog's Final Sign Off," *Wall Street Journal*, January 19, 2015, https://www.wsj.com/articles/moondogs-final-sign-off-on-alan-reed-1421710119.

8. Bordowitz, *Turning Points in Rock and Roll*, 66.

9. Richard Wagoner, "Radio: How a Disgraced DJ Made His Way to KDAY," *Los Angeles Daily News*, December 23, 2019, https://www.dailynews.com/2019/12/23/radio-how-a-disgraced-dj-made-his-way-to-southern-california-airwaves/.

10. Jackson, *Big Beat Heat*, 260.

11. James F. McCarty, "Alan Freed's Ashes, Evicted From Rock Hall, Have a Final Resting Place of Prominence in Cleveland," Cleveland.com, February 29, 2016, https://www.cleveland.com/entertainment/2016/02/alan_freeds_ashes_evicted_from.html.

12. Tom Feran, "Alan Freed, 'Father of Rock,' Gets a Memorial in Stone," Cleveland.com, May 8, 2016, https://www.cleveland.com/metro/2016/05/alan_freed_father_of_rock.html.

CHAPTER 4

1. Dennis Eisenberg, Uri Dan, and Eli Landau, *Meyer Lansky: Mogul of the Mob* (New York: Paddington Press, 1979), 248.

2. Andy Newman, "Gigante Pleads Guilty to Obstructing Justice," *New York Times*, April 7, 2003, https://www.nytimes.com/2003/04/07/nyregion/gigante-pleads-guilty-to-obstructing-justice.html.

3. Andy Newman, "Mob Boss Admits Insanity An Act, Pleads Guilty; Mafia 'Oddfather' Gets 3 More Years," SFGate, April 8, 2003, https://www.sfgate.com/news/article/Mob-boss-admits-insanity-an-act-pleads-guilty-2623607.php.

CHAPTER 5

1. "Gary James' Interview With Jimmie Rodgers," ClassicBands.com, https://www.classicbands.com/JimmieRodgersInterview.html.

2. "Gary James' Interview with Jimmie Rodgers."

3. "Jimmie Rodgers: How the Mob ended his career. (Jerry Skinner Documentary)," YouTube, https://www.youtube.com/watch?v=0Oysq_h2r8w.

4. "Jimmie Rodgers: How the Mob ended his career. (Jerry Skinner Documentary)."

5. "Jimmie Rodgers: How the Mob ended his career. (Jerry Skinner Documentary)."

CHAPTER 6

1. Jeff MacGregor, "Teen Idol Frankie Lymon's Tragic Rise and Fall Tells the Truth About 1950s America," *Smithsonian Magazine*, January 2018, https://www.smithsonianmag.com/history/teen-idol-frankie-lymon-tragic-rise-fall-tells-truth-1950s-america-180967506/.

2. "How Does Heroin Kill You?," Monarch Shores, https://www.monarchshores.com/drug-addiction/how-does-heroin-kill-you/.

3. Roger Ebert, "'Why Do Fools Fall in Love' Review," RogerEbert.com, August 28, 1998, https://web.archive.org/web/20170315115904/http://www.rogerebert.com/reviews/why-do-fools-fall-in-love-1998.

4. Merchant v. Levy, 92 F. 3d 51 - Court of Appeals, 2nd Circuit 1996, https://scholar.google.com/scholar_case?case=17363566383284114372.

5. Don Rhodes, "Widow of Frankie Lymon Dies," *Augusta Chronicle*, April 14, 2019, https://www.augustachronicle.com/story/news/2019/04/14/legal-widow-of-50s-rock-star-frankie-lymon-dies-at-au-medical-center/984722007/.

CHAPTER 7

1. William Knoedelseder, *Stiffed* (New York: Harper Collins, 1993), 36.

2. "Special Report—MCA and the Mob (1988)," YouTube, https://www.youtube.com/watch?v=clEdex3WDxXk.

3. Dan E. Moldea, *Dark Victory: Ronald Reagan, MCA and the Mob* (New York: Viking Penguin, 1986), 100–101.

4. Knoedelseder *Stiffed*, 63.

5. Knoedelseder, *Stiffed*, 63.

6. Knoedelseder, *Stiffed*, 156.

7. William K. Knoedelseder Jr., "Salvatore Pisello: A Shadowy Figure in Records Deals," *Los Angeles Times*, May 4, 1986, https://www.latimes.com/archives/la-xpm-1986-05-04-fi-3550-story.html.

8. Knoedelseder, *Stiffed*, 246.

9. "Prosecutor Benched After Getting His Man: He Convicted Suspected Mob Figure Twice; MCA Said Rudnick Made Unfair Accusations," *Los Angeles Times*, January 22, 1989, https://www.latimes.com/archives/la-xpm-1989-01 -22-mn-1443-story.html.

CHAPTER 8

1. Maxim W. Furek, "Heroin and the Age of Jazz," The Sober World, October 1, 2018, https://www.thesoberworld.com/2018/10/01/heroin-age-jazz/.

2. "Babania: The American Mafia's Love Affair with Heroin," Global Mafia News, February 4, 2015, https://globalmafianews.wordpress.com/2015 /02/04/babania-the-american-mafias-love-affair-with-heroin/.

3. Bill Wyman and Richard Havers, *Rolling with the Stones* (New York: DK Publishers, 2002), 311.

4. Gary Herman, *Rock 'N' Roll Babylon* (Norfolk, UK: Fakenham Press, 1988), 44.

5. Howard Sounes (from a quote recorded by journalist David Dalton), *27* (New York: Da Capo Press, 2013), 185.

6. Pete Townshend, *Who I Am: A Memoir* (New York: HarperCollins Publishers, 2012), 179.

7. Sounes, *27*, 201.

8. Charles Cross, *A Room Full of Mirrors* (New York: Hyperion, 2005), 335.

9. Cross, *A Room Full of Mirrors*, 237.

10. Sharon Lawrence, *Jimi Hendrix: The Intimate Story of a Betrayed Musical Legend* (New York: Harper, 2005), 142–43.

11. Cross, *A Room Full of Mirrors*, 332–33.

12. "Jimi Hendrix Experience," Rock & Roll Hall of Fame, https://www .rockhall.com/inductees/jimi-hendrix-experience.

13. "Rock Singer Sentenced," *Daytona Beach Morning Journal*, October 30, 1970, 15.

14. David Bourdon, "'The Jim Morrison Story: Behind Closed Doors' by Jerry Hopkins and Daniel Sugerman Review," *Washington Post*, July 16, 1980, https://www.washingtonpost.com/archive/lifestyle/1980/07/17/the-jim-morrison-story-behind-closed-doors/2b44aa3d-9442-4140-b7b3-c2e4a873a751/.

15. Sounes, *27*, 221.

16. Sounes, *27*, 218.

CHAPTER 9

1. Fred Dannen, *Hit Men* (New York: Times Books, 1990), 16.

2. William Knoedelseder, *Stiffed* (New York: Harper Collins Publishers, 1993), 201.

3. "The Mob & The Music Industry: Payola (1986)," YouTube, https://www.youtube.com/watch?v=mkM0NsTXMu4.

4. Knoedelseder, *Stiffed*, 229.

5. Desson Howee, "Payola Probe Deepens: Record Labels Drop Ties with Promoters," *Washington Post*, March 3, 1986, https://www.washingtonpost.com/archive/lifestyle/1986/03/04/payola-probe-deepens/6aae7514-7d38-472c-9ee3-8c6e944b5658/.

6. Knoedelseder, *Stiffed*, 215.

7. Dannen, *Hit Men*, 280.

8. Dannen, *Hit Men*, 186.

9. Chuck Philips, "A Payola Probe With No Payoff," *Los Angeles Times*, April 9, 1996, https://www.latimes.com/archives/la-xpm-1996-04-09-fi-56544-story.html.

10. https://joeisgro.com.

CHAPTER 10

1. Sam Daponte, "Gangsters in Music: From Doo-Wop to Hip-Hop," Culture Sonar, February 20, 2023, https://www.culturesonar.com/gangsters-in-music-from-doo-wop-to-hip-hop/.

2. Gus Russo, *The Outfit* (New York: Bloomsbury, 2001), 433–34.

3. Russo, *The Outfit*, 434.

4. J. D. Chandler, "Frank Sinatra and the Mob," Crime Magazine, October 15, 2009, http://www.crimemagazine.com/frank-sinatra-and-mob.

5. Scott Burnstein, "Motown Sound, Philly Soul Sound Were Helped Off Ground By Mob Figures, Federal Files Contend," The Gangster Report, January 15, 2016, https://gangsterreport.com/motown-sound-philly-soul-sound-were-helped-off-ground-by-mob-figures-federal-filings-contend/.

6. Chandler, "Frank Sinatra and the Mob."

7. Carl Sifakis, *The Mafia Encyclopedia* (New York: Checkmark Books, 1999), 109.

8. Daponte, "Gangsters in Music."

9. Jerry Capeci, "Feds Want Jury to Hear Sonny Talk About Mob Murders," *Huffington Post*, April 24, 2010, http://www.huffingtonpost.com/jerry-capeci/feds-want-jury-to-hear-so_b_470557.html.

10. Daponte, "Gangsters in Music."

11. Ben Westhoff, "Did Suge Knight Really Dangle Vanilla Ice Off of a Balcony?," LA Weekly, November 20, 2012, https://www.laweekly.com/did-suge-knight-really-dangle-vanilla-ice-off-of-a-balcony/.

12. Tim Kenneally, "Suge Knight to Serve 28 Years Over 2015 Hit-and-Run Death," The Wrap, September 20, 2018, https://www.thewrap.com/suge-knight-to-serve-28-years-2015-hit-run-death/.

13. "Suge Knight Sentenced Today to 28 Years in Prison for Fatally Running over Man in 2015," CBS News, October 4, 2018, https://www.cbsnews.com/news/suge-knight-sentenced-today-to-28-years-in-prison-for-fatally-running-over-man-in-2015/.

CHAPTER 11

1. James Feron, "10 Charged With Fraud in Inquiry On Bankrupt Westchester Theater," *New York Times*, June 7, 1978, https://www.nytimes.com/1978/06/07/archives/10-charged-with-fraud-in-inquiry-on-bankrupt-westchester-theatre.html.

2. Jerry Capeci, "Greg DePalma, Pal of Sinatra and Willie Mays, Dies in Prison," *Huffington Post*, March 18, 2010, https://www.huffpost.com/entry/greg-depalma-pal-of-sinat_b_373043.

3. Allan May, "Only in Boston," American Mafia, August 12, 2002, http://www.americanmafia.com/Mob_Report/8-12-02_Mob_Report.html.

4. "Theater's 3D Life Draws to a Close," *New York Times*, October 31, 1982, https://www.nytimes.com/1982/10/31/nyregion/theater-s-3d-life-draws-to-a-close.html.

Bibliography

Books

Bordowitz, Hank. *Turning Points in Rock and Roll*. Citadel Press, 2004.

Bruck, Connie. *When Hollywood Had a King*. Random House, 2003.

Carlin, Richard. *Godfather of the Music Business*. University Press of Mississippi, 2016.

Dannen, Fredric. *Hit Men*. Times Books, 1990.

Jackson, John A. *Big Beat Heat*. Schirmer Books, 1991.

Jackson, Kenneth (editor). *The Encyclopedia of New York City*. Yale University Press, 1995.

James, Tommy, with Martin Fitzpatrick. *Me, the Mob, and the Music*. Scribner, 2010.

Kempton, Murray. *Rebellions, Perversities, and Main Events*. Times Books, 1994.

Knoedelseder, William. *Stiffed*. Harper Collins Publishers, 1993.

Lacey, Robert. *Little Man*. Little, Brown and Company, 1991.

Miller, James. *Flowers in the Dustbin*. Simon & Schuster, 1999.

Sifakis, Carl. *The Mafia Encyclopedia*. Checkmark Books, 1999.

Newspapers and Magazines

Billboard

Esquire

Los Angeles Times

Melody Maker

New York Daily News

New York Post

New York Times

Playboy

Rolling Stone

Spin

MOVIES

Don't Knock the Rock
The Girl Can't Help It
Go Johnny Go!
Mister Rock and Roll
Rock Around the Clock
Rock, Rock, Rock

Index

accountants, 193
Addonizio, Hugh, 199
Adonais (Shelley), 158
Adonis, Joe, 31
Agnew, Spiro, 198–99
AKA, 234
Algren, Nelson, 146
All Music (website), 51
Alo, Vincent "Jimmy Blue Eyes,"
    41–42, 43
Aloi, Vincenzo, 35
Alpert, Herb, 106
Ambrosia, John, 37
A&M Records, 106
Anderson, Raymond, 179
Armed Forces radio, 71
Armone, Joseph "Joe Pinney," 17, 167;
    Gambino crime family relation to,
    154–55, 169, 176; heroin relation
    to, 153–54; Isgro relation to, 170,
    171, 174–75; Rudnick relation to,
    178
Army, 67–68, 122
Arthur Godfrey Show, 20, 63
Arthur Godfrey Talent Show, 102–3
audiovisual jukeboxes, 41–42
Augusta Chronicle (newspaper), 127

Back Door to Hell (movie), 105
Bad Boy Record Label, 209

Bad News Brown, 232
Baez, Joan, 159
Baker, Howard, 130
Bally Manufacturing, 31, 43
Bally Records, 31
Bankroll Fresh, 233
Bannister, John, 162
Barbara, Joseph, 92–93
Barnes, Nicky, 146, 153
Barret, Richard, 66
Bastone, William, 58–60
Baynes, Eugene "Bo," 197
the Beastie Boys, 207
the Beatles, 181
Benny, Jack, 63
Bergen County (N.J.) Record
    (newspaper), 6–7
Berry, Chuck, 22, 75–76, 205
Beulah Grove Baptist Church, 126
Big Apple Records, 68, 123
The Big Beat (television show), 23, 53;
    Lymon, F., on, 23, 67, 79, 119–20
Big Hawk, 232
Bigidagoe, 234
Big L, 231
Billboard (magazine), 53, 168
Billboard charts, 67, 115–16
Biondo, Joseph, 153
Birdland, 47–48, 49
Black Mafia, 196–97

Blade Icewood, 232
"Blue Moon," 194
Bobo, Howard Kenny, 118
Bogart, Neil, 202
Bonanno, Joe, 151
Bonannos crime family, 151
Bone Thugs-n-Harmony, 208
Bordowitz, Hank, 80
Borrero, Carmen, 161–62
Boyle, Michael, 39
Brafman, Benjamin, 97–98
Brancato, Anthony, 227
Bray, Sam, 68
"Break on Through (to the Other Side)," 163
bribes, 78; Armone and, 17; for disc jockeys, 1–3, 25, 30, 155, 202; Freed, A., relation to, 81–82; from Glimco, 38. *See also* payola
Brocco, Sonny, 138, 141
A Bronx Tale (movie), 195
Brooklyn Paramount Theater, 77
Brooks, Delores "La La," 201
Brotman, Stanley, 59
Brown vs. Board of Education, 67
Bubbling Brown Sugar (album), 63
Buddah Records, 55, 201–2
Bufalino, Russell, 32–33
Buonanno, Joe, 57
Burdon, Eric, 161–62
Butts, Calvin, 208

Caan, James, 204–5
Calla Records, 55, 202
Cal Neva Lodge, 188
Camouflage, 232
Campbell, Patrick, 73
Canned Heat, 160
Cantellops, Nelson, 56, 93–94
Canterino, Dominick, 60–62

Capeci, Jerry, 203–4; on DePalma, 221–22
Capitol Industries-EMI, 172
Carfano, Anthony, 94–95
Carlin, Richard, 46, 49, 57
Carson, Johnny, 191, 228
Carter, Terry, 210–11
Caserta, Peggy, 159
Cashbox charts, "Party Doll" on, 63
Castellano, Paul: Armone relation to, 155; drug trafficking relation to, 150; Gambino crime family and, 16–17; Gotti, G., relation to, 147–48; Gotti, J., relation to, 216
Cataldo, Joseph "Joe the Wop," 47–48
Catena, Gerry, 31; Bally Manufacturing and, 43; Reynolds relation to, 41–42
Cava, Erma, 59
Chandler, J. D., 191
the Chantels, 51
Charizma, 231
Checker/Chess/Cadet record catalog, 134
Chicago Defender (newspaper), 194
Chicago Outfit, 2, 37–38, 188; jukeboxes of, 32, 39–40
Chinx, 233
Christian, Sam, 197
Clark, Dick, 81, 227, 228
the Cleftones, 4
Cleveland Plain Dealer (newspaper), 85–86
www.cleveland.com, 84–85
Cobain, Kurt, 165
Coconut Grove nightclub, 108
Cohen, Mickey, 32–33
Coleridge, Samuel Taylor, 145
Colombo, Joseph, 35, 87–88, 204
Colombo, Russ, 77

Colombo crime family, 201–2; Franzese relation to, 203–4
Colombo war, 35
Columbia Records, 24, 120, 180
"Come Go With Me," 195
"Come Together," 205
Commercial Phonograph Survey, 39
Communist Party, 175
Consultants for World Records, 8–9
Cooke, John Byrne, 160
copyrights: Birdland relation to, 49; for "Why Do Fools Fall in Love," 18–19, 125–26. *See also* songwriting credits
Corallo, Tony "Ducks," 152–53
Cosby, Bill, 208
Costello, Frank, 15–16, 95; Gigante, V., relation to, 56, 91–92; Sinatra relation to, 189
Cotchford Farm, 158
counterculture, 27
counterfeit records, 5, 140
the Coupe De Villes, 114
Courson, Pamela, 164–65
Creatore, Luigi, 63
credible deniability, 181
the Crests, 195
Crime Magazine, 191
Cross, Charles, 161, 162
Crown Zellerbach, 100
the Crows, 50
the Crystals, 201
www.culturesonar.com, 208–9
Cultursonar.com (website), 187
Custer, George Armstrong, 179
Cutolo, William "Wild Bill," 203
cutout records, 5–6, 14, 16; MCA Records and, 60, 61–62, 135, 139, 183; Pisello relation to, 9, 10–11, 137

Dales, John, 136
Dalitz, Moe, 190
D'Ambrosia, Salvatore "Sally D," 204
Dannen, Fredric, 30, 168, 176
Dark Victory (Moldea), 136
Davis, Miles, 146–47
Davis, Sammy, Jr., 53, 190
DEA. *See* Drug Enforcement Agency
DeAlesandro, Patricia, 154
Dean, James, 73
Dean, John, 198
Death Row Records, 206, 209; Vanilla Ice relation to, 210; Wideawake Entertainment relation to, 212
DeCarlo, Angelo "Gyp," 197; Nixon relation to, 198–99; Zelmanowitz relation to, 200
DeCavalcante, Sam "the Plumber," 54, 62
DeCavalcante crime family, 3, 14; Levy, M., relation to, 36; Pisello relation to, 129; Vastola and, 4, 53–55, 61–62
Decca Records, 102, 177
DeCicco, Frank, 169, 174
Deep Throat (movie), 205
the Delfonics, 196–97
Dellacroce, Aniello, 133
the Del-Viking, 195
Demaris, Ovid, 227
DePalma, Gregory, 190–91, 217–19, 222; Gambino crime family relation to, 220, 225; Sinatra relation to, 216, 221
Depzman, 232
De Robertis Pasticceria, 154
Desert Inn, 190
DeVito, Danny, 184, 185
Dewey, Thomas, 56
Dick Clark Westchester Theater, 227
DiMona, Joseph, 160–61

Dion and the Belmonts, 195
Direct Vending Machine Company, 33
DiRicco, Dennis, 183–84
disc jockeys, 80–81; bribes for, 1–3, 25, 30, 155, 202; shell companies of, 174; "Why Do Fools Fall in Love" and, 115–16. *See also* Freed, Alan
DiSipio, Fred, 170, 176
DJ Uncle Al, 231
The D.O.C., 208–9
Doe B, 232
Dolla, 232
the Doors, 163–64
The Doors of Perception (Huxley), 163
doo wop, 194–96
Dorsey, Tommy, 201
Dot Records, 105–6
Dragna, Jack, 226
Dragna, Louis, 226
Dragna crime family, 216, 225
Drakeo the Ruler, 233
Dr. Dre, 206, 208–9
Drug Enforcement Agency (DEA), 7, 132–33
drug overdose, 18, 125, 156; of Hendrix, 162–63; of Joplin, 160–61; of Morrison, 164–65
drug trafficking: by Bonannos crime family, 151; of Gambino crime family, 148; Gambino relation to, 153; immigrants relation to, 149–50; of Lucchese crime family, 152
Duffy, Michael, 20–21, 37, 64, 108, 109–10

Eagle, Emira, 68–69, 122, 124, 125–26
Eazy-E, 208–9

Ebert, Roger, 124
Ebony (magazine), 113–14
Eder, Bruce, 51
Ed Sullivan Show (television show), 20, 103
Einár, 233
Eisenstadt, Peter, 48
Electrical Workers Union, 39, 40
Emby Distributing Company, 2, 30
EMI, 177
The Encyclopedia of New York City (Eisenstadt and Ferri), 48
End Records, 118
English, Charles, 39; Lormar Distributing and, 40; McClellan Committee and, 41
Esposito, Olympia, 89
Esquire (magazine), 164
Eversole, Archie, 234
exclusive contracts, 30

Faithfull, Marianne, 164
Falcone, Big Jack, 222
Farone, Rudolph, 61
Fatato, Gaetano "Guy," 202–4
Fat Pat, 231
FBI, 175–76; DeCarlo relation to, 198–99; DeCavalcante crime family relation to, 54; Freed, A., relation to, 79–81; Levy, M., relation to, 69–70; Montiglio relation to, 193; payola relation to, 169; Saperstein relation to, 200; Sinatra relation to, 190–91; Watson relation to, 197; Westchester Premier Theater relation to, 220
Federal Bureau of Narcotics (FBN), 148–49, 154
Federal Correctional Institute, 148
Feis, 233
Ferran, Tom, 85–86

Ferri, Marc, 48
Fillmore East, 159
Firebird, 51–52
Fischetti, Charles, 201
Fischetti, Joseph, 201
Fisher, Eddie, 190
Fisher, Howard, 60–62
Fiske, Robert B., Jr., 217–18
the Five Satins, 194
Flabba, 233
the Flamingos, 51
Fontainbleu Hotel, 201
Fortune (magazine), 43
45 rpm records, 29
Foster, B. Y. (pseudonym), 49
Foundations of Music, 213
the Four Seasons, 197–98
Frankie Lymon and the Teenagers at the Long Palladium (album), 118
Franzese, Sonny, 55, 205; Buddah Records relation to, 201–2; Fatato relation to, 203–4
Fratianno, Aladena James "Jimmy the Weasel," 216, 223, 225, 226; in Witness Protection Program, 222, 224, 227
Freaky Tah, 231
"Free," 38–39
Freed, Alan, 83, 167; Berry relation to, 75; in *Cleveland Plain Dealer*, 85–86; www.cleveland.com and, 84–85; FBI relation to, 79–81; payola and, 21–22, 23–24, 27, 52; radio stations relation to, 3, 71–72; "Rock 'n' Roll Easter Jubilee" of, 77; "The Rock 'n' Roll Jubilee Ball" of, 76; Roulette Records relation to, 22, 78, 82; "Why Do Fools Fall in Love" and, 115; at WINS, 53, 74
Freed, Judith Fisher, 84
Freed, Lance, 84

French Connection (movie), 153
French Connection case, 17, 153–54
Fret, Kevin, 233
Froumin, Itai, 165
"Fuck the Police," 207–8
Fulton Fish Market, 132–33
Furek, Maxim W., 146
Fusco, Richard, 217–20
Fyssas, Pavlos, 232

Gaffney, George, 94
Galante, Carmine "Lilo," 152; Genovese crime family relation to, 151, 155–56
Gallo, Joey, 33–34, 35–36, 204
Gallo, Joseph N., 169
Gallo, Larry, 33–35
Gallo war, 35
Gambino, Carlo, 95, 148–49; Armone relation to, 155; drug trafficking relation to, 153; Galante relation to, 151; Sinatra relation to, 216, 219
Gambino crime family, 6, 14; Armone relation to, 154–55, 169, 176; Castellano and, 16–17; DePalma relation to, 220, 225; drug trafficking of, 148; Genovese crime family relation to, 90; Marson relation to, 190–91, 215; Montiglio relation to, 193; payola and, 25; Pisello relation to, 129; Profaci relation to, 35; Sinatra relation to, 216–17, 219, 225–26; Westchester Premier Theater and, 25–26
Gang Land, 203
gangs, 195–96, 208
gangsta rap, 206, 212–13; *Straight Outta Compton* as, 207–8
"Gangsta Rap Made Me Do It," 208
Garcia, Joaquin "Big Jack," 221–22

Gate of Heaven Cemetery, 200
Gaudio, Bob, 197
Gavarante, Baba, 201
Gee Records, 3, 50, 115
Genovese, Vito, 15–16, 56–57, 93; Costello relation to, 91–92; Gigante, V., relation to, 90; heroin relation to, 156; Valachi relation to, 94–95
Genovese crime family, 14; Catena and, 41; DeCarlo relation to, 197–98; Galante relation to, 151, 155–56; Gambino crime family relation to, 90; Gigante, V., and, 3, 88; LaMonte relation to, 140; Levy, M., relation to, 36, 177; McCalla relation to, 55–56; Pisello relation to, 129, 133; Roulette Records and, 22, 50, 69; Saperstein relation to, 200; Scandore relation to, 201; Strawberries Record stores relation to, 57–58; Tieri relation to, 224
Giancana, Sam: Kennedy, R., relation to, 188–89; Villa Venice Restaurant relation to, 190
Gigante, Louis, 58–60, 87; Colombo and, 88
Gigante, Vincent "the Chin," 3–4, 14–15; Costello relation to, 56, 91–92; Freed, A., relation to, 79; Genovese crime family and, 88; LaMonte relation to, 140; Levy, M., relation to, 15, 57, 89–90, 98, 156; low-income housing and, 87; Mauskopf relation to, 97; at Roulette Records, 56
Gioielli, Joseph "Joe Jelly," 34, 204
Giovanelli, Frederico, 133
Glass, Phillip, 74
Glimco, Joseph, 37–38
Global Music, 212

The Godfather (movie), 148, 151, 213
Godfrey, Arthur, 20, 63, 102–3
Goldner, George, 3; End Records of, 118; Firebird and, 51–52; Lymon, F., relation to, 50–51, 117; the Teenagers relation to, 50, 66–67, 115–16, 117; "Why Do Fools Fall in Love" and, 19, 69, 126
Gonzalez, Hector, 44
Goodman, Benny, 73
Goodman, Murray, 164
"Goody Goody," 117–18
Goonew, 234
Gordon, Waxey, 56
Gordy, Berry, 196
Gotti, Gene, 147–48
Gotti, John, 16–17, 90, 97, 131; Castellano relation to, 216; DeCicco relation to, 169, 174; Knight compared to, 209; Rudnick relation to, 178; Vastola relation to, 55
Graham, Bill, 159
gran mal seizures, 107
"Great Balls of Fire," 77
Greelish, Thomas W., 61–62
Greenberg, Sam, 40
Greene, Danny, 226
G-Slimm, 231
guilt-by-association, 175–76

"Hanky Panky," 36
Hardin, Louis Thomas, 73–74
the Harlemaires, 114
Harlem Renaissance, 146
Harris, Greg, 85
Hayes, Richard, 81
Heller, Jerry, 208–9
Helmsley Palace Hotel, 168
Hendrix, Jimi, 161; drug overdose of, 162–63

Herman, Gary, 158
heroin, 25, 145, 152; in French Connection case, 17, 153–54; Genovese relation to, 156; Hendrix relation to, 162; jazz musicians relation to, 146–47; Joplin relation to, 159–60; Luciano relation to, 148–49; Lymon, F., and, 18, 66, 119, 121–23; Morrison relation to, 164–65
Heroin Family. *See* Bonannos family
"Hey Girl," 4
Hip Hop Caucus, 206–7
The Hit Man (movie), 185–86
Hit Men (Dannen), 30
Hoffa (film), 185
Hoffa (movie), 184
Hoffa, Jimmy, 31–32
Holiday, Billie, 159
Holmes, Geoffrey, 172, 173
"Honeycomb," 36, 63, 100, 103; Merrill relation to, 102
Hoover, J. Edgar, 93, 191
Hot 100, 192
Hotel Di Paris, Monte Carlo, 7
Houdini, 233
House of Sounds, 137
House Select Committee on Crime, 4
Houston, Johnny, 118
Howe, Desson, 171–73
Huey, 233
Hussle, Nipsey, 233
Huxley, Aldous, 163
Hypo, 234

"Ice Ice Baby," 187, 209–10
"I Cried," 38–39
Ideman, James M., 184
immigrants, drug trafficking relation to, 149–50
"I'm Sorry," 124

Internal Revenue Service (IRS), 179–80; Freed, A., relation to, 24; Pisello relation to, 7–8, 130
International Brotherhood of Electrical Workers, 40
International Brotherhood of Teamsters, 31–32
"In the Still of the Night," 194
IRS. *See* Internal Revenue Service
Isgro, Joseph, 170, 174–75; DiSipio and, 176; Justice Department relation to, 171, 177–78; in *Los Angeles Times*, 182–84; payola relation to, 178–80, 184; Raging Bull Productions of, 185–86
Italian American Civil Rights League, 35, 87–88
Italian National Police, 7, 130
"It's Over," 106
"I Want You to Be My Girl," 116

The Jacka, 232
Jackson, Henry, 199
Jackson, John A., 22, 77
Jagger, Bianca, 206–7
Jagger, Mick, 157, 158
James, Tommy, 36, 109; *Me, the Mob, and the Music* of, 21, 37, 111
Jam Master Jay, 231
jazz musicians, heroin relation to, 146–47
Jersey Magazine, 70
"Jesse," 168
Joe and Mary's, 151–52
Johnson, Bumpy, 153
Johnson, Mario, 209
joint marketing promotions, 174
Jones, Brian, 157–58
Jones, Tom, 228
Joplin, Janis: heroin relation to, 159–60; in 27 Club, 161

jukeboxes, 2, 28; audiovisual, 41–42; of Chicago Outfit, 32, 39–40; 45 rpm records and, 29; labor unions relation to, 32–33; Lansky and, 30–31; Leonetti on, 38–39
"Just A-Sittin and A-Rockin," 194
Justice Department: Isgro relation to, 171, 177–78; Lynch relation to, 184; MCA Records relation to, 9–10; payola relation to, 11–12, 182–83; Pisello relation to, 130–31, 132, 133, 142–43, 183; Rudnick relation to, 10, 136–37, 144; Tele-A-Sign and, 42

Kadafi, Yaki, 231
Kass, Art, 202
KDAY, 83
Keats, John, 158
Kennedy, John F., 191
Kennedy, Joseph, Sr., 188
Kennedy, Robert, 33, 188–89
Kenner, David, 210
Kenny, John J., 199
King Von, 233
Kiss, John, 165
"Kisses Sweeter Than Wine," 36, 103
Knight, Marion Hugh "Suge," 206, 208; Carter relation to, 210–11; in RJ Donovan Correctional Facility, 212; Vanilla Ice relation to, 187, 209–10
KNOB/97.9, 83
Knoedelseder, William, 10, 60–62; on Ross, B., 168–69; *Stiffed* of, 15
Knox, Buddy, 62–63
Kolsy, Joe, 115
Kozhokin, Roman, 165

labor unions, 31; Electrical Workers Union, 39, 40; jukeboxes relation to, 32–33; McClellan Committee relation to, 38
Lacey, Robert, 31
"La La (Means I Love You)," 196–97
LaMonte, John, 61–62, 137; Levy, M., relation to, 11, 12, 138–39, 143; Pisello relation to, 10, 139–40; Vastola relation to, 16, 141
Landmark Hotel, 160
Lansky, Meyer, 2; Alo relation to, 41, 43; Cantellops relation to, 94; Costello relation to, 92; jukeboxes and, 30–31; Luciano and, 56; Sinatra relation to, 189
LAPD. *See* Los Angeles Police Department
Larner, Hyman, 40
The Last Mafioso (Fratianno and Demaris), 227
L. A. Weekly (newspaper), 210
Lawrence, Sharon, 161
Leach, Lillian, 195
Lee, Spike, 208
Lele, 232
LeMonte, John, 62
Lennon, John, 205
Leonetti, Tommy, 37, 38–39
Levy, Irving, 47–48
Levy, Morris, 14, 45–46; Birdland and, 47–49; Buddah Records relation to, 202; Checker/Chess/Cadet record catalog relation to, 134; FBI relation to, 69–70; Freed, A., relation to, 22, 23, 78, 79, 82–83; Genovese crime family relation to, 36, 177; Gigante, L., relation to, 59–60; Gigante, V.,

relation to, 15, 57, 89–90, 98,
156; Knight compared to, 209;
LaMonte relation to, 11, 12,
138–39, 143; Lennon relation to,
205; in *Los Angeles Times*, 60–62;
Lymon, F., relation to, 118–19;
McCalla and, 55–56, 202; "Party
Doll" and, 62–63; Pisello relation
to, 9; record stores of, 5; "Rock 'n'
Roll Easter Jubilee" and, 77; "The
Rock 'n' Roll Jubilee Ball" and,
76; Rodgers, J., relation to, 19–21,
103, 105; royalties relation to, 3–4,
36–37; songwriting credits and, 3,
49–50, 68–69; Sugar Hill Records
relation to, 206; Vastola relation
to, 11, 16; "Why Do Fools Fall in
Love" and, 18–19, 125–26
Levy, Rachel, 45
Levy, Zacharia, 45
Lewis, Jerry Lee, 22–23, 77
Liberty Records, 63
Licavoli, James, 226
Licensed to Ill (album), 207
Lil Phat, 232
Lil Snupe, 232
"Lily Maebelle," 4
Lincoln Savings Bank, 228
Lindeloff, Robert, 38
Little Anthony and the Imperials, 50
"Little Bitty Pretty One," 119
The Little Shepherd of Kingdom Come
(movie), 105
LL Cool J, 207
Lobrano, Billy, 118
LoCicero, Charles "the Sidge," 34
Lormar Distributing, 40
Los Angeles Police Department
(LAPD), 20–21, 37, 65, 109–11
Los Angeles Rams, 209

Los Angeles Times (newspaper), 10,
143; Levy, M., in, 60–62; MCA
Records in, 12–14; Phillips in,
181–84
low-income housing, 87
Lubinsky, Herman, 30
Lucas, Frank, 153
Lucchese crime family: drug
trafficking of, 152; Profaci relation
to, 35
Luciano, Lucky, 30, 90–91; Costello
relation to, 92; heroin relation to,
148–49; Lansky and, 56
Lucky Luciano (movie), 185
"Lullaby of Birdland," 49
Lulu's Bar, 154
Lymon, Frankie, 3, 17, 116–17, 125–
28, 153, 193; on *The Big Beat*, 23,
67, 79, 119–20; in *Ebony*, 113–14;
Goldner relation to, 50–51, 117;
heroin and, 18, 66, 119, 121–23;
Levy, M., relation to, 118–19; in
Rock and Roll Hall of Fame, 124;
Roulette Records and, 67; royalties
and, 36, 230; songwriting credits
of, 69
Lymon, Howard, 114
Lymon, Jeanette, 114
Lynch, William S., 184
Lynchpin of Bensonhurst
(documentary), 193

Mac Dre, 232
Magnolia Shorty, 232
Malatesta, Peter, 198
Mamet, David, 185
Man of Honor (Bonanno), 151
The Man With The Golden Arm
(Algren), 146
Maranzano, Salvatore, 90

Marshall, Consuelo B., 184
Marson, Tom, 190–91, 215; Fratianno relation to, 223–24; Sinatra relation to, 216
Martin, Dean, 191
the Marvels, 194
"Mary Lee," 194
Masseria, Joe "the Boss," 90
Mastrangelo, Johnny, 195
Matsushita conglomerate, 12, 143
Mauskopf, Roslynn, 16, 97
"Maybellene," 22, 75
Mays, Willie, 221
MCA Records, 12, 172; cutout records and, 60, 61–62, 135, 139, 183; Isgro relation to, 178–79, 180; Justice Department relation to, 9–10; Pisello relation to, 6–7, 8–9, 11, 13–14, 129–31, 133–35, 140–41, 143, 177; Reagan relation to, 135–36, 144
McCalla, Nate, 55–56, 202
McCarthy, Joseph, 175
McCaw, J. Elroy, 74
McClatchey, Colleen, 100–102
McClellan Committee, 31–33; English and, 41; labor unions relation to, 38
MC Daleste, 232
McKinnon, Pearl, 128
McQuire, Phyllis, 189
Me, the Mob, and the Music (James), 21, 37, 111
the Mellows, 195
the Melodies, 100
Mennen, Ghaskar, 172
Merchant, Jimmy, 3, 128; "Why Do Fools Fall in Love" and, 19, 69, 115, 126–27
Mercy College, 228
Merrill, Bob, 102

Messy Mya, 232
Metropolitan Correction Facility, 55
Michel'le, 208–9
Miller, Chuck, 102, 104
Miller, Mitch, 24
Minnelli, Liza, 228
MO3, 233
mob. *See specific topics*
Moldea, Dan E., 136
money laundering: Buddah Records relation to, 202; heroin relation to, 147; Roulette Records and, 4, 89–90, 96
Monka, Jeffrey, 179
Monte Carlo, Hotel Di Paris in, 7
Montiglio, Dominic, 193
Moondog, 22, 73–74
The Moondog Rock and Roll Matinee (radio show), 73
"Moondog's Symphony," 73
Moretti, Willie, 191–92, 197, 201
Morgenthau, Robert, 43
morphine, 149
Morris, Harold, 31
Morrison, Jim, 158, 163; drug overdose of, 164–65
Motown Records, 177
Motown Sound, 196
Mr. 3-2, 233
MTV, 174
Music Operators, 38
Mussachia, Rocco "the Butcher," 133
"My Daddy Rocks Me (With One Steady Roll)," 22, 72
"My Girl," 118
"My Man Rocks Me," 72

National Crime Syndicate, 30, 90, 148
Nava, Gregory, 124
Neiman, Leroy, 222
Nelson, Ricky, 103

the Network, 169–70, 173; payola and, 11–12

Nevada Gaming Commission, 188

Nevada Gaming Control Board, 216–17

New Jersey State Commission of Investigation, 43

Newsday (newspaper), 31–32

New York City Housing Authority, 96

New York Daily News (newspaper), 76, 203

New York Times (newspaper), 48, 223; on McClellan Committee, 33; Westchester Premier Theater in, 217–18, 228–29; Zottola, S., in, 43–44

Nicholson, Jack, 185

Nixon, Richard, 191; DeCarlo relation to, 198–99

Nobles, Gene, 106

Noguchi, Thomas, 160–61

"No One Here Gets Out Alive," 163

The Notorious B.I.G., 231

N.W.A., 207–8

O'Donnell, William T., 43

opium, 145

Oppenheimer, J. Robert, 175

The Outfit (Russo), 189

Out of the Past Inc., 61–62, 138

Pablo Escobar (movie), 185

Pace University, 228

Pacho El Antifeka, 234

Pacific Institute for Research and Evaluation, Prevention Research Center of, 208

Palm Springs, Raquet Club Estates, 83

Paramount Theater, 22–23

Paretti, Hugo, 63

Parker, Charlie, 48

"Party Doll," 62–63

Passamano, Sam, 139

Patricia Music, 49

Paul C, 231

payola, 3, 25, 80–81, 167; Armone relation to, 153, 155; FBI relation to, 169; Freed, A., and, 21–22, 23–24, 27, 52; Isgro relation to, 178–80, 184; Justice Department relation to, 11–12, 182–83; Recording Industry Association of America and, 171–73, 180–81

P. Diddy, 209

Père Lachaise Cemetery, 165

Persico, Alphonse, 203

Peters, Art, 113–14

Philadelphia Soul Sound, 196

Phillips, Chuck, 181–84

Philly Groove Records, 196–97

Photoplay (magazine), 101

Pisello, Salvatore "Sal the Swindler," 12; cutout records and, 9, 10–11, 137; Justice Department relation to, 130–31, 132, 133, 142–43, 183; LaMonte relation to, 10, 139–40; MCA Records relation to, 6–7, 8–9, 11, 13–14, 129–31, 133–35, 140–41, 143, 177

Pizza Connection case, 155

PnB Rock, 234

Police Protective League, 110

Polygram Records, 180

Pop Smoke, 233

the Premiers, 114

Presley, Elvis, 106

Prevention Research Center, of Pacific Institute for Research and Evaluation, 208

Profaci, Joe, 34–35, 204

Proof, 232

Queens Booking Agency, 4
quiz show scandals, 80
Quonset Hut, 189

radio stations, 1–2; Freed, A., relation to, 3, 71–72; KDAY, 83; WABC, 81; WINS, 53, 74, 76
Raging Bull Productions, 185–86
the Rainbows, 194
Rama, 50, 51
"Rapper's Delight," 206
Raquet Club Estates, Palm Springs, 83
Rat Pack, 189–90
RCA/Ariola Records, 171–73; Isgro relation to, 180
Re, Donald, 180, 183
Reagan, Ronald, 9, 183; MCA Records relation to, 135–36, 144; Sinatra relation to, 191; Wasserman relation to, 178
Recorded Music Service Association, 40
Recording Industry Association of America, 171–73, 180–81
record stores, 5, 14–15, 57–58, 96
Reich, Steve, 74
Reno Bar, 154
respiratory depression, 123
Reynolds, Debbie, 41–42
Rhodes, Don, 127
Richards, Keith, 157
Rickles, Don, 191, 201
Rimbaud, Arthur, 163
RJ Donovan Correctional Facility, 212
Robbins, Freddie, 81–82
Robinson, Joe, 6–7
Rockabilly Hall of Fame, 63
Rock and Roll Hall of Fame, 24–25; Berry in, 75–76; Freed, A., in, 84, 85; Lymon, F., in, 124

Rock Around the Clock (movie), 120
"Rock 'n' Roll Easter Jubilee," 77
"The Rock 'n' Roll Jubilee Ball," 76
Rock & Roll (album), 205
Rodgers, Archie, 99, 107–8
Rodgers, Jimmie, 99, 107; Arthur Godfrey Talent Show and, 102–3; Dot Records relation to, 105–6; LAPD relation to, 65, 109–11; McClatchey relation to, 100–102; Roulette Records and, 19–21, 63–64, 100, 105, 108–9, 112; royalties and, 19–21, 36–37, 64, 104, 230; spasmodic dysphonia and, 65, 111
Rodgers, Katrine, 99
Rodgers, Mary, 99–100, 112
Rodriguez, Danny "D-Boy," 231
Rohatyn, Felix, 130
Rolling Stones, 157–58, 181
Roma di Notte, 7, 132
Ronay, Alain, 164
Roots (album), 205
Ross, Brian, 25, 168–70; on Armone, 155, 176; Isgro relation to, 178–79; Levy, M., and, 69–70
Ross, Diana: at Westchester Premier Theater, 219; "Why Do Fools Fall in Love" and, 18, 51, 125
Roulette Records, 3, 52, 192; cutout records relation to, 14; Freed, A., relation to, 22, 78, 82; Genovese crime family and, 22, 50, 69; Gigante, V., at, 56; Isgro relation to, 177; Lymon, F., and, 67; money laundering and, 4, 89–90, 96; "Party Doll" and, 62–63; Rodgers, J., and, 19–21, 63–64, 100, 105, 108–9, 112; Vastola at, 53–54
Royal Roost, 47
royalties, 2, 30, 127; accountants relation to, 193; counterfeit records

relation to, 5; for "Ice Ice Baby,"
187, 209–10; Levy, M., relation to,
3–4, 36–37; for "Party Doll," 63;
Rodgers, J., and, 19–21, 36–37, 64,
104, 230; from Roulette Records,
192; the Teenagers and, 66, 206
RS, 233
Rudnick, Marvin, 6, 133, 140–41,
143; Justice Department relation
to, 10, 136–37, 144; MCA Records
relation to, 12, 183; Reagan
relation to, 178
Run-DMC, 207
Russo, Gus, 189

Sabotage, 231
SAG. *See* Screen Actors Guild
Sahara Club, 34–35
Salerno, Fat Tony, 16
Salerno, Ralph, 56, 153
Samuels, Eddie, 106–7, 111
Santiago, Herman, 3, 128, 195;
Lymon, F., and, 66; "Why Do
Fools Fall in Love" and, 19, 69,
115, 126–27
Santoro, Salvatore "Tom Mix,"
152–53
Saperstein, Louis, 200
Saul, Sidney, 33
Savoy Records, 30
Scandore, Joe, 201
Schiffman, Bobby, 228–29
Schlesinger, Lee, 48–49
Scopitone, 41–43
Scott La Rock, 231
Screen Actors Guild (SAG), 9,
135–36
"Seabreeze," 124
Seagram, 231
Securities and Exchange Commission
(SEC), 218, 220

Senate Permanent Committee on
Investigations, 199
sexual connotations, 72–73
sexual revolution, 73, 78–79
Shakur, Tupac, 206, 231
Shangri-Las, 202
Shaw, Georgie, 102
Shearing, George, 49
shell companies, of disc jockeys, 174
Shelley, Percy Bysshe, 158
the Shondells, 36
Simon, Carly, 168
Sinatra, Frank, 77, 177, 200–201;
DeCarlo relation to, 198; DePalma
relation to, 216, 221; FBI relation
to, 190–91; Fratianno relation
to, 224; Gambino crime family
relation to, 216–17, 219, 225–26;
Giancana relation to, 188–90;
Moretti relation to, 191–92, 197;
at Westchester Premier Theater,
215–16, 228
Singer, Jerry, 106
Sipiora, Ted, 37
"16 Candles," 195
skimming operation. *See* Westchester
Premier Theater
Slick, Grace, 160
Sloan, Cle "Bone," 211
Slotnick, Barry, 224
Smith, Fred "Jukebox Smitty," 39–40
Smith, Joe, 80
Smith, Trixie, 22, 72
Smoke Dawg, 233
Snoop Dogg, 206
Snootie Wild, 233
songwriting credits: Levy, M., and, 3,
49–50, 68–69; for "Maybellene,"
22, 75; Vastola relation to, 4, 16; for
"Why Do Fools Fall in Love," 19,
66–67, 68–69, 115, 126–27

Soulja Slim, 232
Sounes, Howard, 160
Sparks Steak House, 147–48, 216
spasmodic dysphonia, 65, 111
Spector, Phil, 201
Squires, Billy, 229
Stanley, George, 209
Stanley, Lynwood, 209
Stans, Maurice, 198
Stefanino's, 177
Stewart, Terry, 86
Stiffed (Knoedelseder), 15
St. John Roman Catholic Cemetery, 205
St. Mary Abbots Hospital, 162
St. Nicholas Arena, 76
The Stone Pony (movie), 185
Straight Outta Compton (album), 207–8
Strawberries Record stores, 5, 14–15; Genovese crime family relation to, 57–58; money laundering and, 96
Stretch, 231
Strollo, Anthony, 94–95
Sugar Hill Records, 6–7, 13, 133–34; Consultants for World Records relation to, 8; Levy, M., relation to, 206
Sullivan, Ed, 20, 63
Sultans of Swing, 71
Sunnyview Farm, 70
the Supremes, 181
Sylvia, Margo, 195

Takeoff, 234
Taylor, Major Robinson, 121
Taylor, Mick, 158
Taylor, Zola, 120–21, 125–26
the Teenagers, 3, 17–18, 36, 114, 127–28, 195; Goldner relation to,

50, 66–67, 115–16, 117; royalties and, 66, 206
The Teenagers Featuring Frankie Lymon (album), 116
Tele-A-Sign, 42
The Texas Chain Saw Massacre (movie), 205
Thaw, Zayar, 234
This Thing is Ours (movie), 204–5
"Thuggish Ruggish Bone," 208
Tico, 50, 51
Tieri, Frank "Funzi," 224, 225
Tiger Lilly, 58
"Tonight's the Night," 118
Top 40 hits, 29
Topsy's Chicken Shack, 47
Toronto International Airport, 162
Torres, Chico, 195
Toscanini, Arturo, 73
Townshend, Pete, 158, 160
transistor radios, 28
Trombino, Anthony, 227
Trouble, 234
the Tune Weavers, 195
turntable hits, 168
20th Century Fox Records, 120
27 Club, 156; Jones, B., in, 157–58; Joplin in, 161; Morrison in, 165

Umberto's Clam House, 35–36
Unione Corse, 149
Universal, 101
University of Nevada Las Vegas (UNLV), 209
US District Court for the Southern District of New York, 19
US Medical Center for Federal Prisoners, 16

Valachi, Joseph, 94–96, 149
the Valentines, 4
Valli, Frankie, 198
Vanilla Ice, 187, 208, 209–10
Van Zandt, Steve, 86
Varda, Agnes, 165
Vastola, Gaetano "Corky," 5, 12, 14, 143; DeCavalcante crime family and, 4, 53–55, 61–62; LaMonte relation to, 16, 141; Levy, M., relation to, 11, 16; songwriting credits relation to, 4, 16
Vengeance is Mine (Fratianno and Zuckerman), 227
Vesparax sleeping pills, 162–63
Village Voice (newspaper), 58–60
Villa Venice Restaurant, 189–90
VL Mike, 232

WABC, 81
Wagoner, Richard, 81
Wala, Sidhu Moose, 234
Waldorf Astoria, 155, 169, 176
"Walking on Sand," 202
Wall Street Journal (newspaper): *The Big Beat* in, 79; Tele-A-Sign in, 42
Ward, Eric, 128
Warner Bros., Isgro relation to, 180
Warner Communications, 171–73; Isgro relation to, 178–79
Washington Post (newspaper), 171–73
Wasserman, Lew, 9, 135–36, 143; Matsushita conglomerate and, 12; Reagan relation to, 178
Waterfall, Thomas "Red," 40
Watergate scandal, 199
Waters, Elizabeth Mickey, 120, 125–26
Watkins, Viola, 50
Watson, John "Stan the Man," 196–97

Weisman, Eliot H., 217; Westchester Premier Theater relation to, 225
Weiss, George David, 49
Westchester Gannet Newspapers, 223
Westchester Premier Theater, 25–26, 191, 219, 222–23, 226; Clark relation to, 227; FBI relation to, 220; in *New York Times*, 217–18, 228–29; Sinatra at, 215–16, 228; Weisman relation to, 225
Westhoff, Ben, 210
Whisman, Raymond Virgil, 65, 110
"Whispering Bells," 195
Why Do Fools Fall in Love (movie), 124
"Why Do Fools Fall in Love," 3, 36; on *Billboard* charts, 67, 115–16; copyrights for, 18–19, 125–26; disc jockeys and, 115–16; Ross, D., and, 18, 51, 125; songwriting credits for, 19, 66–67, 68–69, 115, 126–27
"Why Don't We Do It in the Road?," 73
Wideawake Entertainment, 212
Winehouse, Amy, 165
WINS, 53, 74; "The Rock 'n' Roll Jubilee Ball" and, 76
Witness Protection Program, 143, 180; Fratianno in, 222, 224, 227
Wohlin, Anna, 158
Wood, Randy, 106
Woodstock, 159–60
Woodstock (movie), 160
Wopo, Jimmy, 233
Wordsworth, William, 145
World Development Report, 208
Worthington, Herbie, 161
WQAM, 83
The Wrap, 210–11
the Wrens, 4

Wurlitzer. *See* jukeboxes

XXXTentacion, 233

Yardville State Prison, 43
"You Baby You," 4
"You Can't Catch Me," 205
Youngan, JayDa, 234
Young Dolph, 233
Young Greatness, 233

Zapata, Adán, 232
Zelmanowitz, Gerald, 200
Zottola, Anthony, 43–44
Zottola, Sylvester, 43–44
Zuckerman, Michael, 227

About the Author

JEFFREY SUSSMAN IS THE AUTHOR OF eighteen books, eight of which are about boxing and organized crime. He lives in New York City.

- *Max Baer and Barney Ross: Jewish Heroes of Boxing*
- *Rocky Graziano: Fists, Fame, and Fortune*
- *Boxing and the Mob: The Notorious History of the Sweet Science*
- *Holocaust Fighters: Boxers, Resisters, and Avengers*
- *Big Apple Gangsters: The Rise and Decline of the Mob in New York*
- *Sin City Gangsters: The Rise and Decline of the Mob in Las Vegas*
- *Tinseltown Gangsters: The Rise and Decline of the Mob in Hollywood*
- *Backbeat Gangsters: The Rise and Decline of the Mob in Rock Music*